Doris Stokes was a celebrated clairaudient who confounded sceptics with the uncanny accuracy of her readings. In Australia she filled the Sydney Opera House and was mobbed in the streets. In America, 'Charlie's Angels' was removed from a prime television slot to make way for her. In this country her appearances on radio phone-ins caused an avalanche of mail.

Praise for Doris Stokes

'[A] psychic superstar . . . warm, amiable and chatty'
Sunday People

'Doris radically updated spiritualism with her brilliant dismissal of the myth which normally surrounds death. There was never any feeling of death around Doris . . . just the living . . . cheerfully crowding in to convey their love, messages and the joy of living'
Spiritualist Gazette

Joyful Voices Omnibus

Voices of Love

&

Joyful Voices

Doris Stokes
with Linda Dearsley

sphere

SPHERE

First published in Great Britain in 2007 by Sphere

Joyful Voices Omnibus copyright © Doris Fisher Stokes 2007

Previously published separately
Voices of Love first published in Great Britain by Macdonald & Co in 1986
Copyright © Doris Fisher Stokes 1986
Joyful Voices first published in Great Britain by Macdonald & Co in 1987
Copyright © Doris Fisher Stokes 1987

A CIP catalogue record for this book
is available from the British Library.

ISBN 978-0-7515-4004-8

Papers used by Sphere are natural, recyclable products made from
wood grown in sustainable forests and certified in accordance with
the rules of the Forest Stewardship Council.

Typeset in Goudy by Palimpsest Book Production Limited,
Grangemouth, Stirlingshire
Printed and bound in Great Britain by Clays Ltd, St Ives plc
Paper supplied by Hellefoss AS, Norway

Sphere
An imprint of
Little, Brown Book Group
Brettenham House
Lancaster Place
London WC2E 7EN

A Member of the Hachette Livre Group of Companies

www.littlebrown.co.uk

'You can't die for the life of you . . .'
Doris Stokes

Voices of Love

I opened the *Daily Mirror* and there he was – on page three. Not a page three girl, but a sad little face peeping over a piece of sacking, one furry paw propping up his chin and a pair of mournful dark eyes staring out hopelessly. The message in those eyes was plain to read: I'm not really bad. Please won't somebody love me?

The pup had been named Boots after the scruffy mongrel in the *Mirror*'s popular strip cartoon, The Perishers, and he was desperate for a home.

Now I didn't intend to have a dog. Not me. Ever since we lost Matey, our ginger cat, I'd said never again. No more pets. We've had a succession of dogs and cats over the years and when Matey finally went out and failed to come home, I said enough's enough. The worry when they're ill, the anxiety when you go away, the sadness when they pass; I couldn't take it any more.

But Terry had other ideas. From the moment we'd moved into our new house he'd been pestering me about having a dog.

'When we've got all the building work done,' I kept saying, playing for time because I've discovered that the extraordinary thing about having your own house is that it seems to mean one building job after another. No matter what you do there's always something else that needs attention. Sometimes I wonder why we don't just make up a bed for the builders and have done with it! They practically live here as it is.

Anyway it could be years before we'd finished with the builders at this rate, I thought, and by then Terry would have forgotten the idea.

So much for good intentions. One look at that poor little face in the *Daily Mirror* and I was lost. The puppy, a Jack Russell/dachshund cross, was only ten weeks old, yet he'd been abandoned twice in his short life. His second 'owner' had tired of him after two weeks and left him at Maidstone Police Station. The police sent him to an animal sanctuary but, said the paper, time was running out as they tried to find him a home.

Poor little soul, I thought looking at the bewildered face again, and that was it. Oh well, we'll manage somehow I sighed as I dialled directory enquiries for the number of Maidstone Police.

The police passed me on to the Viking Animal Sanctuary.

'Oh yes, the puppy in the *Daily Mirror*,' said the man who answered the phone. 'We've had two or three hundred calls about him. We'll be deciding in the next couple of days who he'll go to.'

Two or three hundred calls? We didn't stand much chance then, I thought as I gave the man my name and telephone number, and the funny thing was that although half an hour before I'd had no intention of having a dog, I was suddenly disappointed.

Never mind I told myself, at least that poor little pup will get a good home, that's the main thing.

I put the paper away, got on with my work and pushed all thoughts of the dog firmly to the back of my mind.

'It's no good, Terry,' I said that evening as we were eating our tea. 'I've done everything I can but there were two or three hundred people after that dog.'

Terry was quite upset. He was still far from well, suffering from the effects of a head injury caused by an accident, and diabetes brought on by the shock. He'd obviously set his heart on this dog to cheer him up. I hadn't realised how much it meant to him. Oh dear, I thought as I cleared away the tea things, we'll have to go to Battersea Dogs' Home or something and find him another one.

Then the next morning when I was in the middle of my huge pile of mail, the phone rang.

'It's for you, love,' said John.

'Mrs Stokes?' said a vaguely familiar voice. 'This is the Viking Animal Sanctuary. I just wanted you to know that we've decided to place Boots with you. That is if you still want him.'

'Oh yes. Yes of course we do,' I said, astonished. I'd completely given up hope of getting Boots.

'It was my wife that insisted,' the man went on. 'She's a fan of yours and as soon as she heard you'd phoned, that was it!'

I was delighted and Terry looked really cheerful for the first time in weeks. It was amazing to think that in twenty-four short hours, I'd gone from being adamant about never having another pet, to making arrangements to collect our new dog. I don't know, Doris, you ought to know better at your age, I told myself.

Tony Ortzen, our old friend and the editor of *Psychic News*, presented us with a large dog basket. Someone else gave us some old baby blankets, I got in a good supply of chicken pieces and we were all ready to collect the new arrival to the Stokes family.

Laurie, who as I explained in my last book, is friend, manager and general sounding board, drove us down to the Viking Animal Sanctuary. It was a friendly place, clean and efficiently run and while John and I chatted in the house over a cup of tea, one of the helpers went off to get Boots.

A few minutes later a tiny little scrap was put into my arms. Scarcely one foot long and weighing 5lbs, he was a warm, wriggling black and tan bundle, so full of affection and joy he didn't know whether to kiss my face, chew my fingers or dance round and round in my lap.

'Now Boots, keep still!' I laughed. 'Let's have a look at you.'

Two soft brown eyes, a pair of folded over black ears outlined faintly in gold, one white sock and a funny squiggly little tail that was currently going like a high speed wind-screen wiper.

'Oh he's beautiful,' I cried. It was love at first sight.

The sanctuary gave us a little cage to take him home in. 'Use it whenever you take him out in the car,' they advised. And Boots was as good as gold, sitting perkily in the cage balanced on my lap.

Back home I found Terry slumped in an armchair watching television. He'd been feeling quite poorly that day. I didn't say anything. Quietly I opened the cage and put Boots on his lap. The change was dramatic. Within minutes Terry was laughing and pretending to protest as Boots clambered all over him licking his face, chewing his hair, chasing his slippers as if they were a pair of rats. From that moment on, Terry improved rapidly.

Within a very short time Boots ruled the house and I'm afraid to say he's spoiled rotten. All our good resolutions flew away within days.

'He stays downstairs in his basket at night,' I said. And so he did for about a week.

Then John and I went away for a couple of days and when we came back we found Boots wandering up to Terry's room at bedtime as if he owned the place. He'd got accustomed to sleeping with Terry and that was that.

'He stays in the cage when he goes out in the car,' I said. And so he did at first.

But then Terry opened the cage because he thought Boots was unhappy and from then on Boots had to sit on the passenger seat.

'He stays in the playpen in the garden while the builders are here,' I said. And so he did for ten minutes.

'Well he was crying you see, Mrs Stokes,' said one of the builders sheepishly, 'so we brought him out for a bit.'

It was hopeless but Boots is such a lovable little thing that you can't be cross with him. At first he chewed everything he could get his paws on. He chewed the carpet and my new rug, he chewed our slippers and any shoes left lying around, he chewed almost everything he could get his teeth into.

'Boots! No!' I yelled sometimes. 'I'll have your guts for garters!'

His only reply was to leap straight onto my knee and plant kisses all over my face as if I was speaking words of love. It was impossible to scold him.

Young as he was he seemed to have a long memory. I don't think he's ever forgotten the kindness shown to him at Maidstone police station, because he loves policemen. The first time Derek our local bobby dropped in, in uniform, for a cup of tea, Boots greeted him like a long lost friend. Now whenever Derek comes round he sits between his boots and looks up at him adoringly. And no matter how we spoil him

I think there's still a lingering insecurity at the back of his mind. He's perfectly happy to go out for a walk but on the way back, the minute he sees the house he's off like the clappers and can't stop until he gets inside the gate. No matter what they say I'm sure that dogs and all animals have feelings. They know where they're safe. They know where the love is.

These days of course Boots is quite a celebrity. I seem to do a lot of magazine and newspaper interviews and whenever there's an interviewer there's usually a photographer to go with him. As soon as Boots came along the photographers realised his potential and now he appears in just about every picture. Boots loves it. He's only got to see a camera and he automatically falls into an appealing pose, his ears prick up, his head tilts to one side and he arranges his paws neatly. Talk about star struck!

It was only a matter of time I suppose before Boots appeared on stage with me, but the night he made his debut it was just as much a surprise to me as it was to the audience.

We were at Birmingham Odeon one very hot day in September 1985. I always enjoy going to Birmingham because the people are so warm and friendly that they send out a tremendous wave of love to me on stage and it's an incredible help. The messages always flow faster when there's a good atmosphere.

Anyway this particular evening I finished the demonstration and was just about to move on to a little surprise I had for the audience, when the chairman suddenly sprang a surprise on me.

'Ladies and gentlemen, I've just had a note passed to me,' he said mysteriously. 'Will you please all welcome Doris' personal security.'

Personal security? I can't have heard that right, I thought, because although these days I have a manager, I certainly don't have any security, unless you count John of course. Puzzled, I glanced from the chairman to the audience, where a lot of tittering had started at the back.

To my amazement I saw an American cop, in full uniform with a gun on his hip and dark glasses covering his face, striding purposefully towards the stage. He was over 6 foot tall, as wide as a barn door, and he was holding something. I peered over the stage lights for a better view and when I saw what it was I began to laugh. This huge man was holding a long, extended lead and at the end of the lead was Boots, now grown to about 13 inches long and weighing about 6lbs. The contrast between this enormous man and the tiny puppy was the funniest thing I'd ever seen and the audience were falling about.

Boots thought it was wonderful. As soon as he saw me he darted onto the stage, tying himself into knots and falling over his paws in his eagerness to reach me. The audience went wild and Boots played up to them outrageously. His tail wagged dementedly and he kissed everyone in sight. There was a terrific din of laughter and applause but it didn't worry him in the slightest. He took to it like a star.

Terry had planned the whole thing. While I thought he was safely at home looking after Boots, he was in fact tearing up the motorway to Birmingham. Throughout the evening he and Boots were hidden in a dressing-room upstairs, and Laurie's brother Alphi was persuaded to dress up in his American cop costume (don't ask me how he got it – I haven't the faintest idea) and lead Boots onto the stage.

Funnily enough, all evening I'd sensed that something was going on, but I couldn't think what it could be. The spirit world didn't want to spoil the surprise by telling me the secret but there was no mistaking the feeling of anticipation in the air.

Alphi was so taken with Boots, in fact, that he wrote this lovely poem about him which sums him up perfectly!

Boots

Today I bit the postman
and then I chased the cat
Went into my mum's wardrobe
and chewed up her best hat
I tore up Daddy's slipper
and ate the morning post
Then jumped up on the table
and ate the breakfast toast.

I nearly caught a sparrow
As it landed in the yard
But now I am exhausted
Because I play so hard.

I think I'll have a little nap
Maybe I will snore
And then when I wake up
I will chase the boy next door.

Alphi O'Leary

That visit to Birmingham was very special for many reasons. Most of all I think because my first appearance (I did two) coincided with those terrible riots in Handsworth and at the end of the evening we had to warn people not to travel home through that part of the city. Yet while all that violence and destruction was going on just a mile or two up the road, hundreds of people were generating so much love and warmth and compassion for each other. It just shows the two extremes we're capable of.

When we arrived at the stage door that night we found three ladies standing outside, drenched in tears.

'Oh Doris, can we just give you this letter,' sobbed one of them. 'We wanted to make sure you'd read it. We've left one at the front door too, just in case we didn't see you.'

Laurie quickly took the letter from my hand.

'I'm sorry, ladies,' he said, 'Doris can't stay now, she mustn't be seen talking to anyone, but I'll come back and speak to you in a minute.' And he hurried me inside.

'Oh Laurie,' I said, 'they obviously need help desperately.'

'I know, love, I'll sort something out, but you know what it's like.'

Laurie can be a worrier at times but I understood his concern. The more well-known you get, the more people there are just dying to criticise and if I stood chatting at the stage door with members of the audience before a show I'd be accused of cheating. It's the same with letters. Quite often people will send letters to the theatre where I'm appearing, appealing for me to contact their loved ones during the evening. I couldn't read them even if I wanted to, it would be called collusion. Instead I hand them, still sealed, either to Laurie or the chairman and I don't look at them until I get home.

Naturally I couldn't read this particular letter but the sight of those distressed ladies worried me.

'We're all right now, Laurie,' I said as soon as John and I were settled in the dressing-room. 'See if you can have a word with those ladies.'

They were still there at the stage door. Laurie explained as gently as he could why I couldn't read their letter until after the show but he promised that I would see it eventually.

'Are you going to the demonstration?' he asked.

They shook their heads. 'No, the tickets were sold out ages ago. We only came to deliver the letter.'

'Well would you like to go?' Good old Laurie often keeps back one or two tickets for special emergencies.

The ladies were thrown into confusion. They obviously hadn't come hoping for preferential treatment.

'We haven't got ourselves ready to go in!' they protested.

'How ready d'you have to be!' laughed Laurie. 'You look all right to me.'

That did it. They all accepted the tickets and in a much more cheerful frame of mind they hurried round to the front of the house to find their seats.

I'd known from the moment I'd set eyes on those ladies that it was important I should speak to them and the spirit world was clearly organising the whole thing.

Later during the demonstration a determined Brummie voice said in my ear, 'I'm Ellen but everyone calls me Nelly, and I'm looking for Pat.'

'I've got an Ellen called Nelly looking for Pat,' I repeated out loud. 'Is Pat here?'

Immediately a middle-aged woman came hurrying down to the microphone. There was something a bit familiar about her but I didn't twig at first that it was the sobbing lady from the stage door.

'Nelly's my mother,' said Pat eagerly.

Even then I didn't take a good look at her because I was concentrating so hard on what Nelly was telling me. It was bad news and I'd have to phrase it very carefully.

'Well, love, your mother's telling me she's very concerned about Mary. She's in the hospital, isn't she?'

'Yes she is,' said Pat.

Nelly told me that they were preparing to fetch Mary very soon but I didn't like to come straight out with it.

'Mary's *very* poorly. You know that, don't you,' I began tactfully.

'Oh yes Doris, we know she's dying,' said Pat and as she drew out her handkerchief to dab her eyes I recognised her. 'She was so disappointed not to be able to come tonight,' Pat went on. 'She's always been to see you when you've been at the Odeon. She hasn't missed one show.'

'She's only young,' put in Nelly sadly and as she said it I felt a terrible pain around my liver. I recognised the signs.

'The poor child. It's your sister, isn't it?' I said. 'Is it in the liver?'

Pat confirmed that her sister was indeed suffering from cancer of the liver.

'Well look love, never mind about her not coming tonight. If I can find the time tomorrow I'll go and see her in the hospital to make up for it!'

Pat was a bit astonished, I think, but she left her sister's full name and the address of the hospital with Laurie and at the end of the evening when I was presented with a beautiful bouquet of flowers I held them up for Pat to see.

'Where are you, Pat?' I called out into row upon row of faces. I had no idea where she was sitting but it didn't matter. 'I'll take this bouquet to Mary.'

The next day I was recording a programme for Ed Doolan on BBC radio and there was another demonstration at the Odeon in the evening, but there was just enough time between the two for a visit to Selly Oak Hospital.

Unfortunately it wasn't visiting time but a nurse came out of the ward to speak to us.

'Is it possible to see Mary Woodley?' I asked. 'I promised

her mother I'd come and see her but I'm so busy this was the only moment free. I've got a theatre appearance tonight you see.'

I didn't even attempt to explain that Mary's mother was on the other side when I'd made my promise. I felt that could complicate things immensely.

'Just one moment,' said the nurse, 'I'll ask sister.'

A few moments later she was back. 'Yes that's all right but you mustn't stay too long.'

Clutching the huge bouquet, I was shown into a beautiful ward. Long and airy with huge windows pouring sunshine into the room, it was in no way a gloomy miserable place.

Mary was at the far end and she wasn't expecting me, yet she heard my voice, recognised it immediately and tried to get off the bed. Sadly she was too weak but the sister saw her struggle and hurried forward.

'It's all right, sister,' I said. 'I won't stay long. I just want to give her a message.'

Poor Mary was only thirty-five and she was such a smart girl even in bed. She'd gone very thin and her skin was sallow with the illness but she was wearing a pretty nightdress and she'd had her hair cut stylishly.

'Doris!' she cried as I sat on the bed. 'I knew that was your voice but I didn't believe it!'

She was a brave girl. She admired the flowers and chatted brightly even though she was probably in pain. Nelly arrived within minutes.

'Your mum's here, Mary love,' I said. 'She's never far away from you.'

'Tell her not to be afraid, Doris,' said Nelly. 'It won't be long now and I'll be there to take her hand.'

Mary's face lit up when I gave her this message.

'There's nothing to it, love,' I went on, 'there's nothing

to be afraid of. Your mother'll be with you every step of the way.'

By the time we left I truly believe that Mary's fears had been eased. Her face had a great peacefulness about it and I knew that it had been worth every minute of my afternoon off to bring a little comfort to a very special girl. If I achieved nothing else in Birmingham, that visit to Mary made the whole trip worthwhile.

Afterwards I received a lovely letter from Pat telling me that the message from Nelly was the best medicine Mary could have had and that she was a changed girl since the visit.

But if I thought I could rest on my laurels in the remaining couple of hours before the evening's show, the spirit world had other ideas.

Our terrible summer had turned into a beautiful autumn and the centre of Birmingham was stifling. We opened all the windows in our hotel room but somehow we couldn't seem to catch a whiff of a breeze.

'Come on, love, put your feet up and rest,' John kept urging me, but I couldn't. Two young spirit boys were plaguing me, in the nicest possible sense of course.

One of them, a poor, mixed-up lad before he passed, told me he'd shot himself in the head and whenever he came close I got a searing pain through my temples. He was so unused to communicating that he didn't know how to talk to me without flooding me with his last impressions.

'I'm sorry, Doris,' he said, 'but I'm going to get through tonight even if I give you a blinding headache. I must tell Mum I'm sorry.'

No sooner had he moved away than another boy was mentally tugging at my sleeve.

'It's Paul,' he said. 'You won't forget, will you?'

Paul was rather forlorn because he'd come through the night before at the Odeon and the young woman over whose head his light was hovering refused to acknowledge him. I discovered later that she was related in some way to Paul but she was either too shy or too bewildered to come forward so Paul's messages were wasted. But Paul wouldn't give up.

'You will try again tonight, won't you?' he kept asking. 'They'll be there tonight. You won't forget?'

'I'll do my best, love,' I promised, 'but if they don't turn up or they won't answer, what can I do?'

Paul wandered away but every half hour or so his voice drifted back . . . 'Don't forget . . .'

I'm not likely to with you pair around all the time, I grumbled to myself as I abandoned all hope of having a nap and changed into my long dress for the stage. But I wasn't really cross, and besides this was to be a special evening.

For some time now I'd been supporting a charity called PHAB which stands for Physically Handicapped and Able Bodied. It's an organisation in which the physically handicapped and able bodied mix together socially; the able bodied to help the handicapped and the handicapped to enrich the lives of the able bodied. As well as social evenings PHAB likes to organise outings for its members but they were always in need of new minibuses fitted with wheelchair lifts to carry the handicapped.

Now as I've said before, my old dad always used to tell me: 'Cast your bread upon the waters, Doll, and it will come back buttered' and I've tried to carry out his words ever since. Every year I do as much work as I can for charity and in the past I've simply handed over the cheque to whichever charity I'm supporting, and that's the end of it. Wouldn't it be nice if for a change I could actually see what the money had paid for? I thought. If I gave something they really needed instead. And that's how the idea for the bus arose.

It took a while to raise the necessary £15,000, but at last we got the money together, ordered the bus and made arrangements to hand it over at Birmingham on September 11th. Unfortunately in the end the bus we'd chosen wasn't ready in time; it was still being fitted with the special lifts and painted pale blue, the healing colour, with the words 'The Spirit of Love' on the side. So instead, the company lent us an identical bus to present on the night.

There were quite a few PHAB members in the audience that night and the presentation was to be a surprise for them, but Paul nearly gave the game away in the very first message.

'Now I must start with a message I got last night,' I explained to the audience. 'This Paul Wilson or Wilcox came through and gave me a lot of names but his people weren't there to accept them and he's been on at me all afternoon to try again tonight. He tells me he was in a wheelchair and the address Shepherds Road is important. I do hope someone's here tonight for him.'

This time Paul was in luck. Almost at once a bright, bubbly young girl came down to the microphone.

'It's Paul Wilkins,' she said, 'and I'm Paul's oldest sister.'

Paul, who'd arrived the minute I set foot on stage, breathed a sigh of relief.

'That's Carole spelled with an "e",' he said happily.

He was clearly very fond of Carole.

'Are you Carole with an "e"?' I asked.

'Yes,' she said grinning, 'and I live in Shepherds Road.'

I knew we were spot on now and Carole didn't seem a bit nervous which helped things along nicely. What's more, Paul was getting quite good at communicating now, having practised the night before, and the evidence came pouring through.

'He's giving me a name which sounds like Suliman,' I said.

'That's right, my married name's Suliman,' said Carole.

'And someone called Rashid, I think that was.'

'My husband.'

Paul evidently approved of Rashid. 'He's a good bloke,' he said.

Carole giggled when I passed this on. 'Yes he is.'

Paul went on to explain a bit about himself. He was only twenty-seven when he passed, a physically handicapped boy who sometimes got frustrated and irritated because he couldn't do all the things he wanted to do.

'At times I used to cry because I felt so useless,' he said. 'But then I joined PHAB and it helped me help others. I'm glad I did something worthwhile.'

If you've got to go there can't be a better way than the way Paul passed. 'It was very quick,' he said. 'I went to bed, Mum kissed me goodnight, I said "I love you, Mum" and then I went to sleep and woke up over here. That's the way to do it.'

After he passed he said his mother cut off a lock of his hair. Mrs Wilkins, who'd shyly come forward to join her daughter at the microphone, confirmed that this was true.

'I'm going to put it in a locket,' she said.

Paul went on to mention his stepfather Alan, his uncle Brian and the fact that he'd left £42.16 in his wallet. Then he started muttering something about a tea caddy or teapot and I couldn't make it out at all.

'I think he's saying something about a tea caddy,' I told Carole. 'I don't know what he means. Why's he telling me that?'

Carole's hand flew to her mouth in amazement.

'Oh,' she gasped, 'I thought I was imagining that. I keep my keys in the teapot in the kitchen and just lately when there's no-one around, they've been rattling. I thought it must be my imagination.'

'No, it was Paul,' I assured her. 'He's trying to tell you he's there.'

Paul gave one or two more details, then he mentioned someone called Barr. I had no idea as I passed this name on that Paul was naughtily hinting about the special surprise.

'Mr Barr. Oh that's the man who drives the handicapped bus,' said Paul's mother.

Paul chuckled wickedly, 'And I hope he'll be the first to have the pleasure of driving the new one.'

'Paul! You're giving secrets away,' I scolded.

'He says he hopes he'll be the first to have the pleasure,' I paraphrased, 'and only we know what he means.'

Paul got the evening off to a good start and when he finally moved away to let the other spirit people have a turn the messages came rushing along. The boy who'd shot himself explained that he didn't know what came over him. He was moody and depressed and believed that no-one understood how he felt.

'I finally got a job and I was only there a week when they kicked me out,' he said, 'so I thought bugger it.'

He mentioned some family names and his friends Stephen and Peter, particularly Peter. 'I wish I'd talked to Peter,' he said. 'He would have stopped me.'

There was six-year-old Claire, the image of her daddy.

'There's my daddy Martin,' she cried as her parents came to the microphone. Claire was perfectly happy in her new life, only one thing bothered her.

'I never got to unpack my presents from you,' she said, still annoyed because she'd passed on just before Christmas.

Then there was Gary, the boy who'd been killed giving some friends a lift home; a little toddler who'd drowned in a swimming pool; a husband who knew that his wife had had her kitchen remodelled since he passed and that there wasn't room in it for her washing machine; and so on and so on. Back they all came, husbands and wives, fathers and mothers, sisters, brothers and little children . . . until at last I had to rest and it was time to make the presentation.

The mini bus was already on the stage, hidden from the audience by a thick curtain, and Ed Doolan from Pebble Mill came to the theatre specially to make the announcement.

He talked a little bit about PHAB, then two members of the group came onto the stage: Hayley a little blind girl with two stumps instead of legs, was pushed on in a wheelchair by her helper Scott. She couldn't see and she couldn't walk, but she had beautiful skin, dark glossy hair and the sweetest smile. She presented me with a bouquet of flowers and that, she thought, was the end of it. But I knew better.

'Do you enjoy going to the PHAB club, Hayley?' I asked.

'Oh yes. I live for club evenings.'

'And what d'you think your club would like most in all the world?'

Hayley thought for a moment. 'Well . . . we need a new mini bus because ours keeps breaking down,' she said.

So I opened her hand and put the keys in her palm.

Puzzled, she felt the cold metal. 'What are these?'

'They're the keys for your new bus, darling,' I told her. 'Here it is.'

And the curtain rose and there was the bus in all its splendour. But Hayley of course couldn't see it, so we pushed her up close so that she could feel it instead. Silently she ran her hands over the sparkling paintwork.

'Oh isn't it shiny, Scott,' she whispered.

'Yes,' he said, 'that's because it's brand new.'

The look on their faces was the best reward I could have hoped for. I can't describe the feeling I got that night. People keep saying to me, 'Why on earth are you spending all this money?' But what's the point of being the richest body in the cemetery? If I can make those kids happy it makes me happy too and whenever I think of them enjoying their bus in the years to come I get a warm glow.

A wealthy friend of mine was going on at me about it just the other day. She had recently separated from her rich husband who had spent his health to gain his wealth and was currently trying to spend his wealth to buy back his health. This lady stood there in her mink coat, with her Mercedes sports car parked outside and her large house all paid for out of her husband's company, and between scolding me about giving my money away she complained bitterly about the pittance her mean husband gave her to live on.

'D'you know I'm supposed to manage on £19.50 a day,' she moaned.

'For goodness' sake listen to yourself,' I said, losing patience. 'You're talking exactly like your husband. You've been with him so long you think like him. Stop counting how much this cost and how much that cost. Would you rather be miserable with a millionaire or have your self respect and make do? And as for my money, I'd much rather see it being used by some child that needs it than locked up in a bank.'

There was a stunned silence. I hope she wasn't offended but I couldn't help coming out with it.

There was a postscript to my Birmingham visit. A few weeks after we returned home I was arranging some flowers in front of the photographs of my spirit children, when suddenly I saw the face of Mary, the girl I'd visited in Selly Oak Hospital. I only caught a tiny glimpse of her but her complexion was a warm rosy colour and her face was shining with health.

'I'm safe with Mum now, Doris,' she said.

And Nelly's voice chimed in, 'Will you tell our Pat?'

Laurie was dropping in that day and I knew he had Pat's number somewhere in his office so I asked him to pass the message on. Sure enough, when he phoned, he discovered that Mary had just passed over.

But even that wasn't the end of the story. A few months and many many communications later we were invited back to the Odeon at Birmingham and Pat was in the audience once more. There were hundreds of other people present of course and the messages were flying in all directions so when Nelly and Mary came back yet again I didn't recognise them at first. But then Mary said, 'You came to see me in hospital you know,' and it all fell into place.

'Tell Pat I'd had enough,' said Mary. 'I got so weak and sick I kept saying, "Come on Mum, take my hand." And one day I went to sleep and Mum came and took me home. I wasn't sorry. I'd had enough.' She went on to tell me that Pat had got her ring but that most of her other things were still just as she'd left them.

'I don't know why, because I'm not going to come back and use them,' said Mary. She was particularly concerned about her new red sweater. She was very fond of it and didn't want it given away. She wanted someone in the family to wear it.

She also talked of her husband. 'He was a good husband in one way,' said Mary, 'but we couldn't live together. We parted, so in the end all I had was my family but they are a wonderful family. When I took the final step there were four of them round my bed.'

Most of all I think she was concerned about Pat.

'She's under a lot of stress at the moment and things are difficult at home. She's worrying she's going to get cancer like me. Tell her not to worry and not to be a doormat.'

Finally Mary wanted Pat to know that she was healthy and fit once more. 'Remember the last time you saw me, how I looked?' she asked.

'Yes,' said Pat, 'terrible.'

'Well I'm not like that any more. Forget it. I'm back to normal.'

By the end of the evening Pat was smiling and cheerful.

'I'm a different person now,' she wrote to me afterwards, 'I no longer feel sad and downhearted, and strange as it might sound I feel happy for Mary.'

Yes, all in all, when I look back on my visits to Birmingham, I think I can safely say it was time well spent.

2

The girl was young and pretty with long red-brown hair falling over her shoulders and she was sobbing her heart out. She sat hunched up on the back stairs at the SAGB (the headquarters of the Spiritualist Association of Great Britain) crying as if the end of the world had come, and not caring a bit who saw her.

My friend Nancy and I had just stepped out of the lift on our way back from a quick sandwich lunch and we stopped dead.

'Whatever's the matter, love,' I asked gently.

'I've just lost a very good friend,' she gulped between sobs, 'and I can't get into the demonstration. It's full.' And the tears started falling again.

'Come on, love,' said Nancy, 'we'll get you in if you have to sit on the floor.'

It was one of those days. I don't often get the chance to do a full day at SAGB and when I do it's usually packed out. I'd had to leave home before 10.00 that morning for the first session and there was only time for a quick bite and a cup of tea before I had to start all over again. They'd got them wedged like sardines in that hall and the central heating was going full blast despite the fact that it was a mild day. It was like stepping into a turkish bath.

Nancy had a word with the man on the door and a box was pushed in beside the grand piano for the young girl. It didn't look very comfortable but it was the best we could do.

I started to work normally and then to my surprise a faint light flew directly over the girl's bright hair and a young male voice said, 'I was found dead in bed yesterday.'

Yesterday, I thought, no wonder the poor girl's in such a state.

'I've got a young man here who was found dead in bed yesterday,' I told her. 'Does that mean anything to you, love?'

'Yes!' she cried and burst into tears again.

The young man tried to tell me his name but it was difficult for him to communicate so soon after passing and I could hardly hear him.

'Was that Gary, love?' I asked.

'Yes,' said the girl, 'his name's Gary.'

He was trying to give me his surname too but I couldn't catch it. It was something like Alton or Almon.

'No I don't think I've got that right,' I said to him, 'try me again Gary.'

To my surprise he laughed and started whistling instead. What on earth's going on I thought? If I can't make out what he's saying, how's whistling going to help? Then I realised that the tune sounded familiar. It was like a pop song, yet it wasn't a pop song because I'm not very good at those and I knew this tune well. Then I realised where I'd heard it before. It was the theme tune of one of my favourite TV programmes, *Auf Wiedersehen Pet*.

'It can't be,' I said out loud in shock. 'Surely it can't be Gary Holton from *Auf Wiedersehen Pet*?'

'Yes it is,' said Gary and his friend simultaneously.

Gary Holton was the talented young man who played a popular cockney character called Wayne in the TV series. His sudden death the day before had been all over the morning papers but I'd left too early to see them and I'd known nothing about it. The episode really shook me. I come across tragedy all the time in my job of course but to have someone you watch every week on TV turn up suddenly amongst the spirit voices when you didn't even know they'd passed, is quite a shock.

Gary went on to mention a few more names but the girl was so distressed I felt it would be kinder to move on to another contact. Making a mental note to have a word with her at the end, I continued with the demonstration. It passed smoothly enough with no more unpleasant shocks. Afterwards I collected up my things and looked around for the young girl, but she'd gone.

'Oh she left you this,' said the man on the door handing me a slip of paper.

It was a hasty note thanking me for my help and signed Melanie – no address, no telephone number. Oh well, never mind, I thought, that's the end of that and I went home, sad that we'd lost a bright young talent but certain that I'd heard the last of the affair.

Which just shows how wrong you can be even when you're a medium!

Gary Holton was quite determined to come back for a long chat because unknown to me, he'd made an unofficial appointment three weeks before he passed and he still intended to keep it even though he was now on the other side!

It happened like this. A friend of mine met Gary Holton and his girlfriend Jahnette in Marbella, Spain, where the *Auf*

Wiedersehen Pet team were filming the Spanish scenes for the series. Over drinks in the hotel bar my name was mentioned and Gary and Jahnette said how much they'd like to meet me. The upshot was that my friend agreed to bring them over for a cup of tea on my first day off after Gary had finished filming. No one could have guessed then that Gary Holton, apparently fit, healthy and full of life, had only three short weeks left on this earth.

The TV crew stayed on for an extra week or two, then they returned to Nottingham to shoot the final scenes. It was a hectic schedule for them because they were up against a deadline and every minute counted. Everyone was working very hard indeed but Gary didn't seem to be showing any more strain than anyone else. On the Thursday afternoon he finished his work in the Nottingham studios and set off for London to be ready for the read through at the rehearsal rooms the next morning. He never got there. On Friday morning Jahnette found him dead in bed.

Yet Gary obviously hadn't forgotten that planned meeting with me and I believe that one of the first things he did when he found himself over there, was to set about organising it.

First he prompted Melanie, a young actress he'd worked with who knew a lot about spiritualism, to come to the SAGB at short notice despite the fact that there were no places left. Then he made sure that Nancy and I were returning from lunch at just the right moment to bump into her and he also made sure that he got a message through. He's clearly a very determined young man when he puts his mind to it.

Jahnette of course quickly got to hear of Melanie's message, and remembering the discussion in Spain she was keen to keep the appointment.

She arrived one grey winter morning with her friends Brian and Susie. She was still suffering from shock. She was wrapped in a thick fur coat, the collar pulled up to her ears, yet she looked frozen, just the same.

'Come in and have a cup of tea, love,' I said, getting her quickly indoors and turning the fire up. Her friend Susie looked almost as cold. Only Brian seemed calm and unruffled.

Gary came through almost at once but it was difficult to keep up with him. His voice was instantly recognisable, that broad cockney accent and the language at times! Well it's a good thing I'm unshockable. But despite this, there was a great deal of confusion around him and at times his voice was so faint I could hardly hear a word he said.

At this time Jahnette was still waiting for the outcome of the inquest and we didn't know the official cause of death, although the papers were full of speculation.

Shortly before the tragedy it was revealed that Gary had been a heroin addict and of course now everyone was saying that it was a drug overdose which killed him.

Gary was very annoyed about this.

'I didn't do it. It wasn't drugs,' he insisted. 'I'd kicked heroin. Don't let them say that.'

Then great waves of confusion would come flowing in, he didn't seem to know how he'd ended up on the other side. It had been a great surprise to him at first.

'I was very angry, very bitter when I realised what had happened,' he said, his voice getting agitated again. 'I was just making it. Finally I was making it and then this had to happen. It's not fair.'

'Don't upset yourself, love,' I said gently. 'Tell me about something else.'

'It's okay, I'm at peace now,' he said calming down, but

he changed the subject all the same. He mentioned the names John and Tony.

'John's his manager and Tony is a reporter who's writing about him at the moment,' said Jahnette. 'And now he's talking about Amanda and Lisa,' I explained.

'They're girlfriends of his,' said Jahnette who didn't seem at all bothered or jealous of them.

'I borrowed a tenner from Brian before it happened,' Gary went on. 'Sorry mate, you won't get that back.'

Brian smiled ruefully. He clearly didn't begrudge Gary the money.

But talk of events leading up to the tragedy set Gary reassessing his life again.

'Five years. I wasted so much time . . . I was f . . .' I hastily censored the last word.

He went on to talk of his wife Donna and his long time girlfriend Sue and predicted that there would be a lot of confusion and nastiness over the funeral.

'But I had good friends in Brian and Jahnette,' he added. 'We understood each other, we could tell what each other was thinking. There was nothing we couldn't talk about.'

But he was slipping into sadness again. 'I lived my life and made a mess of it . . .'

'All right, love, don't go on about it,' I said. 'What's been happening lately?'

At first I didn't think he was paying attention but after a second or two, very faintly, I heard something about a house in the country, near Little something. There was the hiss of an 's' sound but that's all I could make out.

'It must be Little Saxham,' said Jahnette. 'We went to look at a house out that way because we wanted to open a centre to help heroin addicts.'

'That's what's going to happen,' said Gary determinedly.

'With Pip. I'll still help you. Just put out your hand and I'll be there.'

Then he started to laugh. 'I'm thirty-three you know but the papers said thirty-two. Don't take any notice of the bloody papers. You can't believe a word they say. And never mind what they said about Brian and Jahnette. The happiest time of my life I have them to thank for. They're true blue. We loved each other. I had a lot of girls on the side but we understood each other.'

He was still very concerned about his friends.

'You've been a very mixed up little girl,' he told Jahnette, 'but now you're beginning to get yourself together. The tears you've shed. We've cried in each other's arms, talking about wouldn't it be better if we went. Promise me you'll learn something from this. Do something positive.'

And as for Brian he was worried that he wasn't making the most of his talent.

'Brian's the sort of bloke who gives up if things don't go right,' he said. 'Lazy bugger. He has so much talent but he doesn't use it. He can write. I love Brian as a soul mate and I don't want him to fritter his life away. He's got lyrics in the drawer that have never been used. Get on with it mate and I'll help you.'

By now Gary was wandering back and forth between the two of them.

'That girl held me in her arms and I sweated and shook,' he said, 'but I'd sorted myself out and then this had to happen. It's not f . . . fair. I would have shown them. I frittered away a lot of money but I was also screwed out of a lot of money. I trusted people. I had no business head.'

After his passing, the papers had been full of terrible stories about Gary and he was particularly upset about one report which linked him with an 11-year-old girl.

'I had three children. I wouldn't have touched an 11-year-old, I've got three kids of my own. Oh I'm well off out of it,' he finished angrily.

This puzzled me because I could have sworn I'd read somewhere that Gary had only one child, but Jahnette explained.

'Yes I know what he means. He's talking about Max, Sue's son from a past marriage, and Danielle my daughter as well as his own son. He loved them and thought of them as his own children. He would say he's got three kids.'

'I always supported the baby,' Gary went on, 'but Brian listen, I have creditors. I owe money. My kid won't get anything unless we're careful.'

By now the power was fading badly and it was a strain to make out his words, but still Gary went on, remembering his friends.

'Amanda. She's only nineteen. Give her my love. I was a bit of a sod but I loved her. There's one thing, Jahnette. They said they loved me and I wondered if it was because I was famous but I never thought that about Jahnette. She loved me for me, warts and all. I took advantage of all those others. But then who wouldn't?'

He talked of his friends Steve and Melanie and finally of Ben.

'Oh I'm glad he's mentioned Ben,' said Jahnette. 'Ben's Keith Moon's son and Gary helped him through a very difficult time in his life. He thought the world of Ben.'

But Gary was gone and I was exhausted. Yet the sitting wasn't quite over. Jahnette's friend Susie had been sitting quietly curled up in an armchair throughout the conversation. The poor girl seemed very subdued and it wasn't until Gary had finished that she shyly mentioned that one or two of the names Jahnette hadn't been able to place might have been intended for her. It turned out that young as she was, she had been recently widowed and she was still suffering badly.

I couldn't let her leave without some word of comfort, so I tuned in once more, gathering up the last shreds of power. Fortunately it wasn't a struggle. Her husband John had been hovering close trying to get a word in throughout the sitting. In fact one puzzling comment I'd heard soon after they'd arrived now became clear.

In the middle of the confusion surrounding Gary, I made out the words, 'We parted on bad terms. I'm sorry. I forgive you,' and the words were spoken very definitely to Susie. There was no question of the message being intended for Jahnette or Brian.

Susie however was puzzled. 'No it can't be for me. I never met Gary,' she said.

No one present could understand it and we let it go but now I realised that it had been Susie's husband trying to interrupt right at the beginning. The story was particularly tragic because they'd parted company unhappily, the husband had gone abroad and been killed in a car accident.

'It was two days before I was due home,' he said. 'Just two days that's all.'

He talked of the accident, the sons he'd left behind and some of the problems of the marriage. It was only a mini sitting because by now I was exhausted, but it seemed to cheer Susie quite a bit.

Afterwards over a cup of tea, Jahnette explained a little more about poor Gary's mixed-up life. Apparently he'd had quite a wild time. He'd been a child actor, then a pop singer and he'd got involved in drink, drugs and goodness knows what else. Then came his unexpected success in the first series of *Auf Wiedersehen Pet* and instead of bringing him pleasure, it seemed only to create more problems. Work poured in and to cope with the work he leaned more heavily on drugs. His relationship with his girlfriend Sue, the mother of his son, began to suffer and soon he was in a pretty bad way.

Jahnette found him in her local pub in a distressed state as he tried to escape the unwelcome attentions of a group of fans. She took him home and soon he was more or less living with her and her steady boyfriend Brian. It might be a funny idea to an old lady like me, but it seems to have suited them. Gary had other girlfriends and Jahnette had Brian but the three of them lived together without jealousy.

'Gary managed to kick heroin,' said Jahnette, 'and he was really getting himself together. We had great plans. He was just starting to realise what he could achieve. He was very concerned about drugs and young people and he felt he could use his fame to do so much to help drug addicts because he'd been through it himself. He wanted to open a special centre in the country.

'The only problem was money. The way he'd been living he'd run into debt. He'd earned a lot of money but he'd spent even more, so he was working very hard to get straight. He'd come out of a year in a play which is very tiring in itself, straight into the second series of *Auf Wiedersehen Pet*. It was such a tight schedule and everybody had to work incredibly hard, but as soon as filming was over Gary was getting ready for a season in pantomime.'

The week before the tragedy was particularly unhappy. Sensational newspaper reports seemed to follow Gary wherever he went and that week his heroin addiction was revealed.

'He was very upset about it,' said Jahnette, 'he thought that no one would believe he was cured and that his career would be ruined. Then that last day, Thursday, something changed. It was as if all the fight went out of him. I'm sure

Doris Stokes

deep down, he knew he was going to die. I was with him at the studios in Nottingham and he went round saying goodbye to everybody. He even tried to see his little Nottingham girl-friend to say goodbye to her. We came back to London and Gary had a few drinks in the pub but he wasn't at all drunk. Afterwards we went to visit some old friends of his and we sat up very late talking. We were too tired to drive home so they let us sleep on a mattress on the floor.

'The next morning when I woke up, Gary was gone. He was still there lying beside me, but I knew as soon as I looked at him that he was dead.

At the inquest it was revealed that traces of alcohol and heroin had been found in Gary Holton's body, enough to have killed him. I found the heroin part strange, because Gary had been adamant about not taking drugs when I spoke to him.

Jahnette too finds it hard to believe.

'I can't understand it,' she said. 'Gary wasn't a saint but he hadn't had much to drink that night and he certainly didn't have another drink after leaving the pub. As for drugs, they said he must have taken the heroin an hour before he died. But I found him at about 9.00 in the morning. We were sleeping on a single mattress and my arm was still across his body. He couldn't have got up without me knowing. I think he died because he'd had enough. He lived very fast and he was worn out.'

Well it's a sad story. Gary Holton was a confused boy and the confusion surrounds him still. It's such a pity. He was so talented and when I was talking to him I realised that he was one of those rare people who have the gift of making people love him. Yet in the end it wasn't enough.

It's a great shame he was too busy to come to see me before he passed. Who knows, perhaps I could have given him some reassurance. But it was obviously not meant to be. I firmly believe that there's a time to be born and a time to die and it was clearly Gary Holton's time to die. At least he won't be lonely on the other side. There are so many other tragic young actors and pop musicians already there, he'll have plenty of company.

3

'Come on Doris, up here.'

The rain was lashing down and it was a terrible night but I picked my way carefully up the rickety steps, now dripping with water, and onto the platform. They'd rigged up a canopy over our heads but the rain leaked through anyway and there were puddles on the chairs.

What a shame, I thought, they couldn't have picked worse weather.

Out on the sodden cobblestones the brass band was playing gamely and a damp Father Christmas wandered around trying to inject a bit of festive spirit into the proceedings. Considering the awful weather a surprising number of spectators had braved the elements and they stood about patiently under streaming umbrellas.

'I think we'd better get on with it, don't you?' I asked the mayor.

So after a very few words I pulled the lever mounted on a box in front of me and bright fairy lights sprang out all over the centre of Halifax. Despite the weather it was a terrific thrill. I've always wanted to switch on the Christmas lights and in Halifax I had my big chance – although I must say I've got a suspicion that it wasn't me who actually activated the current. When I threw that switch there was a little pause, someone waved to someone else and then the lights came on! But why quibble, it was much more exciting than plugging in the Christmas tree lights at home.

I must say though that on such a night you couldn't exactly get carried away with the glamour of it all. Afterwards I noticed a mother standing there with her two children, one in a pushchair and the other standing next to her with water pouring all down his face.

'Hello Auntie Doris,' they chirped looking like a pair of swimmers emerged from the deep end.

Bless their hearts, I thought, and searched in my bag for some pound coins.

'Doris, can you do an interview now?'

It was a radio reporter, with all the equipment but nowhere to use it.

'Well I really don't want to stand out here in the rain, love,' I explained.

We looked around for somewhere dry and ended up doing the interview in the toilet!

Halifax was particularly memorable, not only because I switched on the lights but because I stepped straight into a controversy.

Christmas '85 was one of my busiest ever. My last book *Whispering Voices* was published at the beginning of December and suddenly I was plunged into a whirl of theatre appearances, interviews and events. Halifax was just one stop on my tour but while I was there I was honoured to be invited to switch on the lights.

It seemed a harmless enough invitation but it apparently infuriated the local Pentecostal church, which didn't think I should have anything to do with the lights, the theatre, or Halifax for that matter.

There were angry quotes in the local papers but I didn't fully realise what was going on because I don't have time to study papers when I'm travelling. It only began to dawn on me when I arrived at the theatre to find a great bustle going on. There were people queuing for tickets, people queuing to get in and people wandering amongst them handing out pamphlets.

We were actually making our way round to the stage door when I noticed one particular man who had a lady pushed against the railings and was waving a leaflet at her.

'Laurie, what on earth's that man doing?' I asked. 'Stop a minute, I want to talk to him.'

Laurie stopped the car and wound down the window.

'Will you excuse me, I want to go in,' we heard the woman protesting.

'You mustn't go in,' the man was telling her vehemently. 'You must not go in there. It's evil.'

'Excuse me, love,' I called sweetly. 'D'you think I could have one of those pamphlets?'

The man turned immediately. 'Certainly madam,' he said passing a leaflet through the window as if glad to find someone with a bit of sense. 'I hope you're not going to go in there.'

'It'll be hard cheese if I don't, love. My name is Doris Stokes and it's me they're waiting for.'

For a split second he looked stunned, then he recovered quickly.

'I've been waiting to have words with you,' he said eagerly. 'Do you know that you're the tool of the devil?'

He gave me the usual tirade that I've heard a hundred times before, but he wasn't allowed to finish. People standing close by heard what was going on and tried to push him away from the car.

'Don't listen to him Doris, we love you,' they cried and one woman turned on him furiously.

'Now you listen to me,' she shouted. 'The church has done nothing for me and I've come here as a last resort to see if I can get some comfort. So don't you start about the church. The church hasn't helped me.'

I didn't need to say a word in my own defence, the crowd did it for me. It was marvellous but Laurie was getting anxious.

'Come on, love, we must go or you won't be ready in time,' he said.

'There's 50,000 people around the world praying against you tonight,' yelled the leaflet man as a parting shot.

'If you were a Christian you'd be praying *for* me,' I said as the window rolled up and we moved off to the stage door.

'I can't understand it,' I said to Laurie and John, 'I don't interfere with their churches or decry their religion, so why do they interfere with me? And if they've got something so wonderful, why aren't the people queuing to get into their churches?'

Fortunately the disturbance didn't affect the demonstration and I was specially glad when one of the women who'd defended me so stoutly got a message from her little girl on the other side.

I don't want to give the impression that I cause chaos wherever I go but there had been noisy scenes a few days before when I visited Leeds. I was doing a book-signing in a big store in the city. It was a huge place on a corner and as we drew up I could hear the sound of chanting. The pavement was packed with people and they were holding a big black strip on which was written in luminous print: 'I'm back by public demand!' They waved this home-made banner in the air and chanted 'Doris Stokes! Doris Stokes!'

It made me feel like a pop star.

We went into the shop, the doors opened and soon the queue stretched right round the block. How my arm ached after that session but it was nice to meet such lovely people. As we left they were back on the pavement waving their banner.

'See you in Manchester!' they shouted as the car pulled away. And sure enough they turned up in Manchester a few days later.

One of the nicest things about my trip to Manchester was meeting Julie Goodyear face to face for the first time. Julie Goodyear of course is the actress who plays Bet Lynch in *Coronation Street* and we've been friends for ages, but all our conversations have taken place on the telephone. Somehow, until last Christmas our schedules had never allowed us both to be in the same place at the same time, but at last we were able to manage it.

Laurie had booked John and I into Manchester's Piccadilly Hotel and it was arranged that Julie would come over and join us for dinner on the Saturday night. Saturday night was about the only good night for going out because she didn't have to work the next day.

I was looking forward to it immensely but unfortunately by Saturday evening I wasn't feeling too well. I'd caught a slight chill from getting so wet in Halifax and my mastectomy scar had swollen up. I was sore and uncomfortable and couldn't stand anything tight across my chest. The thought of sitting for an hour or two in the restaurant in smart clothes was unbearable.

'Oh dear, Laurie, what am I going to do?' I moaned. 'I can't call the whole thing off now but I just can't face going down there like this.'

'Don't worry, love, it's not the end of the world. You can have dinner sent up here. Julie won't mind.'

So Laurie got on the phone to the restaurant and I went and changed into my best satin nightie and negligee. Loose nightclothes were the only garments that felt comfortable. I was glad I'd treated myself to a couple of glamorous sets. I mean you can't entertain the stars in an old plaid dressing gown and carpet slippers can you!

I was just combing my hair when the telephone rang. It was the receptionist from the front hall.

'Mrs Stokes? I've got a Miss Goodyear for you.'

'It's all right, I'll go and fetch her,' said Laurie, 'and I'll explain about dinner.'

Good old Laurie. John and I had a quick bustle round the room, tidying magazines and straightening cushions. We'd just about finished when the door opened and in walked Julie Goodyear.

I did a double take. I'd only ever seen her on television as the flamboyantly dressed Bet Lynch, and out of character I wouldn't have recognised her. Her long blonde hair, worn piled on her head on screen, hung loose round her shoulders and she was wearing a very demure dress in black and white floaty material with a big white collar instead of one of Bet's plunging necklines. She looked slim and elegant and anyone less like Bet Lynch would have been hard to imagine.

Then she opened her mouth and the old familiar voice came out, 'Eee love! It's grand to see yer!' and she put her arms round me and gave me a big hug. She did the same to John and the ice was broken. Underneath that cool chic exterior was the same old Julie I'd chuckled with many a time on the phone.

Laurie was right of course. Julie didn't mind a bit about cancelling our table in the restaurant and the dinner was a great success. Normally when you order meals from room service in a hotel, everything you order is brought on one tray and you're left to get on with it. But this time the management realised it was a special occasion. They laid on a waiter and waitress just for us and every course was served separately. It was like being in our own private restaurant.

The food was very good and it was a marvellous evening. We laughed and laughed. I haven't laughed so much in a long time and it did me the world of good.

Julie had arrived at 8.30 in the evening and we were enjoying ourselves so much she didn't leave until 3 am. She's so witty she kept us in stitches and we can't wait until we get another free night so that we can do it all over again.

My appearance at Manchester's Free Trade Hall wasn't nearly so successful. The crowds were very kind and many people wrote to me afterwards to say how much they enjoyed the evening but as far as I was concerned I made a right mess of it. It brought home to me the fact that I'm not as young as I used to be and that it's pointless to attempt too much. Rest is vital to me.

The problem was that terrible wet night in Halifax. We were due to drive on to Manchester immediately after the switching on of the lights ceremony. This would give me the whole of the next day to rest before my demonstration in the evening.

Unfortunately we changed our plans. We were staying at a very comfortable hotel in Halifax. Holesworth Hall is a lovely old country house set in its own grounds with olde worlde furnishings and an atmosphere of peace. Anyway after the lights ceremony I was damp, chilled to the bone and feeling very tired. The last thing I wanted to do was climb back in the car and drive for miles and miles through the torrential rain. I longed for my cosy room at Holesworth Hall.

'Quite honestly all I want to do now is crawl into bed,' I said to John and Laurie as we squelched back to the car.

'I'm glad you said that,' said Laurie sounding relieved, 'because I'm not sure of the route and I really don't feel like driving on a night like this. It's bad enough trying to see out of the windscreen without having to watch for road signs as well.'

Even John who is easy going and doesn't mind what we do as long as everyone's happy, admitted that he too felt like an early night.

That settled it. We abandoned the journey to Manchester and went back to Holesworth Hall.

Our unexpected return put the staff in a bit of a tizz.

'Oh no you couldn't possibly have your old rooms back,' they said. 'They haven't been serviced yet.'

We didn't mind we assured them, but the management did. New rooms had to be found for us to move into but it didn't take long and as we relaxed with a cup of tea by the fire listening to the rain pattering down outside we told each other we'd made the right decision.

The next day I wasn't so sure. By the time we'd packed up, travelled and unpacked again the other end, most of my rest day had gone. There wasn't even time for a nap before getting ready for the theatre.

Oh well, I told myself optimistically, I'll get through it somehow, and I suppose I did, after a fashion, but the whole thing was a nightmare.

I started off well enough, but then half way through I lost control. Names were pouring in from different directions so fast that I couldn't make out which part of the hall they were intended for. I struggled very hard to make sense of it but the audience, in their eagerness to help, made things worse. Usually I hear a name, then I have a moment or two to concentrate on that voice and I get one or two other details to go with it. That night in Manchester I was slow to pick up and the audience unusually fast.

'I've got a Margaret here,' I said and just as I was asking Margaret who she wanted to speak to, half a dozen members of the audience started shouting and waving.

'Here Doris, here! That's my mum.'

'No here Doris! It's my Auntie Margaret.'

'No it's my *sister* Margaret.'

And so on until my head was spinning. Margaret herself was drowned out in the din before she'd had a chance to explain which Margaret she was and other spirit voices poured into the vacuum.

Finally in desperation I called on Ramanov to come to my rescue and together we managed to sort it out. The correct recipients were found in the end but it was a worrying experience.

I apologised to the audience and vowed that never again would I take on two consecutive engagements, unless it was absolutely vital. My power is just like a car battery. If a car battery runs down the car won't work and so it is with me. I must have time to recharge my battery.

December continued busier than ever but it wasn't all work. On December 20th the Spirit of Love Bus was finally ready for the official presentation and Laurie, John and I went along for the ceremony in Tavistock Square, London.

We drove through the archway into the courtyard where the proceedings were to take place and there in all its glory stood the bus. It was lovely. Pale blue and beautifully painted, the words 'The Spirit of Love' stood out like a beacon along the side. On a dull winter's day it was a ray of sunshine and I was filled with pride at my achievement.

The special lift was down and a group of people were clustered round admiring it. The big-wigs from the PHAB organisation were there, along with the kids in their wheelchairs and Baroness Trumpington who was going to receive the bus on behalf of PHAB.

It was wonderful for me to see at long last the end result of all that hard work, but I think it was the kids who had the most fun that day. They wheeled their wheelchairs onto the lifts and rode up and down and back again. Within minutes they knew how to operate it better than the driver did.

Baroness Trumpington was very kind and gracious and she told me how marvellous she thought it was that someone as old as me should be involved in this way. I wasn't quite sure how to take that but I know she meant it kindly so I decided to be flattered.

After the presentation we went upstairs where they'd laid on a buffet of smoked salmon and wine. John and I exchanged glances because we don't really go in for fancy food, but one of the PHAB people noticed it and laughed.

'Now come on Doris,' he said, 'we know you only have a cup of tea normally but do try. It's a special occasion.'

So we did our best and it was very nice. The only thing I regretted was that I couldn't mingle with all the people. Since my stroke last year I've found I can't stand on my feet for very long and at these sort of dos I have to sit at the side and watch it going on instead of walking round and talking to everybody.

At around the same time as the PHAB presentation came one of the nicest events of my year, The Woman's Own Children of Courage Awards at Westminster Abbey.

Apparently they've been holding these awards since 1975 when Mrs Mary Wilson presented the ten children judged to be the most courageous kids of the year with a special trophy. Over the years it's become more and more of a star studded occasion. At first the presentations were made by people with a political association like Mary Wilson, Audrey Callaghan and Margaret Thatcher. Then gradually a royal flavour crept in. Princess Alexandra, Princess Michael of Kent, Princess Anne and The Queen Mother made the presentations backed up by as many celebrities as could make it on the day.

But no matter how famous the names, nothing can steal the limelight from those ten brave little kids. They are the true stars of the occasion.

Call me soppy if you like but there's something about that day – the abbey all decorated for Christmas, the sweet sounds of the carols and those special children all dressed up in their best, their eyes shining with excitement – that never fails to bring a lump to my throat and I wouldn't miss it for the world.

This particular year the ceremony was even more thrilling than usual because Princess Diana was presenting the awards. I have to admit that I'm an unashamed royalist and like a lot of other people there I was dying to see Princess Diana close up. All the celebrities were milling around. There was Ernie Wise and Peter Bowles, Shakin' Stevens and his wife who was expecting a baby in January. There was Su Pollard in all the colours of the rainbow, Claire Rayner and Lenny Henry, Rod Hull and the uncontrollable Emu (a great favourite with the kids), Dennis Waterman and Rula Lenska – oh and so many famous people it was very difficult not to stare.

Yet no matter how well known and famous the guests,

everything stopped for the Princess of Wales. She outshone the lot of them.

When she walked in there was a sort of gasp. She looked absolutely breathtaking, and goodness me how slim that child is! She was wearing a violet suit with a fitted jacket, padded shoulders and puffed sleeves and a neat little pillbox hat to match. The deep colour emphasised the blue of her eyes and the fairness of her hair and she looked truly beautiful.

What's more she really is as marvellous with children as the papers say she is. You only had to watch her with those little ones for five minutes to see that it was true.

Quite spontaneously she picked up the smallest of the children, four-year-old Jamie Gavin, a tiny little mite and the youngest person to have undergone a heart and lung transplant, and she held him in her arms as naturally as if he'd been one of her own sons.

The atmosphere was terrific and those kids, well they were an example to us all. There was Sulas Kulkarni, a boy who'd gone blind at the age of seven, yet he played football, swam and went on a 700-mile bike ride to raise money for his school. There was Jodie Woodward who was shot in the face by a mad gunman and subsequently lost an eye. There was Sharon Allen, a leukaemia sufferer, and Sean Hedger who was only eight yet had saved his friend's life when the boy had fallen onto a live railway track. Then there was Joanne Baron who saved an old man from that terrible fire at Bradford Football Club when the spectators' stand went up in flames in minutes, Julie Malton who saved a friend from injury during a terrorist attack in Greece, Darren Durn who defied a gunman and ran for the police when the robber held up his mother's baker's shop and poor little Samuel Heenan from Northern Ireland who lost his mother from a stroke and then saw his father murdered before his eyes outside their farm-house.

The most moving moment came when Steven Clarke, a tiny six-year-old with brittle bone disease, received his award from Princess Diana. He'd suffered over thirty fractures in his frail little legs and he hardly dared move in case he should fall and break another bone, yet he was determined to walk to the Princess. There he sat in his wheelchair, smart in a miniature suit and bow tie, with callipers on his legs, waiting patiently. Then when it was his turn he pushed himself out of that chair and slowly and painfully, each callipered leg an effort to lift, he walked the few yards to Princess Diana. It was the greatest distance he'd ever covered in his life.

'Well done Steven, well done,' said Princess Diana, her voice full of emotion and I found that tears were pouring down my face. I looked across at editor Iris Burton's aunt who was sitting next to me and she was crying too. It was one of the bravest things I've ever seen.

Afterwards talking to Ernie Wise I said, 'It makes you ashamed the way we moan and carry on about the least little cold, doesn't it? Here are these kids cheerfully accepting pain and operations and goodness knows what terrible things. They can teach us a lesson any day.'

I went home reminded once more that we should be thankful for every day that comes along and so what if we've got a cold or a bad back? We don't have to make everyone else miserable too. It's a difficult lesson to learn and I'm as guilty as the next person about forgetting it. I seem to suffer from all sorts of aches and pains these days, I catch every bug that's going and I'm ashamed to say that there are times when I'm low when I moan about it. I whine on to John or Laurie or anyone who'll listen as if no-one else has ever had flu before. Then something like the Children of Courage

Awards comes along or I meet some brave soul in the terminal stages of cancer and I'm brought up sharp. I'm glad Ramanov sends me so many reminders because I certainly need them!

I was very glad to get back home after dashing about the country for weeks, but it was only days to go until Christmas and once again I just didn't feel up to the preparation. I was exhausted. True luxury for me would have been to go to bed until New Year.

Fortunately Patrick, my dear friend who is also a chef, volunteered to cook the Christmas dinner for me on Christmas Eve, just as he'd done last year. It was such a relief. Patrick did the lot and he's such a good cook I didn't have to worry about how it would turn out. I knew it would be delicious.

And what's more, the spirit world had arranged a nice little Christmas present for Pat too. Patrick, who's Irish, lost his mother a few years ago and the previous year when we were setting the table I'd suddenly seen her face in a candle flame. Patrick's hair is darkest brown but his mother had a head of rich red chestnut and as her face swam through the flame, she said, 'Tell Patrick the candles are burning cleanly.'

The candles *were* burning cleanly but the message had a special significance for Pat. Apparently his mother who was a devout and superstitious woman always remarked when the candles were burning well: 'The candles are burning cleanly tonight, the souls are happy in heaven.'

This year as Pat was bustling about the kitchen he was obviously thinking back to 1984 and he went very quiet. I didn't want to intrude on his memories so I silently carried on with the mail. The mail doesn't stop just because it's the festive season. But after a while I sensed there was something else on his mind.

'Doris,' said Pat, coming out of the kitchen at last, 'I know you're very tired and I don't want to get you working but I've been so sad I've been dying to ask you this all day. Where's Mum going to be for Christmas?'

He was right. I was tired and I didn't really feel like doing a sitting but he had been so good to me I couldn't refuse.

I started to tune in when all of a sudden the door to the cupboard under the stairs, which Pat happened to be facing at the time, flew open, even though the catch had been left across, and a shaft of light flashed across the room in the direction of the bathroom.

Pat turned white. 'Doris, what on earth was that?' he asked fearfully.

'That was your answer,' I told him. 'There's no need to be afraid. Your mum's here with you.'

'What's the matter with you now child?' said a soft Irish voice distinctly. 'What's the matter with you now? I'm here when you need me.'

And then her voice drifted away. It was only a tiny episode but it cheered Pat immensely and he rushed off to phone his sister and tell her the news. So there were several happy Christmases going on around the Stokes household that year.

4

John was very upset. He wandered round the house turning out drawers and cupboards, opening bags and envelopes and pulling books off the shelves.

'Whatever's the matter, John?' I asked when I came down from the bedroom and saw what he was doing. 'What have you lost?'

'My healing ring,' said John anxiously. 'It's vanished. I'm sure I didn't take it off anywhere but it's gone.'

John's healing ring, a lovely silver affair set with a turquoise, never leaves his finger and his hand looked quite bare without it.

'Are you sure you didn't take it off in the bathroom?' I asked.

'Positive,' said John.

But I checked the bathroom sink and the kitchen sink to make sure. Nothing. There was no sign of the ring at all. We searched the house from top to bottom, we looked round the garden and in the shed, because John had been doing a bit of gardening the day before, but we didn't find a thing. John was very upset about it. That ring was particularly precious to him.

He'd bought it some years before when we were in

America, on the instructions of his Red Indian healing guide, Red Dawn. Now people are always asking why so many guides are Red Indians. Well they're not always Red Indians of course. Everyone has a spirit guide and they can be from any nationality at all. The one thing they have in common is that they are spiritually advanced and they have volunteered to look after a particular soul as he goes through his earthly life.

I don't pretend to have all the answers but I'm sure a lot of them are Red Indians because the Indians are such a spiritual people. They were probably the first spiritualists. Indians often used to go off on their own into the hills to talk to their spirits – perhaps they still do – so it's not surprising that with such a head start over the rest of us in understanding, so many of them should turn up as guides.

Anyway there we were one afternoon sitting in a traffic jam in New York when my eyes were suddenly drawn to a shop across the road. It was a modern place all black glass and red writing and somehow I couldn't stop staring at it. Strange, I thought, it's not the sort of shop that usually interests me, it didn't have any clothes or attractive furniture in the window, when suddenly Red Dawn's voice interrupted my daydreaming.

I hadn't heard Red Dawn's voice for years, yet I knew it instantly.

'I want John to buy something from that shop,' he said.

That was all, but we knew better than to ignore Red Dawn.

I glanced over at John and noticed that he too seemed transfixed by the same place.

'Red Dawn says you're to buy something from that shop,' I told him.

John didn't seem surprised. It was as if he sensed it too.

'Did he say what I'm to buy?'

'No that's all he said. But I expect you'll know it when you see it.'

The traffic was too bad to allow us to stop just then, so John went back the next day while I was doing some interviews. Apparently it was a Red Indian shop, filled with every touristy Indian item you could think of from full top-to-toe feather head-dresses to tiny silver and turquoise tie-pins. John was a bit taken aback by the sheer quantity of stuff on sale and he wandered round and round examining every single thing carefully because he didn't want to make the wrong choice.

At first, he told me later, he didn't know what to make of it. Then he tried the logical approach. Red Dawn obviously wanted him to have something that he would use regularly and that he could take home on the plane, John reasoned. That ruled out the huge feather head-dresses and the broad collars of brightly coloured beads. He wouldn't get much use out of them in London! It's got to be something small, John said to himself and he looked more closely at the tie-pins but somehow they didn't feel right.

He went round the shop so many times the assistant was getting suspicious and each time he ended up in front of a turquoise and silver ring in a glass case.

That must be it, John thought, and he asked to try it on. It fitted so well it could have been made for him and the minute the ring was on his finger he felt happy. He didn't want to take it off.

Convinced he'd found what Red Dawn wanted him to get, he bought the ring and he's been wearing it ever since, particularly during his healing sessions.

And now it was gone. I know John can be absent-minded at times but he'd never lost that ring before. We did our very best to find it but it was no use. Though we turned the whole place upside down we couldn't find so much as a gleam of silver. I was even beginning to wonder if Boots could have swallowed it.

I don't normally bother the spirit world with trivial things unless there's a very good reason, but John was so distressed I asked if they could help.

'Just this once, could you tell us where John's ring is?' I asked.

The reply was immediate. 'It's by the wall in the garden.'

'John come on, it's in the garden,' I told him.

The only problem was that we've got two walls in the garden, one in the back garden and one in the front. We searched along the back wall first and apart from one of Boots' old toys, we found nothing. Then we examined the front wall and there under a bush against the bricks, lay John's ring. It must have slipped off his finger as he was weeding and he didn't notice it was gone until several hours later.

I must stress that I don't often use the spirit world in this way, but by coincidence I'd called on them for help just a month or so before this episode. For several weeks I'd been suffering from pain at the base of my spine. We all have backache from time to time but instead of getting better with rest, this got worse and worse.

The doctor didn't know what to do with me and I began to fear cancer of the spine. Day by day I grew steadily more uncomfortable until in the end I was literally crying with pain. It felt like red hot pokers being forced up my backbone. What on earth am I going to do? I wailed to myself, I've got a demonstration on Wednesday and I can't do it like this. I can hardly sit down.

In the end, desperate for some relief from the pain, I called on my dad.

'Dad, what on earth am I going to do? I can't go on like this,' I told him. 'What's wrong with me?'

For a moment I thought nothing would happen and then at last I was aware of my father's presence. His love flowed out to me and I heard that dear old voice.

'Don't worry Doll, it's not cancer,' he said. 'You know your coccyx goes into a tail? Well the tail's turned in and it's trapped a nerve.'

'What should I do about it, Dad?' I asked. I couldn't face another operation.

'It's easy,' said Dad, 'and not at all painful. Get yourself a rubber ring and use it whenever you sit down. All you've got to do is lift the weight off the base of your spine and give the nerve a chance to heal.'

I was delighted. John went out and got me a couple of rubber rings. I covered them with pillow cases and put them on my chair in the sitting room and the other on my seat in the car. I even took one to the theatre with me the following week and placed it on my armchair on the stage.

The doctor, bless him, didn't scoff. 'Well your dad could be right,' he said noncommittally, 'it's worth a try. But if it doesn't work I think we'll have to get you into hospital for some tests.'

No fear, I thought silently.

And as if to confirm I was on the right track, a few days later I was clearing out a cupboard and I came across my photograph of Harry Edwards. I hadn't seen the picture for about two years. I knew I hadn't thrown it away but along with a number of other things it had 'gone missing' rather mysteriously when we moved and I was beginning to give up hope of ever seeing it again.

In case you haven't heard of him, Harry Edwards was the

greatest healer I've ever known in my lifetime. He had such faith in what he believed the spirit world wanted him to do that he gave up his job as an insurance man and bought a beautiful mansion in its own grounds to serve as a healing sanctuary. The house cost £8,000, a great deal of money in those days and Harry had only £18 in the bank. Nevertheless he was so convinced that this was what the spirit world wanted him to do that he went ahead.

Donations came in to help him and every time he got desperate, something happened to get him out of the jam. Harry was obviously doing the work God wanted him to do. He never charged a set fee, he simply asked people to give what they could afford.

Harry's healing became famous, people travelled from all over the country to be treated by him and I have particular reason to be grateful to him. Years ago John became ill with cancer of the stomach and the hospital sent him home to die. In desperation I appealed to Harry for help and Harry managed to bring about a cure.

It's not surprising he had a special place in our affections.

Throughout the years Harry sent out little printed postcard pictures of himself with his healing letters, but I was honoured to receive what he called a 'real' picture – a large glossy portrait. I put it in a nice frame and for years it stood on the shelf in my sitting room. Whenever I felt under the weather I looked into Harry's smiling face and asked him to help get me back on my feet. Even when Harry passed over I felt that he was still healing from the other side and the photograph suddenly turning up like that just when I needed a bit of help seemed more than coincidence. As if to confirm it, a few days later I opened a letter to discover that someone had sent me a copy of Harry Edwards' healing prayer.

Harry's picture went back into the sitting room, I put Dad's advice about the rubber ring into practice and soon my back was vastly improved. The doctor had been so concerned about it he'd been on the point of making an appointment for me at the hospital, but now I told him it wouldn't be necessary. With the spirit world's help my back problem was nearly cured.

These incidents may seem trivial in themselves, but they show how close the spirit world is at all times. You don't need flying chairs and dramatic events. The spirit world makes itself known in the smallest ways.

Earlier in the year Laurie asked me what I'd like for my birthday. It's always a difficult question because people are so kind, they give me flowers and little trinkets and bath goodies throughout the year to such an extent that come birthdays and Christmas I can't think of anything I need.

'Oh dear, Laurie,' I said, 'I don't know what to suggest.'

Then suddenly I remembered something. A few years ago I did a sitting for Yolande Finch, the ex-wife of the late Peter Finch, a sitting that was memorable because they actually started having a row through me! Despite this Yolande was very pleased and afterwards she'd had some perfume made up specially for me. Apparently she went to an exclusive shop called Floris where they make perfume, and ordered some.

'Think of apple blossom and fields of buttercups and daisies,' she told them, which I thought was rather lovely.

Anyway the perfume was gorgeous and just before she left to live in California, Yolande gave me some more.

Sadly that was several years ago and I'd long since run out.

'Hang on a minute, I've thought of something,' I said. 'I'd love some more of that perfume Yolande gave me.'

So Laurie went to the shop in Jermyn Street, London but they couldn't find a trace of the order. They checked their files very carefully but there was nothing under Doris Stokes. There was a perfume recipe by Yolande Finch's name so Laurie ordered that. It must be the one, he thought.

I unwrapped the handsome blue box on my birthday and took a long deep sniff of the perfume. Beautiful . . . it was so long since I'd smelled the original I couldn't tell if this was exactly the same but it was lovely anyway.

A few weeks later I woke up suddenly in the middle of the night feeling very hot and restless and found myself facing the mirror doors of the fitted wardrobes. It was still very dark but the light from the street lamps slipped through the curtains and glowed on the surface of the glass. How those doors reflect the light I thought sleepily. Then my eyes opened a little wider.

I could see a face in the mirror and it wasn't my own.

'Oh dear who's that?' I asked.

Very deliberately I closed my eyes, counted to ten and then looked again. The face was still there but more clearly defined now. It was Peter Finch.

'Peter!' I said startled, 'What do *you* want?'

'You haven't got the right perfume you know, darling,' he said in a distant voice.

'But Laurie went to the shop specially.'

'It's the *wrong* perfume,' he insisted and even as he spoke the face faded from the mirror and he was gone.

At that time of night I couldn't care less anyway, so I rolled over and went back to sleep, but when I woke the next morning I tuned in to check. I don't know if it was Peter Finch, or my father who answered my query but once again I caught the words, faintly like an echo . . . 'the wrong perfume . . .'

It was only a trivial matter of course but by now I was

thoroughly intrigued so I rang the shop myself to see if I could get to the bottom of it. Manager Dominic Browne more or less confirmed what Peter Finch had told me.

'No, I'm afraid we couldn't find anything at all for Doris Stokes,' he said and he thought it was very likely that I'd got the perfume Yolande bought for herself.

'But Mrs Stokes,' he went on, 'I'm a great admirer of yours and we would like to make up some perfume specially for you with our compliments and from now on it will be on file so that you can order it whenever you like.'

I was thrilled. It makes you feel really special to have your very own perfume, particularly when you can order all the bits to go with it: the talcum powder and soap, the toilet water and bath oils, all matching.

I discovered that the shop is pretty special too. Apparently it was established in 1730 and it has preserved its genuine old world look. Inside it's all thick red carpet and glossy mahogany. The show cases came from the Great Exhibition at Crystal Palace in the 19th century and the lamp fittings are all solid Victorian brass. Not many shops in London can boast that sort of history.

What's more there's a 'by appointment' sign over the door, so who knows – perhaps Prince Charles buys perfume for the Princess of Wales at Floris, or maybe the Queen Mother pops in for her talcum powder! It makes me feel pretty grand to think we might buy our toiletries from the same shop. Whatever would my old mum have said to think of her little Doll Sutton who thought a box of bath cubes from Woolworth's was the last word in luxury, going shopping in the Royal Family's shop, just up the road from Buckingham Palace?

It brings it home to me just how far I've come from Grantham, that's for sure.

But as I said before, these things are of little importance

in themselves except that they show how close to us the spirit world is at all times. I don't have to do a sitting or a big public demonstration in order to talk to spirit people. They are around us in our daily lives and half the time it's more difficult for me to shut them out for the sake of a little rest than it is to talk to them.

Yet no matter how hard I try to switch off, little bits still come creeping through. One day Patrick brought his friend Tony over to see me and unknown to me Tony was hoping I'd say something about his father. He didn't like to ask because he knew it was my day off but he was hoping just the same.

Of course his father on the other side picked up the signals that Tony was unconsciously sending out and came straight to my sitting room where we were chatting over a cup of coffee.

The first I knew of it was when I heard a persistent voice repeating the name Harry in my ear. I tried to close my mind to him but he was determined and I found my eyes swivelling continuously to Tony even when it was Patrick or Terry or John talking. What's more I was seized with an overpowering urge to sniff. I sniffed a couple of times but the impulse remained as strong as ever.

'What's the matter Doris, have you got a cold?' asked Tony.

I shook my head but I knew when I was beaten.

'Tony,' I said, 'does the name Harry mean anything to you?'

'Yes,' he said, 'that's my father's name.'

'And Pomp, Pom.' What on earth was Harry trying to tell me – it sounded like a pet's name of some sort. 'Pom . . . could that be Pomeroy?'

Tony was delighted. 'That's his second name.'

He was very pleased because it was such an unusual name I'd never have guessed it in a month of Sundays.

'I started him off in his job,' Harry told me proudly.

'Yes he did,' said Tony. 'He took me up for my interview.'

'And I bought him his first typewriter,' said Harry.

'Yes that's right,' said Tony, more and more amazed.

Harry went on to say how proud he was of his son because Tony is now an underwriter at Lloyds. It was only a few words, not a sitting at all really, but it meant a lot to Tony and by the time his father had finished speaking, he was in tears.

These things happen quite spontaneously and sometimes they seem so silly I feel a fool to mention them. He'll think I'm off my trolley if I say that, I think, but as often as not I get no peace until I do and then it turns out that the message was correct after all. Even that compulsive sniffing was wonderful evidence to Tony because his father had suffered from an habitual sniff.

I remember once when I was doing a demonstration in Brighton, Laurie and his wife, Iris, came down to stay for a couple of days. The first morning we decided to have breakfast together in our room and all the time I was getting ready, this tune kept running through my mind.

'I'm Henery the eighth I am, Henery the eighth I am I am . . .' sang this irritating voice over and over as I soaped myself in the bath, and dressed.

Laurie and Iris arrived. The breakfast was brought up and still the tune went on. It got stronger and stronger until I could hardly concentrate on the conversation round the table. Every time I looked at Iris the volume seemed to increase until in the end I thought my head would burst.

'It's no good,' I said laying down my toast. 'Who the hell's Henry? It's been going on ever since I got out of bed this morning: "I'm Henery the eighth I am, Henery the eighth I am I am." It's driving me mad.'

'That's my dad,' said Iris almost dropping her cup in surprise. 'His name was Henry and we were always singing that song to him.'

That's all it was, just a tiny little scrap but Iris' dad had obviously heard she was coming to breakfast and he wanted to let her know that he was close. His 'signature tune' was the best proof he could give her that he was really there.

We had a wonderful time in Brighton. The weather was reasonably warm considering the terrible summer we had last year and it always makes me feel better to be beside the sea. What's more I had a marvellous contact against all the odds during one of my demonstrations.

The evening had been going fairly well and lots of spirit people came back. There was a father who knew that his daughter always had £50 kept by for emergencies, apparently her mother had bought her a £50 ring on the understanding that if she was short of money she could always pawn it. There was a husband who knew that his wife kept his pyjamas under her pillow and touched them for comfort every night before she went to sleep, and there was a particularly tragic case of a poor man who'd walked in front of a train.

'Please forgive me,' he begged his wife, 'I can't really explain. I'd been worried and I'd had words with someone but I don't know what came over me to do a thing like that. After I'd done it I looked down at my body and thought, what have I done to my lovely wife and children?'

He'd left two children, he told me, and his wife, who was a nurse, confirmed this. Then he told me the gruesome details of his injuries, but they were so dreadful I couldn't bring myself to say them aloud.

'Oh dear I can't say that,' I told him. I turned to his wife. 'Look, love, you as a nurse know what happened, don't you?'

'Yes,' she replied. 'I know he was decapitated.'

So it was out. But at least I didn't have to say it and risk upsetting her if she didn't know.

The poor man just wanted to know that his wife forgave him and to make her understand that despite his terrible brainstorm, he loved his family.

There were lighter moments of course. There were grannies who wanted to wish grandchildren a happy birthday and one particular lady who said to her daughter:

'Give my love to Jim although he'll never believe I've been back when you tell him.'

And the recipient laughed because as she said, her husband Jim would never believe it.

Then towards the end of the second half a young man's voice cut in very clearly, drowning all the other clamouring voices.

'I'm looking for my dad. He's called Norman,' he said.

It was so positive that I apologised to the man I was talking to at the microphone who'd been in the middle of a message from his wife, and called out:

'I've got a young man here who's looking for his father, Norman. Have we got a Norman here who's lost a son?'

There was a resounding silence. Then one man stood up.

'I'm Norman,' he said, but he hadn't lost a son. He was hoping for a message from his father.

'No, I'm sorry, love,' I told him. 'This is definitely a boy looking for his father Norman.'

Nothing. No one claimed him.

'I'm sorry, son, he can't be here,' I told the lad. 'Just wait at the side and we'll see what happens.'

The minutes passed and more voices displaced him. Then as always happens towards the end of the evening when I'm getting tired, the power begins to fade and as it ebbed away the voices grew fuzzy. I strained to catch the faint words. It was getting more and more difficult and I glanced across at Tony Ortzen who was taking the chair.

'Not long now,' he mouthed.

Then suddenly the boy came back.

'My mother Barbara's here,' he insisted with unusual clarity at this stage of the proceedings. 'She's sitting over there. Please find her before it's too late.'

He directed my eyes to a bank of seats.

'Is there a Barbara sitting over there?' I asked.

There was a small pause, then a woman stood up. 'Yes I'm Barbara.'

'Come on down then, love,' I told her.

Tony was making signs that I'd have to bring the evening to a close, but somehow I knew it was important to speak to Barbara.

'Do you know Norman?' I asked her.

'Yes,' she said, 'he's my husband but he's gone outside for a smoke.'

'And have you lost a son?'

'Yes we have,' she said.

Thank goodness for that, I'd got the right family. It was difficult to hear what the boy was saying by now but I could just make out something about an accident. He was thrown, he said, and the back of his head and his neck got it.

'He went over very quickly, love,' I said gently. 'He went out and didn't come home again. He was killed.'

Barbara nodded.

'I feel as if he was thrown and the back of his head and neck got it.'

Barbara confirmed that this was true.

Then the boy went on to talk of someone called Anne.

'Anna,' Barbara corrected, 'his sister.'

There was so little power left by now that it was getting

very hard for me to pick up anything at all, but the boy was still struggling to get through. He said something about his father.

'If only Dad could talk about it,' he said, 'if he could have a cry and let it out it would help. And if only they'd get my pictures out.'

I passed this on to Barbara. 'Don't shut him out of your life, love,' I said, 'he's still part of the family. Oh dear he's not been over very long, has he? Less than a year.'

'Only four months,' said Barbara.

Tony Ortzen was making quite urgent signs to me now to wind things up and the power was diminishing by the second but still the boy hung on.

'He hasn't mentioned his other sister,' said Barbara.

Faintly I heard the name Caroline.

'It's not Caroline is it?' I asked.

'Yes that's right!' said Barbara, delighted.

Then there was a stir at the end of the aisle and I saw a compact, stocky man with a sheaf of papers under his arm striding purposefully towards the stage. Such was his air of determination I thought he was about to deliver a writ or something.

'There's Norman!' cried the boy in my ear. 'Come on Dad. I want to tell him I'm here.'

Norman reached us just as the power evaporated altogether. His son only managed to get one last message through to him.

'Dad wears my sweater in the garden.'

Norman was astonished.

'This is incredible,' he said. 'Yes I do wear his sweater in the garden.'

Barbara quickly relayed to him all the things their son had said and Norman looked quite dumbfounded.

'Well if all this is true, I'm staggered,' he muttered.

Afterwards they came forward to talk to me and Norman explained why he hadn't been in the room when the message came through. Apparently ever since their son had been killed in an accident they'd been trying to find proof that he lived on somewhere. Sadly they'd found no evidence at all. Reluctantly Norman had come to my demonstration as a last resort but by the second half he lost patience.

'This is a load of rubbish,' he said in disgust, 'I'm going out for a smoke.' He went outside and paced around the foyer smoking cigarette after cigarette and telling everyone he saw what a load of nonsense it was.

He was gone so long he didn't hear his son calling his name and by the time he got back into the hall the whole thing was nearly over.

Nevertheless Norman was delighted with the evidence that had come through, even though he heard most of it at second hand.

So interested did he become that the following Saturday when we arrived for my next demonstration, we found Norman and his whole family waiting at the stage door.

'You're an amazing lady, Doris,' said Norman. 'It was so good we've decided to come again.'

Sadly their son didn't manage to get through a second time but the family wasn't too disappointed. When we finally emerged from the theatre much later that night, there was Norman waiting to say goodbye.

'I just wanted to give you this, Doris,' he said and he pressed some money into my hand to buy flowers for my spirit children, together with a letter. This is what it said:

Dear Doris,

We were absolutely devastated by Joseph's accident and we decided that we had to consider the possibility that he was not gone forever. As a cynic this contradicts my logical approach to life, but I felt that now was the time to find out once and for all.

My disillusionment increased as I was told by various mediums and clairvoyants that I was enjoying a particularly pleasant and happy period!!

I finally determined to go to the top as a last attempt (your meeting) and then if I could get no confirmation that Joe was still with us, we would drop the quest for all time and seek to repair our shattered lives.

Knowing the great relationship that we had with Joe would, if possible, establish a basis for contact, we willed Joseph to be at your meeting because we were going to attend it as well.

The first half of that evening was hard work for you and as it progressed I began to fear that once again we had achieved nothing – so much so, that I left the hall for a smoke.

That's typical of Joe! He attempted to befuddle your performance and then waited until I had left before he really made known his presence.

We were seeking confirmation that life does not cease at death. You do not know us and had never met us until last Thursday. You had no association nor any information about us from any source whatsoever. You could have received nothing from us mentally – I was not even in the hall, yet you told us precisely, when Joe contacted, that:

1. He asked for Norman (that's me – his father).
2. After some time he asked for Barbara (his mother).
3. He named Anna (not Anne) his sister.
4. He named Caroline, his other sister.
5. His main injury was to his neck (broken) by going forward.
6. He went out and did not come back.
7. He asked us to replace photographs that we had put away.
8. He was fond of himself (yes, he believed he was God's gift to Sussex).
9. He now had lots to do – intended to travel, 'And it will not cost you a penny'.

Throughout his life I had always begrudged him spending and never ever paid him cash for his work and efforts.

You conveyed nothing that was evasive – we carefully (unkindly) gave you no prompting.

We are now in no doubt that Joseph lives and we can resolve our sadness and despair knowing that in due course we shall walk along the road again with him beside us.

I thank you Doris for all of us – myself, Norman, his mother Barbara and sisters Anna and Caroline and of course Joseph.

I hope we shall see you again but being aware of your commitments it may have to wait until we all pass over.

Don't forget – the invitation stands – cup of tea, a smoke and a nice chat, *wherever*.

Our kindest thoughts for all time.

Norman Knight

5

I finished my last book, *Whispering Voices*, from my hospital bed, propped up against the pillows or sitting in the armchair beside the window looking down at London rushing past below, and playing music on my tape recorder for inspiration. It was an odd ending to a book I suppose, and since then a lot of people have written expressing concern, so I'd just like to say I'm much better now thank you.

The problem was a slight stroke. It came on one evening as I was watching television.

Strange really because the book was practically finished, I had my presentation to Princess Anne to look forward to and everything was going well. But that day, when I should have been full of energy and celebrating the end of months of work, I felt distinctly peculiar. I was so tired I could have gone back to bed for a sleep almost from the moment I got up.

Don't be so lazy Doris, I told myself. You can't lie in bed all day. And I forced myself to get on with the chores.

By evening I was more tired than ever with a nagging headache, but an hour or two relaxing in front of the television would soon put me right, I thought. I reached out to glance through the *TV Times*.

'You know I think that film we wanted is on the other side,' I said to John. At least that's what I tried to say to John.

'You what, love?'

'That ffff . . . ffff film wwwwww . . . w.' I stopped. It felt as if I was trying to speak through a mouthful of glue.

'What's the matter, love, is something wrong?' John was trying not to look alarmed, but suddenly I was pretty alarmed myself. The whole of my right side had gone strangely heavy and I could hardly lift my right arm from the chair.

'I th-th-th-think yyy . . . yy.' I was trying to tell him that he'd better call the doctor but I couldn't get the words out. It didn't matter, John was at the phone and dialling the number even as I stuttered.

Fortunately I have a marvellous doctor and he lives close by. He arrived at the house in minutes.

'Well Doris,' he said once he'd given me an examination and got me to bed, 'I think you've had a slight stroke. I want you in hospital right away.'

I was horrified. I was being presented to Princess Anne the next day, 'but ddd . . . ddd.'

John interrupted, 'She doesn't want to miss Princess Anne,' he explained.

Some doctors might have been difficult but my doctor has always been marvellous and well understands the importance of morale boosters to general well-being. He agreed that since I could more or less stand upright and since the presentation was taking place in a hospital, the outing would probably do me more good than harm. Afterwards however I must go straight into hospital.

It was a deal!

The day was exhausting of course but as I described in my

last book, I enjoyed it immensely and afterwards I went into hospital with no complaints. But if I thought I was going to have a rest in hospital, it just shows how wrong a medium can be.

First of all I had to go for brain scans. Terry had had a brain scan after his head injury and when I told him on the phone one day that I was to have one too, he frightened the life out of me.

'Oh it's dreadful,' he said, 'You feel as if your head is going to burst. It's terrible. You're clamped into this headrest and you have to keep absolutely still. You can't move a muscle. It's awful.'

He frightened me so much that I got myself into a state and I thought, I'm not going to have it done. They can't make me. I'll refuse. I knew I wasn't being sensible of course and as an ex-nurse I should have known better, but I suppose I wasn't well and I was feeling over emotional. Fortunately a kind male nurse named Tim came to my rescue. I told him of my fears and he was very sweet.

'I'm sure it's not that bad Doris,' he said, 'but I'll ask sister if I can come with you.'

Sister must have agreed because Tim came with me and held my hand throughout the whole operation. The rays were coming down but Tim never left my side. And I discovered the brain scan wasn't nearly as bad as Terry had led me to believe. I suppose he was so ill when he'd had his that it seemed dreadful to him, but in fact I've had far worse tests in hospitals than that.

The brain scan was only the beginning, of course. My leg dragged and my right arm was pretty useless and I was put on physiotherapy twice a day, including Saturday and Sunday, to get my muscles working again. They worked me very hard but I didn't mind. I was determined to overcome this stroke.

When I got back to my room after physio I sang along to the radio to help my speech and I sat for hours, flexing my fingers and then making a fist with my right hand and twirling my right foot and lifting my leg.

'You won't catch me walking with a stick,' I said as my joints ached, and I ran through all the exercises again.

It was frustrating at times of course. I wouldn't let anyone cut up my food for me as if I was a baby, so I struggled for ages with pieces of meat and as often as not the meal was stone cold by the time I got it to my mouth.

My speech was still infuriatingly slow and well-meaning visitors kept trying to help me out by finishing sentences for me – often with the wrong words.

'No, no,' I'd splutter, 'that's nnnnnn not w . . . w . . . what I m-m-meant . . .' and I'd have to start all over again.

Nevertheless I was improving every day and the flowers and cards that arrived constantly cheered me up no end.

One Sunday morning I went down to physio at 10.00 for my first hour of exercises. Thirty minutes into the session I was laid out on the table kicking my legs, when suddenly a porter came in.

'You have a visitor, Mrs Stokes,' he said.

There was something about the look in his eye, a kind of suppressed excitement, that made me say, 'Is it Freddie Starr?'

'Yes,' he said, a bit miffed that I'd spoiled his surprise.

'Oh well, could you ask them to give him a cup of coffee because I haven't finished yet.'

'Don't worry, Doris,' laughed the physiotherapist, 'I'll let you off just this once,' and she helped me down from the table.

'I'll take her back,' said the porter.

'No, *I'll* take her back,' said the physiotherapist and I had to hide a smile because they both wanted to meet Freddie Starr.

In the end they both came up in the lift with me and as we approached my room I found we were trailing a line of nurses as well. The whole pack of us squeezed into the room and there was Freddie looking as freshly scrubbed and bright-eyed as a choirboy.

'I've asked them for some toast and coffee,' said Freddie after giving me a big hug, 'because I came out without any breakfast. Not for anyone else would I get up at this time on a Sunday morning when I'm not working.'

Freddie and I have been friends ever since I did a sitting for him and gave him messages from his old mates Alan Lake and Diana Dors. I've seen the loving, serious side of Freddie but I also know his sense of humour so I wasn't at all surprised when he suddenly walked around the bed, turned back the covers, undid his belt and started to drop his trousers.

The nurses stared at him in amazement, which is just what Freddie wanted.

'What are you looking at?' he asked innocently. 'I'm going to take Doris to bed and give her a cuddle and I'll do more good in five minutes than you can do in ten days!'

He was only joking of course but he was right in one way. That visit from Freddie was a real tonic and probably did me more good than a whole bucket of medicine.

Soon I felt so improved I was pestering the doctor to let me go home. It was particularly important because I'd promised Jimmy Young that I'd appear on his new TV current affairs show and I was determined not to let him down.

Reluctantly the doctors agreed that I could leave on

Thursday. This was cutting it a bit fine because the show was being recorded on the Friday, but I knew I could make it.

Anxiously the producer phoned me.

'Don't worry,' I told him from my hospital bed, 'I'll be there.'

Shortly afterwards Jimmy Young himself phoned.

'Jimmy, I promise you I'll be there in the studio tomorrow night,' I assured him.

'But Doris you're still in hospital.'

'I know but I'm going home tonight and I promise you I'll be there.'

'Well we'll have a nurse waiting for you and a room for you to rest in,' said Jimmy because he's a thoughtful man.

'That's marvellous,' I said, 'see you tomorrow.'

Yet even as he put the phone down, I'll swear, he wasn't convinced.

The next day, as promised, I got myself on the train for Leeds. To be honest I was feeling a bit grey and fluttery and very tired, but I'd recovered pretty well. My speech was almost back to normal, my arm was pretty good and the worst problem with my leg was that it had spells of shaking uncontrollably. It still does I'm sorry to say but I've had to learn to live with it. I simply warn people that it's not a sign I'm about to go into a trance or do something spooky and then I tuck it under my chair as far out of sight as possible. It's a nuisance but I know I can count myself lucky. Some people are paralysed after a stroke. At least I can get about almost as well as before.

Anyway when I got to Leeds I was whisked to the Queens Hotel where the programme was being recorded and sure enough, there was a nurse and a comfortable room waiting for me.

Jimmy and the producer were very good. They needed

to talk about the show but instead of asking me down to the studio they came to my room to avoid putting any strain on me.

'We won't take you onto the set until the moment we need you,' they promised. 'The air conditioning's broken down and it's like an oven out there.'

There was just time for a rest, then I diddled myself up as best I could and went downstairs. I was looking dreadfully pale and drawn but it couldn't be helped. At least I kept my promise to Jimmy.

It was an interesting show. Jimmy wanted to discuss the question, 'Is there life after death?' I was there of course to argue that there was. Claire Rayner was there to disagree and there was a studio audience with a wide range of differing views.

Claire doesn't believe in what I do at all but she's always very sweet to me. She kept saying:

'Doris bless her this . . .' and 'Doris bless her that . . .' but we had some heated discussions all the same and despite the fact that she's opposed to me, she is always very fair.

At the end of the debate she said, 'It doesn't matter if we stayed here till midnight, there'll always be some that believe and some that don't,' and of course she was absolutely right.

What I like about Claire is that although she doesn't agree with me, she respects my point of view and she's never abusive. When we meet she's always polite and friendly and just as she respects my opinions, so I respect hers. I can't understand why so many people fall out over differing beliefs, there is really no need for it at all.

Isn't it funny how, when you come out of hospital, you discover that you're not quite as well as you thought you were when you were in there demanding to be allowed out?

I'd been fighting like mad to go home because I felt so

much better but that appearance on the *Jimmy Young Show* made me realise that I wasn't as strong as I'd thought. The discussion lasted only half an hour but by the end of it I was shattered.

'Right,' said my doctor the next day, 'no more work. You're to have a complete rest.'

And so I spent the next few weeks pottering about at home and concentrating on my exercises. The physiotherapist had been very strict about that.

'You must maintain your progress,' she'd said. So I bought an exercise bike and every morning to this day I cycle a few miles to get my bad leg working.

But I can't stand being idle for long. The letters were piling up and we had so many requests for demonstrations that as soon as I was well enough, Laurie booked one or two theatre dates, widely spaced so that I'd get a good rest in between. And around this time I met an old lady who really put me to shame.

One morning I opened a letter from a woman in Sussex. Her aunt was coming up to her hundredth birthday, she explained, and her dearest wish was to meet me. Was there any chance that something could be arranged?

I was touched. Fancy an old lady like that wanting to meet me, I thought, so I rang her up for a chat.

Maudie Smith was amazing. A little bit deaf but sharp as a razor. No sitting nodding off in rocking chairs for her. She was still active, alert and full of fun. I did the tiniest of sittings over the phone and got a few scraps from her husband Charlie who sent his love, and also from her grandchild who'd been tragically killed. Maudie had been very disappointed about her husband Charlie. Apparently she'd intended him to live to be one hundred too, but he'd only made it to ninety-five, and she was obliged to get on with the centenary celebrations on her own. Nevertheless she forgave him his lack of willpower and was glad to know that even if he couldn't be there in body, he'd attend her party in spirit.

As it happened, the following week I had a demonstration at the London Palladium.

'Wouldn't it be lovely, Laurie, if we could get Maudie along,' I said. 'I'm sure she'd be thrilled to see the Palladium.'

So Laurie rustled up a couple of tickets from somewhere and we sent a chauffeur-driven car to collect Maudie from her home in Worcestershire. It was too far for an old lady to travel to London and back in one day so we put her and her son Chester up in a smart London hotel for the night.

Maudie was a walking wonder. Neatly turned out with her hair freshly done she was full of bounce and energy. The day before she'd been busy mowing her lawn she told me.

'Well it grows so fast in the summer doesn't it?' she remarked.

She would have been pretty good for seventy, let alone one hundred!

Unfortunately Maudie's Charlie didn't get a look in that night at the Palladium but it was an interesting evening for her nevertheless.

There was a man called Walter who'd had cancer of the bowel and he wouldn't go away. He kept popping up in the middle of everyone else's messages.

'I've come to see my baby,' he told me, wagging his finger in my face, 'and I'm not going till I've spoken to her.'

Fortunately his daughter came forward to claim him after a while and Walter was content to pass on a few messages and wish happy birthday to his two grandsons who were both celebrating birthdays within weeks of each other. This done he went on his way and allowed other people to have their say.

There were two other tragic young men who'd committed suicide, one of them by stepping in front of a train, and there was one lovely married couple – Jack and Margaret I think they were called – who came back together to talk to their daughter.

'They're giving me the name Janet,' I said.

'That's me,' said the girl.

A moment or two later came the surname Bennet.

'Yes I'm Janet Bennet,' she gasped, torn between smiles and tears.

'She was upset because she didn't say goodbye to me,' Janet's mother told me and as she came close I felt a pain in my chest.

'Did your mother have heart trouble?' I asked Janet.

'Yes she'd suffered from heart trouble for quite a while, then she had an accident and a cardiac arrest.'

'I would have been a cabbage if I'd lived,' said Margaret. 'It was so stupid. I didn't even get across the road.'

Then she said something I couldn't quite catch. I could only make out the word 'bank'.

'She's saying something about a bank, Janet,' I explained. 'Do you live near a bank?'

'No, but she had the accident outside the bank.'

'And she says she only had about £200 to leave.'

'Yes that's right.'

Margaret went on to talk of Janet's husband Steven and her son Rob. She asked for some flowers for Janet because her wedding anniversary was coming up.

'Next month,' said Janet in delight.

And she knew about the car they'd recently bought.

'You know what, you don't have to wind the windows down, you just press a button and they go up and down by themselves.' Margaret was highly impressed.

By now Janet was giggling happily. 'Yes the new car's got electric windows,' she confirmed.

And so it went on and on. After the intermission, Tony Ortzen called Maudie onto that famous stage where we presented her with a big bouquet of flowers and a framed photograph from the new book. The entire audience, hundreds and hundreds of them lining the plush red balconies, sang Happy Birthday. It was a wonderful moment and I believe Maudie had the time of her life.

Afterwards she wrote me a lovely letter. She had had a marvellous birthday, she explained, she'd heard from the Queen and Margaret Thatcher and the whole village had organised a special party for her, but the best part of all was coming to the Palladium. Apparently she hasn't stopped talking about it since.

As usual, during that Palladium demonstration, there were several names and messages that fell on stony ground. No one claimed them from the audience and I, along with most people present, had to assume that I'd made a mistake. I am only human after all and I do get things wrong. But not long ago we heard from a woman who'd attended a Palladium demonstration shortly after Maudie's and she was able to throw some interesting light on the subject of unclaimed messages.

I'll let Mrs Howlett from Essex explain for herself what happened:

I lost my husband last year from cancer of the bowel and I went to the Palladium with my daughter Lorraine, more for her sake than anything. I thought it was a load of rubbish. I would have liked to believe it but I couldn't. Yet I was half hoping that Doris would convince me all the same.

Anyway we sat there through the first half and all

these messages were coming through and it was amazing. But I couldn't believe it.

'It must be a set up,' I said during the interval. 'She must know these people. They must have arranged it beforehand.'

I was going on like that when the man behind me tapped me on the shoulder.

'What are you taking that seat up for if that's how you feel,' he said. 'If you don't believe her after what you've seen you'll never believe anything.'

'Look I'm sorry but I won't believe it till she says something to me,' I told him.

After the interval there was question time and then Doris started the messages again.

'I've got a man here who passed with cancer of the bowel and he's asking for Laurie,' she said, and as she spoke she was tapping the side of her chair and rubbing her stomach, just like George used to do towards the end when he was in pain.

At first Doris thought she wanted a boy called Laurie but then she said, 'No, it's a girl's name.'

George always called Lorraine 'Lorri' but neither of us moved.

'He's talking about Annie Winifred,' Doris went on. Annie Winifred was my sister-in-law who died a few years ago.

Then Doris mentioned Rosie or Rosine. Well George's sister is called Rose.

'And he's looking for someone whose name ends in "een".' Doris said, 'I couldn't catch the beginning, it could have been Cathleen, Eileen, een, een. No, sorry, I missed it.'

My name's Gwendoline. She also mentioned baby

Peter who'd been born after he passed. Our Peter was born six weeks after George died. And finally she said she was getting the number 14 very strongly. Well I live at number 14, my daughter lives at number 14 and my other daughter lives at 194 and if you add those numbers together it comes to 14.

'That's Dad,' said Lorraine and she was in tears. 'Come on Mum, let's go down.'

But I couldn't move. I felt completely numb, so Lorraine went down by herself. Unfortunately by the time she got to the front, a big family who took up practically the whole of the first row had got a message and they spent so long at the microphone that when Lorraine eventually got there Doris had lost contact with my husband.

She was very disappointed but I must admit the messages we did get amazed me. I hardly said a word all the way home. There's no way Doris could have known all those things. She'd never seen or heard from me. I'd never even written her a letter. I only went to please my daughter.

Now I wish I'd got up when she first mentioned my husband but I was too shocked to move.

I think Gwendoline's story must be the tip of the iceberg as far as unclaimed messages go. Of course I do get things wrong now and then, it would be dishonest to pretend I didn't, but just as often, I believe, I'm right and people are too shy or stunned to come forward. It's such a pity when you think of all the effort their spirit people have made to contact them – in vain. And it seems that Gwen's husband has been trying to let her know that he's all right almost from the day he went over.

'Yes some strange things have happened,' said Gwen. 'They're only little things but important to me. The day George died, the vicar came round and asked what hymns we would like at the funeral. Now George liked to get up and sing when he'd had a few drinks at the pub and he always rounded off his songs with *You'll Never Walk Alone*. It was like his signature tune, so after I'd chosen a couple of hymns I asked for this song but the vicar advised against it. It wasn't a proper hymn, he said, and since there were going to be so many of George's friends there he felt it would be too emotional.

'Anyway the funeral was in the morning and afterwards I just left the house as it was and went to my daughter's but she couldn't face going straight home either.

'"I want to do something out of the ordinary, Mum," she said. She was expecting a baby at the time, so even though there was snow on the ground and we were still in our black clothes, we went to Southend to buy the baby's pram. And while we were choosing one, Elvis Presley came over the loud speakers singing *You'll Never Walk Alone*. So George got his song on the day of the funeral after all.

'Some time after this I was sitting in the conservatory that my husband finished building before he died, with a couple of friends. Suddenly as we were talking we all heard the front door open and someone walk in. As a joke, I said, "That's my George. Come in George." But my friend's husband was so worried that an intruder had got in he went upstairs to check. There was no one there.

'Just after this everyone started remarking on a strong smell of geraniums. I couldn't smell anything myself because I had a heavy cold but during the evening a neighbour popped in and she too mentioned the smell of geraniums.

'There weren't any geraniums in the conservatory but

while he was building it, George had climbed over the dividing wall between our two houses and trampled our neighbour's geraniums. She had given him a good telling off about it.

'Now I don't know if this makes sense to anyone else but it all seems like more than coincidence to me. What's more, George often worked away from home when he was alive and I used to be afraid on my own in the house. Yet funnily enough, since he died I've never been frightened. It's as if George is still with me.'

Well there's only one thing I can say to that – of course he is! Some people might dismiss all these things as coincidence but to me it's absolutely plain. Gwen's husband, clearly a warm, loving man, is still close to her and has been trying to set her mind at rest by showing her as best he can that he's there.

What a pity Gwen didn't get up at the Palladium – but at least George got a few words in anyway. Now she wants to come to another demonstration in the hope that George will get through again.

'And if he does,' said Gwen, 'you won't catch me staying in my seat this time.'

I do hope she's lucky.

These days I tend to use what energy I've got for big public demonstrations. I do still do a few private sittings when the spirit world tells me that a particular case is specially urgent, but now I'm getting on a bit I can't do as much as I used to and I've had to cut down a little. I can reach as many people in one evening at a theatre as I could reach in two or three months of private sittings, so this seems a more sensible way to use my powers.

I know I'm always running on about how the world would be a better place if everyone learned to love each other. As

Ramanov keeps telling me, if each one of us lit up his own little corner, think what an effect it would have as that light spread around the world.

You see there I go again! But at the risk of being boring, it's true, and it's wonderful for me to know that my words haven't fallen on deaf ears.

At public demonstrations I'm always struck by the love and warmth that's generated and by the unselfish way people not lucky enough to receive messages themselves, nevertheless pour out sympathy and good will to those who have and whose tragic stories unfold at the microphone. I know there are millions of nice people in the world because I meet so many of them at my theatres.

Not long ago I appeared at Lewisham, one of my regular venues because it's not far from home. I was staggered to discover that in bitterly cold weather the people were queuing from four in the morning for tickets. It was so cold that the management set out a trolley with free tea, coffee and hot soup to keep people warm.

'Well, we've learned from you Doris,' said the manager. 'It's the people who count.'

I was really touched, even more so when I received a couple of letters afterwards echoing his words.

'We were queuing for hours,' wrote a lady who'd stood for ages in that freezing wind, 'but there was no anger, no pushing or shoving. We all had a joke and made friends with each other and talked about you and your books and how marvellous the atmosphere was going to be.'

'Despite the weather we had a good laugh,' wrote someone else. '"If we have to stand here much longer we'll be talking to Doris from the other side," joked the woman standing behind me . . .'

And another lady added: '. . . the lovely part was that when we got into the theatre on the night, we were all waving to each other across the auditorium and meeting up with friends we'd made in the queue.'

With such wonderful people in the audience I knew it would be a special night and to cap it all, Freddie Starr turned up during the afternoon as I was getting my hair done.

'Oh Freddie, I'm getting ready for the theatre,' I explained.

'Are you?' he said, his blue eyes clouding for a moment. Then he brightened. 'I know, if I can lie down on the bed for a couple of hours and have a rest, I'll go with you!'

So this big star went up to rest on Terry's bed while the hairdresser battled with my springy hair and then he accompanied us to the theatre, fussing over me like a mother hen. He helped me up and down the stairs, wrapped me in my shawl so that I didn't catch cold and brought me hot tea in the dressing-room. After all that there wasn't even a seat for him. Every single seat had been sold, so he had to sit on a plastic chair in the wings.

There was plenty of variety that night, that's for sure. We had a couple of dogs put in an appearance to prove that pets live on just the same as their human masters. We had a woman who wanted a good moan about her daughter-in-law:

'I never liked her. I always said she was no good,' she gossiped to me though I didn't dare repeat it. 'I'm glad she's not in the family any more. The divorce was a good thing I say.'

Then there was a chirpy voice which announced, 'They called me Whack, you know.'

Whack? What a peculiar name, I thought.

'Well me name was Walter really but they called me Whack.'

'Does anyone here know a Walter called Whack?' I asked doubtfully.

There was no reaction for a moment or two, then Walter's niece emerged from the audience.

'He's talking about the Nags Head pub.'

'Yes that's where he used to drink in his younger days.'

'And he says did you find me bank books?'

His niece laughed. 'Yes we did. There were two of them down the side of the settee!'

The audience enjoyed Walter. He was a bit of fun, but earlier in the evening they'd been just as appreciative for a very special mum.

The spastic boy she'd cared for for 41 years came back to thank her for all her devotion.

'They wanted to put me in the hospital, and they wanted to put me in a home, but my mum wouldn't let them,' he said. 'She looked after me right up until the day I came over.'

He wanted her to know that he was with Richard who'd passed not long after him.

'And oh Mum, if you could see me now. The arms that were twisted are gone and everything is straight now. I always had a good brain but it was just my body that let me down and that's been put right now.'

'Could my mum have some flowers as a thank you for all those years?' he asked me.

'Yes of course she can, love,' I told him. 'She certainly deserves them.'

Then there was a husband who was worried about his wife. She was having trouble with her neighbours who kept a big fierce dog which barked all day long. She was terrified of the dog but whenever she complained about it the neighbours refused to take her seriously.

'I had a breakdown Doris, and was given psychiatric treatment and now they're telling me I'm imagining it. Even the police won't listen.'

'She's not imagining it,' said her husband angrily. 'She's scared to death of that dog. Tell her to throw a bucket of water over it next time it barks. She'll only have to do it a few times and it'll learn.'

More seriously still, I picked up two boys who'd been murdered, both of them stabbed. One wanted to send his love to his fiancée.

'We were going to get married in April,' he told me angrily, 'and then this happened. I left her at 11.30 and not long afterwards I was stabbed in the back. All I had on me was £10.'

The other boy whose name was Pat was looking for his mother Linda. He too had been stabbed late at night.

'What did we do to deserve it?' they both asked pitifully.

And I couldn't answer. We live in a very sick world these days.

It was a sombre note to end on but the power was fading away and I couldn't do much to lighten the atmosphere. Fortunately this particular night I didn't have to, because Freddie Starr was waiting in the wings to do it for me.

'Now don't all rush off,' I told the audience, 'because we've got somebody very special to present the flowers tonight . . .'

Then Tony Ortzen, the chairman, tantalisingly introduced John and then gave Freddie Starr a long teasing build-up.

'A star in more ways than one,' he hinted, but then gave the game away. He mentioned the messages I'd given our mystery guest from Alan Lake and Diana Dors. That did it.

The people in the audience who'd read my book guessed immediately who he was referring to and the place erupted into great cheers and applause.

Freddie, beaming all over his face and clowning about, bounced into the lights. He was marvellous. He handed out the flowers with a kiss for every single recipient, he patiently posed for endless photographs and then right at the end as the recipients moved back to their seats, he sang *Love Me Tender, Love Me True*, in his brilliant impression of Elvis Presley.

Freddie has a beautiful voice and as the moving words soared out over the audience you could have heard a pin drop.

It was a magical end to a magical evening.

But backstage the fun wasn't over yet. All through the evening I'd noticed Tony and Janet Roffey sitting in the front row. Readers of my last book will know that they are the parents of little Hollie Roffey, the youngest child to have a heart transplant.

I'd met them before poor little Hollie was born, I'd tried to comfort them at the funeral and then a few months afterwards I'd almost given away the secret of Janet's new pregnancy. She was saving it as a Christmas present for her husband.

Well Hollie turned up on the stage that night. She was a lot bigger than when I'd first seen her but she was just as gorgeous. She stood there holding on to my knee and smiling up at me, the lights streaming down onto her rich copper head, bright as a new chestnut.

Oh dear, shall I say anything? I wondered. It was so difficult. I didn't know the Roffeys were coming that night but if I spoke up people would remember my book and say it was fixed. So I kept quiet. It's such a shame that you have to take these things into account but there you are. That's what happens when you start getting on television and in the papers. People can't wait for an excuse to criticise.

So I kept silent about Hollie but afterwards I met Tony and Janet in the dressing-room and we had a good old chat.

Janet was looking wonderful. She'd had her hair cut and styled and happiness had turned her into a really beautiful girl. Just as I'd predicted months ago when both those poor kids were in the depths of grief, their second child wasn't long in coming and she was in perfect health.

Little Samantha was born in the summer of 1985. She was just as gorgeous as Hollie, but dark like her daddy while Hollie took after her uncle.

'We want to give you a picture to keep,' said Janet, 'but we didn't know which one to choose so we've brought the lot. Pick out the one you'd like and we'll get it framed.' She put the whole set of photographs into my lap. I sat there looking through snap after snap of the beautiful gurgling baby. They were all lovely, but finally I made my choice and now I'm looking forward to receiving the framed picture for my mantelpiece.

It's nice to have such a happy ending to a story that started with tragedy, and now I am delighted to learn that Hollie has been given the ultimate accolade, which Robert Maxwell, the publisher of my books, put in motion. A rose has been named after her, so she will never be forgotten.

I'm sure that from now on things will go well for Tony and Janet. They deserve it.

6

It was a beautiful day in the middle of summer. Battersea Park echoed with the shrieks of children at play, and a young family on holiday from Essex strolled under the trees.

'Can we feed the birds now, Mum?' the small boys pestered, until at last their mother gave in and produced a packet of stale bread from her handbag.

Soon they were surrounded by fat London pigeons, almost too overweight to get off the ground and the bread was pecked up in minutes.

'Now don't throw that bag on the ground,' said the father sharply as the boys cast about for something else to do. 'There's a bin over there.'

So one of the boys picked up the bag and trotted obediently over to the litter bin.

And that was when their pleasant day in the sun turned to horror.

There was an interesting looking bundle amongst the rubbish in the bin. Wrapped in a thick plastic bag it showed odd lumps and bumps and knobbles. Quite what the shape reminded him of the boy couldn't say. He poked the bundle experimentally.

There was a rustle of plastic, the bag parted slightly and

the boy found himself looking at a small human foot sticking grotesquely into the air.

'Dad . . .' he quavered, 'Dad . . . !' and then he was off and running as fast as if there was a fierce dog at his heels, to the safety of his parents . . .

The new born baby had not died of natural causes, the police discovered later. It had been murdered.

It was a frustrating case. Despite exhaustive enquiries they had drawn a blank.

'Would you mind if I called in a psychic?' asked Debbie Martyr, the reporter on the *Wandsworth and Putney Guardian* who was covering the case.

The police didn't raise any objections so Debbie contacted Nella Jones, a clairvoyant, and then she telephoned me.

Now I don't pretend to be a psychic detective and as often as not although the spirit world does give information about murder cases which turns out to be correct, it rarely leads to the arrest of the culprit. But if, knowing these limitations, people still want my help, I do what I can especially if the case involves children.

The murder of babies in particular is something that makes my blood boil. When I think of the agony I went through when I lost my son and how much I would have given to hold another baby of my own in my arms, I find it very hard to forgive someone who could deliberately hurt such a defenceless little creature.

'Well, Debbie, I'll do my best,' I said, 'but I can't promise anything.'

We live well outside the area covered by Debbie's paper so I knew nothing of the case and Debbie was determined to give little away.

'All I can say is that a baby has been found dead,' she told me.

That was all right by me. I'd much rather people didn't give me any clues at all.

I tuned in. For a moment nothing happened but I could feel the power building up and I knew there would be something. Gradually the outlines of my sitting room began to soften and recede and mentally I was somewhere else. I got the impression of a dank, comfortless public toilet. There was a very young girl close by.

I couldn't see her but I could feel her and she was scared, very scared.

'I think the baby was born inside a toilet,' I said, 'and one of his parents could be coloured or swarthy skinned.'

I paused. A new and horrifying impression was forming in my mind and I didn't like it one bit. I sensed that tiny body swinging through the air and that little head cracking against a wall with a sickening muffled bump. Quickly I blotted it out.

'I'm sure it's a boy and that he was murdered,' I said quickly. 'I think he was hit against a wall and I see injuries to the back of his head.'

I gave Debbie a few more details which we can't print because it turned out to be information only known to the police, and then I was being taken to another location. The feeling that I was being shown the place where the mother lived, flooded through me.

Looking inward, I saw a big building, high and gaunt and ugly. It was a shabby block of flats. In the distance I could hear the rattle of trains so I knew it was near the railway line and there was an overwhelming impression that I was between Wandsworth and Battersea.

Then the block of flats melted into the background and I got a confused view of arches or an archway, I couldn't seem to get that picture into focus, but there wasn't time to dwell on it. I was on the move again. Past the flats I went, to the corner of the road on which stood a pub; something to do with a crown. Perhaps the word crown was part of its name or perhaps there was a crown in the sign, I couldn't tell. I was being led on round the corner.

Here the road opened out a little and I could see an open space or small park not far from the pub. Somewhere on that open space was a public toilet which was left unlocked at night.

'Perhaps that's where the baby was born,' I said, 'and I'm sure the birth was in the early hours of the morning.'

Debbie was scribbling away without making much comment. Then I heard a name, very strongly.

'I'm getting the name Gillian or Julie. Anne might be part of it and also the name Turner.'

Whether this girl was the mother or whether she was connected with the case in some way I didn't know.

When I'd finished, Debbie couldn't really tell me whether I'd been much help or not, but she thanked me most politely for my time. First she had to take my report to the police. Afterwards however she explained that they seemed impressed:

'I must admit that I went into this with a very open mind,' said Debbie, 'but I was amazed at some of the things both Doris and Nella came up with. Although they didn't have any contact with each other their accounts tallied in a surprising number of ways.

'I was fairly cagey about the case but they told me things that I knew to be correct and also things that I thought were wrong but which turned out to be correct when I checked with the police.

'Doris gave details which haven't been released yet, like the exact injuries to the baby and the contents of the plastic bag, because there wasn't just a baby in the bag. She also gave some names which can't be mentioned in case they should turn out to be the suspects.

'Funnily enough she was right too about the name Julie Anne Turner. It meant nothing to me, but later while I was talking to the police, one of them was doodling on a piece of paper and suddenly he said, "Bloody hell. That was the name of the girl who was murdered six weeks ago."

'The case had been solved almost immediately and it got practically no publicity but the investigations into the murder of Julie Anne Turner had been carried out from the same incident room that was now being used for the murdered baby case.

'"One or two things right could be put down to lucky guesswork," said one of the policemen, "but all this is uncanny. It gives me goosepimples."

'As far as I know, they haven't solved the murder yet, but it was a fascinating experience. It certainly opened my eyes.'

There is a lot of debate going on in spiritualist circles about whether a medium's powers should be used in this way but I believe that when it comes to murder, everyone should give what help they can. Some people assist the police by helping in the search for missing children, others phone in with the tiniest scraps of information which might prove useful. My own gifts might not in the end lead to an arrest but it would be wrong of me to refuse to try.

A medium's work is certainly varied! A few months after the murder case I was called in to assist with another small but important aspect of mediumship – earthbound spirits.

It sometimes happens that after a death a spirit is so tied to an earthly location – usually because of some traumatic event that occurred there – that he refuses to cross to the spirit world. He hangs around, sometimes for hundreds of years, making a nuisance of himself, particularly to people with great but undeveloped psychic power. When this happens the place is said to be haunted and receptive people often see ghosts.

Anyway it was journalist Michael Hellicar who drew my attention to the case. In my last book I described how I gave a sitting to one of Michael's readers who was 'haunted' by the 'ghost' of his dead wife. It turned out the poor woman had committed suicide during a depressive illness and she simply wanted her husband to know what happened and to stop feeling guilty.

Apparently, some weeks after the book came out, the husband contacted Michael Hellicar again. He had made his peace with his wife and had suffered no further problems with her, but recently strange things had been happening in the house. There had been flashing lights, objects moving of their own volition and most worrying of all, weird signs burned into the bedroom door. The man had also caught glimpses from time to time of ghostly figures.

It sounded bizarre to me but you can never dismiss this sort of thing out of hand, so Michael and I went down to investigate.

Michael arrived promptly one Monday morning and before we left I dashed into the bathroom for a moment's quiet to tune in, on my own.

Instantly the wife arrived. 'You got my name wrong when you wrote about me,' she complained, and she reminded me of the correct version.

As it happened we'd changed the couple's names to Brian and Janet to protect their identities since it was a distressing case.

'I don't mind you telling people my name's Irene,' she said, 'there's no point in hiding it.'

So from now on I'll refer to the couple by their real names: Irene and Trevor.

Once again Irene was worried about her husband. She feared he was heading for a mental breakdown.

'Please help him, Doris,' she said, 'if he stays in that house I'm afraid he'll go the same way as me.'

'I'll do my best, love,' I promised. 'Let's go and see what's happening.'

It was a grey, gloomy morning and the streets looked drear and water-logged. All you needed was a bit of swirling mist and the ghost film atmosphere would have been complete.

But Trevor didn't live in a remote gothic mansion. His home was a modern airy townhouse built around a grassy square and even the most vivid imagination couldn't describe it as a lonely spot. Trevor's neighbours were many and close and it was the sort of place where children would play football in the summer and leave their bikes on the concrete paths, and where the ice-cream man would call regularly.

Not the sort of location to interest a film director of course but then what most people don't realise is that new houses can just as often be haunted as old.

Inside, the place was neat, freshly decorated and not in any way creepy. Yet Trevor was obviously deeply concerned and his new girlfriend Pam was worried.

He took Michael upstairs to show him the burn marks on the bedroom door while I stayed in the sitting room talking to Pam. She seemed a lovely girl, friendly and open, but suddenly I wondered if Irene could possibly be jealous.

'It's not you doing this is it Irene?' I asked silently.

'No, it's not,' she said indignantly, 'I like Pam. She doesn't mind Trevor talking about me and she doesn't shut me out. They could be happy together if Trevor would leave this house, but they won't be any good till he moves.'

The channels were well and truly open now and as Irene moved away, a little boy came to take her place.

'I'm Kevin,' he said and as he spoke I felt a great rush of love for Pam.

'That's my little boy,' cried Pam in amazement. Apparently she'd been married before and had lost her baby son through a cot death.

The power was gaining in strength now and as I sat in the armchair sipping a cup of coffee, I felt the room slip away and I was looking at four big posh houses, and somewhere close by there was a priory.

'I'm Sarah,' said an elderly female voice. 'I used to live here.'

And then came a name that sounded like Rosenblaum or Rosenberg.

'Is it you doing all this Sarah?' I asked.

'No not me,' she said, 'I just want them to be happy.'

The next second I was pulled back to the present. Trevor and Michael returned.

'I think that years ago there were four big houses on this site,' I told them, 'and there was a priory nearby.'

'There was a priory,' said Trevor, 'it used to be about 250 yards away.'

And as he spoke I could feel the psychic power coming off him in waves, but it was clouded and confused.

'When he's away from home working, he suddenly stops what he's doing and has an overwhelming desire to get back to the house,' said Irene. 'It's as if he's on an invisible thread.'

Trevor confirmed that this was true, but before I could repeat Irene's warning that he should move, another spirit from the old days popped in. Dr Golden, he said his name was, and he too had lived in one of the big houses.

'The towel rail keeps falling off,' he told me, 'and the tap keeps turning on, but it's not me doing it. I couldn't do a thing like that.'

The case was becoming more and more puzzling. The house seemed to act as a magnet for every passing spirit and it could only be Trevor's psychic power that was attracting them.

'You must learn to channel your power properly,' I told Trevor and then my voice trailed off. The atmosphere was changing and suddenly I became aware of outbuildings round the back of the large houses and a feeling of anger and despair. My head was pulled to one side, imitating the position of the head of a hanged man and I realised that someone had hanged himself in one of those outhouses. I caught a tiny glimpse of a man holding his head on one side.

'Sam,' he said. So I took it that Sam was his name.

'That's it,' said Trevor. 'I keep seeing this man on the stairs. He wears an old dressing-gown and he holds his head on one side as if he'd been hanged.'

Sam brought with him such a tide of misery that I was reminded of Irene's words to me about Trevor.

'If he doesn't move I'm afraid he'll go the same way I did,' and I wondered whether she was telling me more than I'd first realised. Could she too have been affected by Sam's unseen presence and have been driven to commit suicide by unconsciously picking up his suicidal thoughts?

'Now listen to me, Sam,' I said firmly, 'you're upsetting these people. You've got to stop. If you look to the right you'll see a light. That's your guide. Just put your hand out and he will help you over. You're earthbound son.'

Black depression rolled over me, then I heard Sam speaking

again in a dull, cracked voice, 'My child . . . my child drowned.'

'Your child drowned?' I asked in surprise. 'But there's no river near here surely?'

'There used to be a pond on the old maps,' said Trevor.

'Well look Sam, it's no good blaming yourself. If you go to the spirit world you'll find your little daughter . . .'

'Madelaine,' said Sam.

'They called her Madelaine,' I explained to the others who couldn't hear Sam's side of the conversation. 'Go where the light is Sam and you will find your daughter grown up and waiting for you.'

There was silence.

'Are you going to do that for me, Sam?'

Nothing. He'd wandered away again. I only hoped he'd taken my advice and was following the light.

The silence grew and grew. There was no point in forcing contact, so while I was waiting I suggested that I have a look at the burned door.

Trevor's house was on three floors. The first and second floors felt pleasant and relaxed but as I climbed the stairs towards the third landing I began to feel distinctly queer. My body was chilled and my legs went all weak and shaky.

'This is where I see Sam,' said Trevor as we reached the top.

Then he opened the bedroom door and showed me the extraordinary marks. Defacing the whole of the centre of the door was a large, crudely drawn star of David scorched into the paintwork and beneath it was the rough outline of the letter 'S'.

It was the strangest thing I've ever seen. The burnt paintwork was quite smooth and silky to touch, apart from a tiny area near the top on which one or two small blisters showed, and the surrounding paintwork was unmarked.

I've seen some weird things in my time as a medium but nothing as weird as this. If it was Sam's work it beats me how he did it.

Shaking my head in bewilderment I followed Trevor back downstairs.

'What d'you think you're up to, Sam?' I asked silently, but there was no reply. Instead I got a picture again, but in more detail this time.

There was a large red brick house, a big gate at the bottom of the garden and two paths going out the back to the outhouses. There was a study with french windows and one of the paths skirted to the right of it and led round to a barn or a shed. This was where Sam hanged himself.

But Sam was silent. I could only hope that he'd taken my advice and was busy greeting his daughter in the spirit world.

'Well, Trevor, I hope he's gone,' I said at last, 'but there are two things you must do. You must develop your psychic power properly to stop them tapping into it like this, because you can't cope with it – and you must move. You're not happy in this house any longer and you won't be really happy again until you move.'

Oddly enough he seemed very reluctant to leave the place but he promised to think it over. There was nothing else I could do.

I hope Trevor's taken my advice and I hope that Sam has gone on his way. At the moment it's too early to be sure. We'll just have to wait and see.

7

Dear Editor,

I have been staying with my sister since November, missing my regular ordered copy of *Weekend*. I have just returned home and I'm catching up on my back copies. I was reading December 10th's copy and with dismay saw the article offering a free sitting with Doris Stokes.

I realise that my chance for that offer has long since gone but I would beg you to continue to read my letter and hopefully you may be able to help us.

My sister Gillian is 35 years of age, she is married with two children aged 9 years and 7 years. Gill has Chronic Myloid Leukaemia and has been in and out of remission since November 11th. Her consultant has now told her that she has only 9–12 months to live. Gill is a wonderfully brave girl and has terrific willpower. When she found out about her illness, indeed when we all found out, it shook our faith. We only regained that faith when we saw Doris on the television. Just watching that one programme allayed all Gill's fears on dying. She knew she would join Dad on the spirit side.

If Gill could have one wish before she died I know it would be to meet Doris Stokes. She still watches the video of that programme.

Dear Editor, I know you must know her home address. Would you please make a dying girl very happy and forward this letter to her. We would travel to the end of the earth for Gill, we love her so dearly.

Thank you so much for sparing the time to read this letter. If my request is impossible to perform please let me know so that I can keep trying myself to contact Doris.

Yours sincerely
Heather Randall
Staffordshire

At the moment I have a backlog of 20,000 letters, most of them asking for sittings and obviously it's not possible for me to do even a fraction of them. I worked it out the other day and I was amazed to discover that if I gave a sitting a day without a break for weekends or holidays, for the next 50 years, I'd be 116 years old and I still wouldn't have worked my way through them all!

Even with the spirit world's help and the best doctor in South London, I doubt if I'll make it to my 116th birthday, let alone be working until then, so sadly we have to tell most of these people that a private sitting's just not possible. But I haven't given up sittings altogether. Now I let the spirit world tell me which of the desperate cases I must see. There's no mistaking the nudge I get from the other side. Suddenly, as I'm sifting through the mail, one letter will leap out at me, its envelope almost burning my hand and I'll know that Ramanov my guide wants me to tackle this particular case.

Heather's letter, printed above, was one of these.

Weekend magazine had approached me some weeks before to see if they could arrange a sitting for one of their readers. Knowing that so many people wanted to see me, they were going to ask their readers to write in saying why they thought they should be chosen.

I was a bit doubtful about the idea at first, but then I realised that some desperate soul would get a sitting and the magazine would handle the letters and make the heartrending choice. Believe me, at times it's agony to have to turn down one tragic case in favour of another. Even with the spirit world's help it's a nightmare task.

Anyway I agreed, a 'winner' was chosen, the date was fixed and then Heather's letter was passed on to me by the magazine. That day I had my usual stack of mail to sort through, but there was something about that deep blue envelope that caught my eye. It wasn't just the colour. No matter how I piled the letters that envelope kept falling into my hand and when I opened it and read Heather's moving words I knew why. Without doubt I must see her sister.

Laurie looks after my diary these days and makes all the appointments for me, so I phoned him at once.

'Laurie put them in,' I said, after I'd explained the situation, 'I don't care where or when, but I must see them.'

'It means working on your day off,' he warned.

'That doesn't matter,' I said. 'This is important.'

So one Thursday morning Heather and her sister Gillian made the long journey down from Staffordshire. Their train was late and they'd been travelling for hours but they didn't complain. Instead they were full of apologies for having kept me waiting.

What marvellous sisters they were. There was Gillian, a lovely child, so brave but so pitifully thin even though she told me proudly she'd put on a stone in weight since going into remission; and there was Heather, compassionate and devoted. Heather was a nurse at the hospital where Gillian was being treated and on one occasion when Gillian was very ill, she'd begged Heather not to leave her.

'I won't,' said Heather taking her hand and she didn't. It's a wonder she didn't get fired because nurses can't stay at a patient's side as they please.

'I wouldn't have cared if I was fired,' said Heather. 'Gillian needed me more than anyone else at that time and that's all that mattered.'

How wonderful to have such love between sisters I thought, as I got them settled with a cup of coffee. So many girls fight and squabble.

It didn't take long to get tuned in. Sometimes I have to struggle for ages to build up the power and make a contact but Gillian's dad was so close to her, I found him immediately. He was so worried about his little girl, he rarely left her side either, and he was soon ticking me off.

'Put that cigarette out,' he ordered, minutes after we got started. 'It affects her lungs.'

Gillian hadn't liked to mention it but I stubbed out my menthol cigarette at once. Her father went on to talk about the family. He'd met Bill his father and Nelly his mother on the other side he said and he mentioned his wife Jan who recently had a gall bladder operation.

'She's worried because she still suffers pain. She thinks it's something serious but it's only adhesions,' he explained.

Then he said something about Gill having three children.

'No only two,' said Gillian.

'Three!' insisted her father firmly. 'Two kids and a dog. The third is the bloody dog. She calls him the baby.'

Gill burst out laughing. 'Yes I do!' she chuckled.

When she smiled her face lit up with such serenity and peace that I could see she had accepted the worst and learned to live with it.

Her father had not. He kept worrying that the illness was somehow his fault. Although he'd passed quickly with a heart attack he worried that Gill might have inherited some tendency through his genes.

'I want to know why,' he said. 'I've asked them over here and they say it's God's will and I say bugger God's will, I want to know why.'

He was also worried about his grandchildren, Christopher and Pippa.

'She hasn't told my grand-daughter,' he said. 'If the worst happens she must explain it to the children. Tell them Mummy had to come and live with Grandpa. But don't give up Gill. You've defied them up till now, because they said you wouldn't be here for Christmas and you bloody were.'

I tried to get him onto a more cheerful subject by asking what he used to do for a living.

'I used to do the buses,' he said.

'Do the buses?' I queried silently. 'D'you mean you were a bus driver?'

'No,' he said impatiently, 'I used to do the buses.'

Puzzled I repeated the odd phrase to Gill.

'Yes that's quite right,' she said, 'he cleaned buses.'

But her father didn't want to waste time on trivia. He gave me the name John.

'That's my husband,' said Gill.

'She's got one of the best,' said her father. 'He's breaking his heart but he tries not to show it. He goes and shuts himself in the bathroom and has a cry.'

I didn't want to upset Gill so I tried to persuade her dad to tell me a bit more about his grandchildren.

'Pippa's a beautiful child. Very graceful. She's always dancing,' he said, 'and as for Christopher, he's a good lad. He runs about after his mother doing things for her but inside he's scared. He could be clever if he applied himself.'

He went on to mention some more family names and the fact that he knew that Gill had recently been talking to someone who was discussing a divorce, but most of all he wanted her to know that if things went wrong and her treatment wasn't successful, he'd be there to take her by the hand and help her over into a new life on the other side.

'We're so proud of her, she's so brave,' he said before the power finally faded away.

Afterwards as the three of us sat chatting I tried to emphasise to Gill the importance of explaining to her children what was going on. I've seen grown men and women in their forties still scarred by the sudden loss of a parent, because they didn't understand what was happening.

'If Mummy suddenly disappears they can't understand it,' I said. 'They think she must have gone because they did something wrong and they carry that guilt for the rest of their lives.'

Gill promised she would do her best to explain.

'I have talked to Christopher,' she said, 'but somehow I haven't managed to say anything yet to Pippa. I will try.'

At the end, just as they were leaving, she put her arms around me and gave me a big hug.

'I feel very bitter because I've got to leave my lovely husband and children,' she confessed, 'but Doris I'm not afraid to die after today. I know my father will be there.'

Tears burned my eyes as I returned the hug. She was obviously one of God's special children and had been chosen long before she was born to take this difficult path.

'Don't give up, love. Miracles do happen,' I assured her, and then they were walking away up the garden path, one frail, one sturdy, two devoted sisters.

I don't know where these marvellous people find their courage. There are so many of them. If you passed them in the street you wouldn't give them a second glance, yet their ordinary appearance hides a bravery that would do credit to the most heroic soldier.

I remember being very taken aback at a demonstration in Brighton when a spirit mother in the course of a message to her daughter said abruptly:

'She's going to join us shortly.'

That can't be right, I thought in horror. The young woman in front of me was only in her early thirties and apparently healthy and strong.

'I misheard you, love,' I said silently to the mother.

'No you didn't,' she replied tartly, 'she's coming over soon. She's got cancer. Tell her to put her affairs in order.'

That's all very well I thought, but how do I say that in front of hundreds of people? Not for the first time I found myself racking my brains for a tactful way to phrase a difficult spirit message.

'There's going to be a parting soon, love, your mum tells me,' I said gently, 'Go and see a solicitor and get things put in order. D'you know what I mean?'

The girl nodded silently, too full of emotion to speak, but afterwards she wrote me a beautiful letter. She too was no longer afraid of death now she knew her mother was waiting for her, she said, and the message had given her the strength to consult her solicitor about all the little details that needed sorting out.

Strange really. Until a few weeks ago I'd always felt that one of my most important tasks was to help parents who'd lost children because I'd lost a baby myself and I could understand that terrible pain. I still believe this of course but more and more recently I've come to realise how much work needs to be done for the terminally ill. Perhaps it's just an illusion but to me it seems that their numbers are increasing and so many of them are desperate for comfort and reassurance.

Gill of course wasn't the winner of the *Weekend* 'competition'. The magazine made their choice and quite rightly didn't publish any details until well after the sitting. They were amazed at the response. Hundreds and hundreds of letters poured into the office and the editorial staff had the agonising task of sorting them out. They whittled them down to a short list of about twenty, then the editor made the final decision.

They kept the contents of the winner's letter secret of course, but afterwards in the report of the sitting, they included the extracts that so moved the editor.

'I would love so much to have a sitting with Doris Stokes to thank her for the comfort my teenage daughter gained from her books before she died in such distressing circumstances,' wrote Helen Bates. 'I believe they helped her not to be frightened when the end came. All her life Alison tried so hard to help and please people, even insisting on doing first aid duty at our local theatre while she was ill. It would be wonderful if Doris could put me in touch with her. I'd just like to tell her how much I miss her and how sorry I am that I didn't do more for her.'

Helen Bates, a comfortable, dark haired, middle-aged lady arrived with reporter Jack Pleasant and the magazine's photographer. All I knew about Helen at that stage was her name, but the moment she walked in the door I sensed great tragedy around her. She had lost a child I was sure of that, but there was something else. She was suffering not only from that awful searing pain, but from a feeling of guilt as well.

We started work almost as soon as the introductions were over. At once I saw a tiny light flickering around Helen. That meant the tragedy was recent.

'I can see a tiny light, that tells me someone hasn't been over very long,' I said slowly. 'It's not a year yet. It was a great tragedy and it's been harder on you love than on anyone.'

Helen swallowed hard and nodded.

Suddenly I heard a young girl's voice, she couldn't have been more than nineteen or twenty and she told me she'd gone over quickly at the end and hadn't said goodbye.

'That's right,' said Helen. 'She was only eighteen actually.'

As she spoke I saw a brief flash behind her head and illuminated in the light was a face that looked even younger than eighteen surrounded by pretty fair hair.

It turned out that the poor child had been suffering from a brain tumour and no one knew. Her behaviour changed and people nagged her for being moody, when all the time she was desperately ill.

'I didn't realise anything was wrong,' she said. 'First my eyes went funny and I got glasses. The doctor told me it was to do with my monthly cycle.'

'Yes,' said Helen her eyes filling with tears. 'She held her head on one side because she couldn't see.'

The young girl, whose named turned out to be Alison, mentioned her grandad Bill, her dad Peter David and her boyfriend Jim. She even talked of a pet.

'It's called Cindy or Sandy something like that,' I said aloud struggling to catch the faint word.

'Cinders,' said Helen. 'It's a cat, born the day she died.'

Alison gave quite a few other names but she was chiefly concerned with easing her mother's feelings of guilt.

'If the bloody doctors couldn't tell me I had a tumour on the brain, how could my mum tell why I was so nasty,' she said. 'Remember me to Iris,' she added pointedly.

Helen gasped. 'That's a woman I work with. She was very cruel to her.'

'Tell her I forgive her,' said Alison. 'She's been worrying about it ever since. I hated her at the time but I don't now. She wasn't to know I was ill.'

But Alison wasn't the only spirit person to pop in during that sitting. Towards the end when Alison had grown tired from the effort of communicating, she moved off the vibration and a man dashed in while he had the chance.

'It's Jack James,' he said and the light whipped round to Jack Pleasant who had been calmly taking notes. Jack's jaw dropped.

'That's my father-in-law,' he said.

'I just wanted to get my two pennorth in,' Jack senior told me, obviously very pleased with himself.

'Oh and tell them I know what they're up to. They're having the builders in soon.'

'They're due next month,' said Jack weakly.

Afterwards he wrote a very nice article about the sitting, and included a verdict from Mrs Bates:

'Marvellous . . . she even mentioned the big coloured photo of Alison I have in my bedroom and that her eyes seem to follow you around the room. It was an experience that will make these last few tragic months a lot easier to bear . . .'

But I wasn't finished with *Weekend* yet. Not long after the sitting they contacted me again. All those heartrending letters had moved them as nothing had moved them for years. They hadn't realised how much grief there was in the world and they wanted to do something for all the hundreds of readers who hadn't had a sitting. Would I mind giving a public demonstration specially for the *Weekend* readers? they asked.

I was delighted to help of course. The editor suggested the 600 seater Mermaid theatre near the Thames in London but Laurie explained that it would be too small, knowing that I would like each invited guest to have a travelling companion. I felt this was especially necessary as I knew some people would be coming from Jersey, Cornwall, Scotland and even Italy. So we hired the 1200 seater Poplar Civic Theatre where I had been filmed for the 40 minutes TV documentary *A Happy Medium*. Once again the response was greater than expected for an afternoon demonstration, so I asked Laurie to hire an even larger theatre.

'We'll pay for it, love, it's only fair to the people. How can we disappoint them?'

So Laurie cancelled the Poplar theatre and booked the lovely Barbican Concert Hall in the Barbican Centre opened by Her Majesty the Queen in 1982. The capacity was over 2,000, yet the demand was so great we still had to disappoint some people. But we had to stop somewhere.

It promised to be a wonderful occasion and I was looking forward to being the first medium to appear at the Barbican when something happened.

A few days before the *Weekend* demonstration a reporter came to see me. I won't mention his name because it must be humiliating for a trained journalist to have to make his living by muck-raking so I won't embarrass him further, but from what I gather he told a few untruths to Laurie in order to get an appointment and then when he finally got into my home he interrogated me for 5½ hours. There's no other word for it. I felt as if I was on trial in my own sitting room. It was quite obvious that he wanted to do a hatchet job.

'I put it to you . . .' he kept saying as if he was Perry Mason, until in the end my head was spinning. Nothing I had to say seemed to satisfy him.

I have to expect this sort of thing, I know. It's sad but true that as soon as you start getting nice things written about you in the paper, other papers want to write nasty things simply to make a change. I know this and yet it still hurts when they do it. It's very hard to ignore.

Worst of all was that 5½ hour grilling. I don't know whether I'm getting old or whether it's the effect of my stroke, but afterwards I felt exhausted and rather sick.

As it happened the story was so full of inaccuracies when it came out that you couldn't take it seriously but I'm grateful to that young man for one thing. He pointed out an error in my first book, *Voices In My Ear*, which I can now put right. Somehow the gremlins got into the works while the books were being put together and I've described a bombing raid in Grantham as happening in 1945, when in fact it happened several years earlier. Sorry about that. Looking back forty years things got out of sequence and my apologies to any readers who were misled.

Anyway suffice it to say that by the time the Barbican demonstration came round I was feeling rather depressed. It's a chilling sensation to know that people bear you ill will and want to believe the worst of you. Nevertheless I was determined not to let the readers down, so I got myself dolled up, pinned a smile on my face and set off for the concert hall.

We didn't get off to a good start.

'You can't park there,' said the security guard as we sat outside the posh doors of this space age building while the driver went to enquire where we were to go.

'We won't be a minute,' I said, 'the driver's just gone to find out the way to the concert hall.'

'Sorry madam, you can't wait there,' he repeated impatiently.

'Well there's nothing we can do about it because the driver's got the car keys,' I said.

Exasperated the guard moved away and a moment later the driver returned.

'Right Doris we go through here to the lift and that should take us right up to the concert hall.'

He opened the door, John got out and turned to help me because I get tangled up in my long theatre dresses if I'm not careful, when the security guard came running.

'Come on now move this car!' he insisted angrily.

The driver tried to argue, but it was no use. I could see that unless the car was moved we'd all end up in the police station.

'Go on, don't worry about us,' I said to the driver. 'We'll find it.'

So the car rolled away and John and I went into the plush building. It was an interesting place, no doubt about that. Huge and very modern with lots of light polished wood and little staircases that went up and down all over the place. Fortunately we were early, because John and I blundered about getting nowhere until at last one of the attendants took pity on us.

'We're looking for the concert hall,' I explained.

'Follow me,' she said.

Well I don't know what we'd have done without her – probably still been there looking for the lift I reckon. She led us up and down some more staircases and through a white walled corridor where there was some kind of arty exhibition going on. It was to do with different sounds I think because there were all these weird objects that produced different notes when struck. There was a rope ladder with hollow wooden rungs down which children dragged plastic sticks; there was a dangling thing twanging round a copper bowl; there were strips of metal that revolved and shook; and a pair of cymbals that were very popular with the kids. The din was indescribable and we hurried through as fast as we could.

The attendant deposited us at the lift.

'You want the second floor,' she said.

So up we went and once again found ourselves in a long corridor looking bewildered. What people must have thought of me in my long dress and gold slippers at 2.00 in the afternoon I can't imagine.

Once again an attendant came to our rescue.

'We're looking for the concert hall,' I repeated weakly.

I was just beginning to think that it was all a joke and that the concert hall didn't exist, when the man opened a door on a scene of frantic activity.

Rows of seats led down to a large stage where Laurie and his helpers were rushing round laying carpet, setting out flowers and arranging chairs.

'Hello Doris,' said Laurie cheerfully. 'It's going to look wonderful.'

But it wasn't the glorious flowers that caught my eye, it was the stage. There were no curtains, no wings for me to stand in while waiting to go on, just rows and rows of seats sweeping right the way round. There was nowhere to hide, just this huge brand new stage of softly gleaming pale wood. It frightened the life out of me.

'This chap will take you to the dressing-room,' Laurie

continued as if nothing was wrong. 'You've got plenty of time for a cup of tea.'

If I was the type to take tranquillisers, I'd have swallowed a handful then, but I'm not, of course. Instead I made do with a very strong cup of tea.

John was just putting the kettle on for another cup when the door opened and a hot and bothered Tony Ortzen almost fell into the room.

'I thought I'd never get here!' he gasped. 'I've been walking around this building for miles following the yellow lines. Follow the yellow lines, the notice says, but when you do you end up where you started!'

Tony was another candidate for a strong cup of tea.

'Tony, we've got to think about this,' I said when he was more relaxed. Tony was chairman for the afternoon and would be preceding me on stage to do the introductions.

'There are no wings for me to stand in, and I can't wait outside the door because it's made of glass and they'll see me through it, so we'll have to go on together.'

It meant rearranging his lines slightly, but Tony agreed it was the only way to do it.

By now I was feeling a nervous wreck. I made my escape to the loo as I always do when I want a bit of peace and quiet and silently I implored the spirit world for help.

'Ramanov, I badly need your help this afternoon,' I said.

Instantly there came a name. 'Craig,' said a distant voice.

'Craig hang on a minute,' I called, 'give me a bit more to go with it. Who are you looking for?'

'Shirley,' said the voice moving closer, and then, 'Wood.'

It wasn't much but it was enough to get me started.

'Okay Tony, I'm ready now,' I said when I came out, and so, bracing ourselves to face that daunting open stage, we went out.

Tony went through the glass doors and I was at his heels and as I crossed the threshold the whole place went up. They couldn't have given me a warmer welcome. Relaxing now I followed Tony up the steps to the stage and then I sat next to him while he made his modified introduction.

Right from the beginning everything went well.

'Just before I came on I heard a young boy called Craig,' I said, 'and he's looking for Shirley Wood. Is there anyone called Shirley Wood here?'

A woman came hurrying to the microphone. 'My name's Shirley, but not Wood,' she said.

'Do you know Craig?'

'Oh yes.'

'Listen Doris,' said Craig moving in closer, 'I didn't say Wood, I said Woodland. It's an address. Oh and I'm sixteen.'

Shirley confirmed that this was true and that she lived in Woodland Way.

'She's got my hair in a locket you know,' Craig told me proudly.

'Well what happened to you, lovey?' I asked him, 'Were you killed?'

'No, I had leukaemia,' said Craig, 'the last two or three years were pretty dreadful.'

'Yes they were,' said Shirley.

Craig mentioned his friends John and Thomas and his aunts Lily and Margaret and he wanted to wish his father happy birthday.

'My father is really my stepfather,' he confided, 'but I love him more than anything else in the world. I used to get a bit upset at times and Dad used to calm me down.'

Then he added, 'Dad's got my watch on you know.'

Out in the audience a man nodded.

'Yes he has,' said Shirley.

Craig tried to give me his dad's name. It was very short, only three letters, but I couldn't catch it properly.

'Three letters,' I said slowly, 'Roy, Ray . . .'

'Ray,' said Shirley.

'That's his dad.'

'Yes.'

Craig was delighted to have made contact so quickly. 'Dad didn't want to come because he didn't believe in this,' he laughed. 'He'll have to now, won't he?'

Not long after Craig had moved on, we had another satisfied visitor from the spirit world. I heard a woman's voice and the name Edie.

'I'm looking for my husband Norman, dear,' she told me. 'Oh and I drowned.'

I repeated this to the audience and suddenly near the back of the hall I became aware of a man struggling to his feet.

'Yes, that's Norman,' said his wife, 'but do watch him on those steps. He's not very good on his legs and he doesn't see very well.'

'Yes that's true,' Norman agreed as he picked his way carefully down the aisle.

'Well take your time, love,' I told him. 'Your wife doesn't want you to hurt yourself.'

When Norman finally made it to the microphone he explained that I'd got his wife's name wrong:

'It's not Edie, it's Ethel,' he said.

Normally I'd have wondered if I'd got the wrong contact but in this case, since all the other details were correct, I knew that the mistake was mine.

'Sorry, love,' I aplogised to Ethel, 'I thought you said your name was Edie.'

Ethel didn't care, she had more important matters on her mind.

'I'm worried about Norman because he's blaming himself,' she told me. 'He didn't hear me go but there was nothing he could have done. I got up at 2.00 in the morning when he was fast asleep. I'd been ill you see and I thought I had cancer. I didn't want to be a burden on him.'

'Yes she was afraid she had cancer of the bladder,' said Norman.

Ethel, who'd been married to Norman for forty years, walked miles until she came to some water, I think it was a river and then, confused and tired by the exertion, she slipped in and drowned.

'But he's still blaming himself and he mustn't,' she said. 'There was nothing he could have done. If I hadn't gone out that night I'd have gone another night.'

On a happier note she wanted Norman to know that she was still close and kept an eye on him just as she always did.

'He's put up clean curtains, just as I always used to at this time of the year,' she said. 'He carries my wedding ring in his pocket and he's moved into a one-room flat now. Oh yes and he's got my picture on his bedside table and every night before he goes to sleep he kisses it and I kiss him back.'

There was so much information coming through that Norman, who'd hardly got over the surprise at hearing his name called, couldn't take it all in.

At one point Ethel mentioned some friends of hers but Norman said he'd never heard of them.

'He has, he has,' said Ethel impatiently. 'He knows them as well as I do. They were in the old people's flats where we used to live.'

Light dawned when I mentioned the flats to Norman.

'Oh yes of course,' he said. 'They were Ethel's best friends there. I remember now.'

It was a marvellous contact and a touching display of the

love between two elderly people. They'd had their ups and downs throughout forty years of marriage but they still loved each other as devotedly as they did on their wedding day. It was clear that Ethel was going to stay by Norman's side until the moment they were reunited in the spirit world.

The second half of the demonstration went just as well with many amusing little incidents to lighten the atmosphere. Earlier in the evening I'd heard the name Sandy repeated now and then and I'd taken it to be a shortening of Sandra. Nothing else came with it though and I didn't follow it up. Back in the dressing-room during the interval however, I got it again, but much more distinctly.

'It's not Sandy for Sandra,' said a Scottish and very male voice, 'It's Sandy for Alexander. I hope you can find my wife. I'm a bit reserved but I was determined to get through because she's come a long way.'

So after the break I asked for Sandy's wife and a neat Scottish lady with a dry sense of humour came forward.

First she confirmed the details. Yes, her husband Alexander had died of cancer in the neck, and yes, the illness only lasted twelve weeks.

But then Sandy mentioned Sarah.

'His mother,' sniffed Sandy's wife.

'They didn't get on very well,' said Sandy.

'No,' agreed his wife, 'she was an old vagabond.'

'Well he wants you to know love, that Sarah's here with him,' I put in.

'God help him,' said his wife tartly and there were roars of laughter from the audience.

Then Sandy asked for some flowers for his wife.

'Oh good,' she said when I told her, 'because he never gave me any when he was here.'

'Well I thought I'd better ask or she'd give me hell when

she comes over,' Sandy confided. 'She's plagued with her back in the winter you know.'

'I'm plagued with it now,' added his wife.

But Sandy was obviously looking at the flowers piled up on the stage and choosing something nice.

'Could you give her one of the bouquets,' he asked, 'and could you give that big centre piece to the bairn's mother back there.'

Behind his wife at the microphone a young woman who'd lost a child waited for her turn.

'He says the bairn's mother behind you should have the big centre piece,' I said.

'He would,' said Sandy's wife, 'he's not paying for it.'

By now the audience were in stitches, but for all the unsentimental exchanges there were tears in that woman's eyes and there was a great deal of affection between the couple.

The afternoon raced by and all too soon Tony Ortzen had to bring the demonstration to an end because there was another function taking place later that evening.

I left the stage to the most tremendous applause and people rushed forward to thank me for their messages, shake my hand or ask for autographs.

It really had been the most marvellous occasion.

But I wasn't quite over the hurt caused by that newspaper reporter. The unpleasant article came out the day before a demonstration at Lewisham, and I was worried to think that people would believe the ugly things that were printed. Now I've got to prove myself all over again I thought sadly.

'Don't worry about it, love,' said John. 'Just do your work and you can't go wrong.'

But my work can be affected by my mental state and if I wasn't careful I knew I could make a hash of things just when I most wanted to do well.

I was pretty nervous by the time I got on stage but fortunately the first contact was marvellous.

'We sent you some flowers,' a man kept whispering in my ear, but I couldn't understand it because there were no flowers in the dressing-room.

It turned out that a beautiful bouquet signed just Lillian and John which had arrived at home some time before was from this man and his wife. I'd been puzzled at the time because there was no accompanying letter and I didn't know any Lillian and John. I assumed I must have given them a message at a theatre some time before and that the flowers were a thank you gift.

It didn't occur to me that the gift was a thank you in advance!

Well the man talking to me was John and he was looking for his wife Lillian. What's more he'd only passed the previous Thursday and they hadn't had the funeral yet.

John wasn't lonely on the other side. He'd met several workmates who'd gone over before him.

'But it wasn't right, Doris,' he told me. 'I wasn't an old man, I was only sixty-three.'

'Actually he was sixty-four,' said his wife. 'He was just sixty-four but he had his birthday while he was in hospital and he refused to celebrate it until he was home.'

'She hasn't washed my pyjamas yet,' said John. 'Silly really. She thinks she'll wash me away if she washes them but she won't because I'm there with her all the time.'

John went chattering on. He told me he'd left £53 in a drawer at home, that he'd pinched his wife from another fellow before they were married, and he even mentioned the budgie Bobby.

I couldn't have wished for a better way to start the evening, but for some reason instead of making me relaxed, it made me worry that I couldn't keep the quality going. Anxious thoughts crept in and the rest of the first half was dreadful. I was hearing things well enough but nothing came together. I got scraps of information all over the place and no one claimed them. I kept hearing something about a pub called The Golden Fleece, and some time-sharing apartments in Spain. But the messages didn't belong to each other and I got myself into a mess.

It's not working I thought in despair.

I went off at the intermission and had a cup of tea and then I went to the loo and had a few tears. What's the matter with you girl? I asked myself sternly. God's on your side. Go out there and show them.

The little pep talk did the trick. Back I went and the second half went like a dream. All the bits and pieces that were such a jumble in the first half fell into place. We found the owner of the time-share apartment who had a message from his wife, we found the reference to the Golden Fleece pub – it turned out that the man who worked there had gone into the gents, and killed himself. He'd only been married five months.

And so it went on. By the time I finished, the audience gave me a standing ovation and I came off walking on air.

'Don't let them bother you, Doris,' people kept telling me as I made my way back to the dressing-room. 'We don't believe a word of it. To hell with them, we love you.'

All my worries dissolved. Once again the spirit world had proved that I was wrong to doubt.

'Just trust in us and we won't let you down,' Ramanov was always telling me and sure enough they'd done it again!

Not long after this I received two lovely poems inspired by that article.

Why oh why, won't they see, when I've tried so hard to
   just be me,
I can't perform miracles, this I can't do
All that I've done is try to help you.
The messages come and in my own way,
I just pass on what your loved ones say,
I don't invent, I don't pretend, I just try to help as would
   any friend,
And if in the end some comfort I give, is that so wrong
   if I help others to live
In the knowledge that somewhere in God's own good
   time
Reunited they'll be in a joy so sublime,
If this I can do then happy I'll be,
Please don't condemn, I'm only me!

Sylvia Mallett dashed that off almost as soon as she heard
of the attacks on my good name and shortly afterwards, John
Wheeler of Sussex wrote this *Letter to Doris* in verse:

> Few they are who have the Faith
> To run the race and hold the pace,
> When hard the track that they must run;
> While others seem to have the fun.
> Some fail by doubt and some by fear
> And others when they've come so near
> The winning post in psychic quest
> Fail only through a lack of zest.
> No sticks or stones can bar the way,
> Nor even what the sceptics say . . .
> For those who run the race for truth
> Eventually they find the proof.
> Hold true to purpose and intent—

For steadfast faith will circumvent
The words of those who scoff and scorn
They are but young Souls newly born.
The lessons of successive life
The effort made, the stress and strife,
Will teach to everyone in turn
The lessons they are here to learn.
Then on that day to Heaven's pleasure,
A knowledge that each one will treasure,
That those who've run the race and won
Are helping now, we who still run.
For on the other side of death,
Running with unceasing zest
Are the keepers of the portals
The gateway twixt passed souls and mortals.

How could I possibly feel downhearted, with such good friends as these?

8

Some years ago when I was in Australia, I happened to appear on the same TV programme as the pop singer Meat Loaf. Now I'm not very well up on pop singers and I was astonished as I was leaving the green room to see this young man walking in. Dressed all in black motorcycle leathers, he was one of the largest men I've ever seen. He was enormous.

'How on earth does he do all the jumping around that pop singers do at that size?' I whispered to one of the TV people as he led me to the set.

'Well I've heard they give him a whiff of oxygen before he goes on, then he does a number, comes off, they give him another whiff of oxygen and throw him back on again!'

It seemed incredible to me if it was true.

Anyway, without the benefit of oxygen myself, I went on, started to do a demonstration for the audience and the whole thing went so well that I ended up staying an hour!

Poor old Meat Loaf was waiting all that time for his entrance and as I came off he said, a little crossly I thought, 'Who *is* that old lady?'

'I might be an old lady, love,' I told him jokingly, 'but they've never had to give me oxygen yet!'

Meat Loaf laughed, the tension evaporated and suddenly we were friends.

Since then I've found that no matter how strange young people might look to my eyes, underneath the peculiar clothes and weird make-up, they are nearly always lovely people. I've had punks queuing at the stage door just to hand me a rose and the most bizarre looking reporters from young magazines writing beautiful articles full of spiritual understanding, about my work. It just shows that you can't judge people by their appearance.

Sadly though, although a lot of pop singers are very nice people they do seem to get themselves into awful messes, and end up passing over long before their time. I've spoken to so many of them on the other side and it seems such a shame that so much talent is cut off in its prime.

One of the most famous stars I've 'met' in this way is Elvis Presley and not long ago I had a chance to renew our acquaintance. I must stress that I can't call up whoever I choose for a cosy chat. I mean I'd quite like a few words with Winston Churchill but why on earth should he want to talk to me? My only chance of contacting the great man is through a sitting with a member of his family or a friend, or if there was some sort of link.

In the case of Elvis Presley there was already a link because I'd spoken to him some years ago during a sitting for Marc Bolan's mother Phyllis. Marc was telling his mother about his new life on the other side and the friends he'd made. He was particularly thrilled to have met his idol Elvis Presley and he brought him along to say hello. Marc introduced Elvis to his mother and Elvis introduced Mark to *his* mother who was with him on the other side. I recall that Elvis was a softly spoken young man and he seemed to be very polite. He kept calling me ma'am.

Anyway it was a pleasant interlude but I thought no more about it until the *Sun* newspaper rang me and asked if it was possible to contact Elvis. Apparently his wife Priscilla had just written a sensational book about their marriage and they wanted to know what Elvis thought of it. Would he like to defend his reputation from these slurs?

I was staying in Brighton at the time because I was doing a few theatre demonstrations and I knew I had a morning to spare.

'Well look I can't guarantee anything,' I said, 'I do know Elvis slightly but I've no idea whether he'll want to come and talk to me or not.'

The *Sun* said that they quite understood but they'd like to try all the same, so reporter Ruth Brotherhood was despatched to Brighton.

She arrived armed with an Elvis album and a wedding picture of Elvis and Priscilla, to help get me in the mood. I looked at the photograph. The couple were so young and eager looking, an apparently well matched pair. Both attractive and healthy, they should have had years ahead of them to live happily and raise a family. What a shame it had ended in bitterness and tragedy.

The hotel was right on the seafront but outside the traffic thundered by, as noisy as on any London street. Laurie closed all the windows to help me concentrate and then keeping that haunting photograph in my mind, I tuned in.

I took a while to make contact because there was no love link, but eventually I realised that a man was standing close by. As I homed in on the light that suddenly appeared in the room, I felt a tide of bewilderment and confusion washing around me. It was a sensation I was becoming used to. So many young people I contact these days carry the same muddled feelings with them, but this man seemed more mixed-up than most. Or at least he used to be when he was on the earth.

Then he spoke and I recognised the slow, southern voice and the quaint good manners.

'Yes it's me, ma'am,' he told me.

'Well Elvis,' I said silently, 'I expect you know what's been going on? So what's all this about you and your wife? Why's she been saying these things about you?'

There was a pause as if Elvis was trying to get his thoughts in order and then it all came tumbling out, a bit disjointed, but then he obviously found it difficult to put his feelings into words.

'I was brought up to treat women with reverence,' he said, 'I wanted my wife to be a virgin. That's why I chose Priscilla. I chose her from the beginning and I groomed her.'

He had clearly been a conceited man, and though he was struggling now to achieve humility it didn't come easily to him. Yet he loved Cilla, he truly loved her, he kept saying and I believed him.

'I made a great many mistakes in my life but the biggest mistake I ever made was with Priscilla. I put her on a pedestal. I treated her as something . . . maybe I was a bit weird, but as something holy . . . I had a very religious upbringing you see. I revered my mother and then I revered my wife and that was where I went wrong. She needed me to be a husband, a friend, and a lover – and I wasn't.'

But for a religious person he had some strange tastes. Suddenly his voice stopped and he showed me a picture. I was looking at a terrific-sized room and everything was black. Black, black, black everywhere, carpet, sheets, everything just black and huge mirrors reflecting it. In the mirrors I could see a bed, yet somehow I knew that this wasn't Cilla's bed. It was Elvis's private room.

'Well they did sleep separately later on,' Ruth explained.

Then the picture vanished and I was looking at another room – the bathroom. The contrast between the bathroom and the bedroom couldn't have been greater. Where the bedroom was all stark and black the bathroom was all pale marble and furs scattered across the floor.

'Sometimes I could be mean in spirit to my wife,' Elvis went on, sounding genuinely sorry. 'But does my daughter realise that when I used to lock myself away for days, that I loved her very much. It's just that I needed to take pills. I'm a hypochondriac I suppose. I used to take drugs for this, drugs for that. I was so frightened. I thought I had cancer. I passed blood sometimes.'

'Does he remember the early days with Priscilla?' asked Ruth because things were beginning to take a morbid turn.

Elvis's voice softened, 'She was only fourteen, just a school girl. I remember her in white. But I thought I was God Almighty. I thought I could take her and mould her. And I did. She was overawed by me. I really thought I was the king. And now I'm over here and I realise that I'm just an ordinary boy with a special gift of making music.'

Looking back over his life he could see the mess he'd made of things and he was full of remorse.

'Forty-two. I was only forty-two,' he said. 'Oh God. I had all that money. What was the use of it? . . . And what upset me was the rows afterwards. Colonel Parker, Vernon – there was plenty for everybody. Why row?'

As to Priscilla's revelations he wasn't worried for himself.

'It doesn't hurt me none,' he said. 'But what about Lisa. Will it hurt Lisa, I'd like you to ask Cilla that. It doesn't hurt me none, I'm out of it aren't I, but why hurt Lisa. She doesn't need the money. Why do it?'

'Yes, but what went wrong, love?' I asked. 'Cilla loved you at first. What happened?'

There was a long silence. I got the impression that Elvis didn't like admitting to his faults.

'When I should have been doing my duty as a husband I was shut up reading the Bible,' he said.

'There must have been more to it than that, love.'

There was another pause.

'I was wrong wrong wrong wrong wrong,' he suddenly burst out passionately. 'After she'd had the baby I thought she was sullied. I confused her with my mother. It was like making love to my mother. I couldn't do it.'

He seemed so upset, I changed the subject and asked him about the people he'd met on the other side. I knew his mother was with him of course but he mentioned that his father Vernon had since joined them and several other names that Ruth couldn't place. He talked of Betsy and Herbert, someone called Mary Ann, or Marian, and also of a preacher. He kept on about this preacher as if the man had had some kind of special significance for him.

It was clear that he was a very weird man in his personal life. Half of him wanted to let rip and go with tarts, but the religious part of his nature held him back. As a compromise by all accounts it seems he liked his wife to dress up in a tarty way to act out his fantasies.

'I thought I was her master,' said Elvis, 'I took her from nothing and I thought she should be grateful. I was wrong . . .'

He had learned a lot since his passing, yet he hadn't quite managed to rid himself of self pity. He knew that he became bloated and grotesque in his last years and yet he was inclined to blame everybody but himself.

'Why couldn't I have met somebody who could have straightened me out?' he asked, his voice rising to a childish whine.

I'm afraid I lost patience a bit with that.

'Everyone gets under pressure you know love and they have to work it out for themselves,' I said rather more sharply than I intended.

Elvis crumbled immediately. 'I know I must have been weak. I wanted to be mothered. I wanted my wife to be my mother and the other half of me wanted to be the master. I was a coward too. I couldn't have borne a painful passing. I couldn't stand that. My mother died a painful death and I couldn't bear it to happen to me . . .'

'D'you mean you took yourself over because you were afraid you had cancer?' I asked him silently because it almost sounded as if he was telling me that his death had been a suicide.

He shook his head vehemently.

'I didn't mean to do it. I got mixed up. I took a lot of pills but I didn't mean to do it . . .'

An impression of his last moments swept over me. I was on the bathroom down on my knees on the fur rug. I was saying my prayers I think, then I felt very sick and there was a terrible pain in my head.

He kept saying something about his toes being black which I couldn't fathom at all.

'D'you mean you had black socks on? Or that you didn't have socks on?' I asked, but the reply was jumbled and I couldn't make it out.

'My mother came for me, ma'am,' he added, 'and I went before my father.'

There was a pause and I gathered that he wasn't best pleased with his father. He seemed to think there had been squabbles over money and he was annoyed that his father had married again. He didn't think he should have replaced Elvis's beloved mother.

On the subject of his daughter Lisa, though, his feelings were plain.

'I'm very proud of her. She's beginning to look like me. I want her to be happy. Tell her to be careful. Tell her to make sure she marries a man who loves her for herself and not for her money.'

He paused, 'I want her to have a normal life and have babies. In fact I'm going to have three grandchildren . . .'

The power was getting very weak by this time. It had been a long and emotional sitting and I was exhausted. I think Elvis was finding it a struggle too.

'Well I think we'll have to stop now,' I told Ruth, 'I can hardly hear him.'

But even as I spoke I heard one last sentence floating towards me before the vibrations went dead.

'Please ask my wife to forgive me . . .'

I felt quite shaken when the sitting was over. What an unhappy man Elvis Presley had been. I thought of all the people who must have envied him his talent, his early good looks, his money and fame. To think he had all those things and yet he had nothing . . . What a terrible, terrible waste.

9

The policewoman looked stern. She'd walked into the party in her severe navy uniform, her hat pulled down low on her forehead and everything had gone quiet. Conversation stopped, the music trailed away and guests watched her uneasily from the corners of their eyes.

'Is there a John Stokes here?' she asked crisply, unconcerned about the effect she was having on the party.

John walked forward, 'Yes love. That's me.'

'John Stokes I've got a warrant for your arrest,' she told him.

Anyone else might have been worried, but John, secure in the knowledge that he couldn't possibly have done anything wrong, was not alarmed. He knew there must be some mistake.

'Oh really,' he said, 'what for?'

'I believe you have a dog?'

'Yes. Boots.'

'Have you got a licence?'

John frowned, 'No, I don't think so, he's not a year old yet. We don't need a licence do we?'

The policewoman took out her notebook.

'I'll have to take down your particulars.'

'All right,' said John, 'what do you want to know?'

She paused, a mischievous grin warming her face.

'Would you like to unbutton my shirt?'

At this point I couldn't control myself any longer and I burst out laughing. The 'policewoman' was a Kissogram I'd organised as an extra present for John on our 42nd wedding anniversary. What's good enough for the executives in London is good enough for my husband I thought and I wanted him to have a really memorable occasion.

To the amazement of the guests, the policewoman slowly peeled off her formal uniform to reveal a leopard-skin leotard, stockings and suspender belt underneath. It was all quite tasteful. There were no rude boobs or anything like that, and John didn't turn a hair. At the end the girl said.

'I have to post the telegram, John,' and she pulled out his trousers and stuck the telegram down the front.

'John wants everyone to play Postman Pat!' shouted a joker amongst the guests and everyone fell about laughing.

It was a marvellous party.

In fact we had two marvellous parties in January. The first to celebrate my 66th birthday and the second, our anniversary, which falls in the same month.

We'd not had a party for years and as my birthday approached I started thinking how nice it would be to have a really good do. The problem was, where? Spacious as our semi seems to us after the small ex-serviceman's flat where we used to live, it's still not large enough to hold all our friends – not if they want to breathe as well that is!

'Well what about the pub?' said Laurie when I mentioned the problem.

As well as looking after me, Laurie also runs a pub in the East End.

'The saloon bar's quite nice and it would certainly be big enough,' he said.

So it was settled. Iris, Laurie's wife, did all the catering; she laid on a magnificent spread. Brendan Blake, an old friend who is also a professional singer and comedian, led the entertainment and we had a real old knees-up. Derek Jameson, another old friend, came along and afterwards he wrote in the paper, 'Top medium Doris Stokes doesn't go to posh restaurants on her birthday – she celebrates in an East End pub!'

Well really, what would I want with a posh restaurant at my age? I'm not out to impress anybody. It was much more fun in the pub. We had a terrific time and people enjoyed themselves so much they said: 'When can we have another one?'

So we did it all over again on our wedding anniversary.

Patrick brought his old grandmother who is ninety-seven to the second party and everyone made a fuss of her. She came along dressed up to the eyes in her little fur coat, and Brendan Blake sang 'When Irish Eyes Are Smiling' specially for her. He had to sing right in her ear because she's rather deaf these days, but she loved it and ninety-seven or not she was up on the floor dancing away with the rest of us.

I have to admit that even though I've been complaining of shaky legs ever since my stroke, I felt as if I could dance all night. It was wonderful.

With the anniversary approaching it seemed a good time to tackle John again on the subject of a new wedding ring. When we were married John bought me a 29s 11d utility ring because the cheap utility rings were all you could get in those days – unless you were a millionaire I suppose.

Well it wasn't very good quality. Over the years it grew

thinner and thinner and on our 30th anniversary I asked John if he'd buy me a new one.

He wouldn't.

'No,' he said, 'it's not the money. I'll buy you anything else but I want you to keep the ring you were married in.'

It was sweet and sentimental and I was rather touched so I kept the ring on my finger and settled for something else. But the next twelve years took their toll. The ring became so thin and sharp it kept cutting my finger. I was forever taking it off, putting on a plaster and replacing the ring when my finger was healed, only for it to cut my finger all over again.

'It's no good John,' I said at last, 'I'll have to have a decent wedding ring. I can't go on like this. I'll have a septic finger.'

So reluctantly John agreed to buy me a new ring, and I chose a beautiful model of intertwined red and white gold leaves. Even John had to admit it was gorgeous. We put the old ring away in a box and I made sure John made a note of where it was kept.

'If I go before you, John,' I told him, 'for goodness' sake don't forget to take the good ring off and put the other one on before you cremate me!'

All in all the early part of the year was a very sociable time. I was highly excited to be invited to Hatchards, the exclusive bookshop in Piccadilly, for their Author of the Year reception.

As it happened I was suffering from the remnants of a cold and I'd been left with a sore throat and an irritating cough every time I opened my mouth. I didn't dare have anything to eat in case it set me off and I only stayed half an hour but it was fun all the same.

It was very posh indeed. There was a toastmaster in red coat and white gloves to announce you as you walked in.

There were cameras everywhere to photograph your entrance and there were so many famous authors it made your head spin. After Dick Francis, Dulcie Grey, Jilly Cooper and Jeffrey Archer, I lost count.

Jeffrey Archer was very nice. I was sitting there sipping my orange juice and watching the dazzling crowd when he came over and sat on the floor at my feet.

'I'm kneeling in front of a superstar!' he said with the most charming smile.

I was amazed. I'd always thought he would be a bit of a stuffed shirt but he wasn't at all. I wouldn't be surprised if he went back into politics seriously and ended up Prime Minister one day!

At the risk of sounding as if I trip over stars every day of the week I must also mention my visit to Thames TV for *An Audience With Billy Connolly*. I was invited to be part of the audience for the television show and I enjoyed it very much.

Billy Connolly was a little bit strong in places, for me, but for all that he drew on his experiences as a child and I found I could identify with him. He talked of the way you had coats piled on the bed in winter because there weren't enough blankets to go round, and the way everything was poshed up when the vicar dropped in and the best biscuits, kept for special occasions, were brought out.

It brought back a lot of memories. We were taught as children that the vicar or priest was something special and everything had to be the best for him. I remember long after-wards when I was staying with friends in Dublin, being very surprised at the amount of whisky the priest put back when he dropped in on Friday evenings. But then I thought, why am I surprised just because he's wearing a dog collar? He's still a man and he has his weaknesses like everyone else.

It was just the way I was brought up. We were taught
that the vicar was above the rest of us. We were very poor,
yet we weren't miserable. I remember going round to Maggie
Roberts' father's corner shop for a halfpenny worth of
broken biscuits. It didn't bother me because it seemed quite
normal. I didn't know anyone who bought biscuits any
other way.

Maggie Roberts of course went on to be Prime Minister
Margaret Thatcher, but in those days she was just Maggie
from the shop, a smart little girl who always did her home-
work. Her father was a preacher too and on Sunday nights
we kids got a poke of sweets if we sat through his sermons
at the chapel. We sat there for hours letting all this hellfire
and damnation wash over our heads, so that we could claim
our sweets at the end of it!

Oh yes, Billy brought it all back. After the show we stayed
for supper and Billy came over to say hello.

'Even if I couldn't have seen your face I would have known
where you were,' he said, 'because you gave off a glow.'

'Well it surely wasn't my jewellery, love!' I joked, but inside
I was touched. What a lovely compliment.

But if I've given the impression that I'm leading a wild
life of parties and shows I must explain that these things are
just the fun highlights and between them there's been a great
deal of solid, hard work.

When I'm not making theatre appearances, Laurie keeps
me busy with a steady stream of personal sittings. They're all
booked through his office and I never know who's coming
until they arrive. I'm very honoured to think that one of my
recent sitters was Benazir Bhutto, daughter of the former
Prime Minister of Pakistan who was hanged by the military
regime. I saw her on television not long ago surrounded by
a quarter of a million people – and to think that she sat

there on the sofa in my sitting room, with me just in my old dressing gown. It's a strange world.

In fact Benazir almost didn't get a sitting. She'd been booked in for some time and I'd had to cancel the first appointment through ill health. By a stroke of bad luck I was ailing again when the second appointment came round and I asked Laurie to postpone the meeting once more. But this time he couldn't contact Benazir. So there I was resting in bed, when there was a knock at the door.

Dragging on my old dressing gown, I went down to find Benazir, her sister, and her friend Jane, all standing in the hall unaware that Laurie had been phoning all over London in an attempt to stop them coming.

'Oh dear, shall we go and leave you in peace?' asked Jane when they saw that I was obviously unwell.

But I couldn't turn them away once they'd come this far.

'No it's all right, love,' I said. 'Come and sit down and we'll have a try, but I feel so rotten I can't promise we'll get anything.'

John put the kettle on and the girls made themselves comfortable. Benazir seemed a very nice young woman. She was slim and dark with pale gold skin and heavy glasses that gave her the look of a young Nana Mouskouri.

She couldn't have been very old, little more than a child to me, and I had no idea as she sat there holding her cup with delicate fingers, that she wanted her father's advice because she had very big plans indeed. Despite the fact that politics had killed her father and her brother, Benazir was planning to return to Pakistan to take over where her father had left off.

It was her father himself who mentioned her plans. At first he talked of family matters. He mentioned his nick-names for Benazir and her sister: Pinky he called her, and her sister was known as Sunny. He also mentioned his first wife, his child wife he said, from Iran. He spoke of his son who had been poisoned, then he talked of the night he himself passed over.

'There were twelve of them,' he said. 'They came for me in the night and they strangled me.'

Whether he meant they strangled him in his cell, or whether he was referring to the fact that he was hanged wasn't clear. Most of all he wanted Benazir to know that she had his support and his blessing.

'Verdie,' he kept saying – that's the nearest I can get to the spelling. I thought it was a name.

'No,' said Benazir, 'in our language it means I promise.'

'I promise I'll always stand by you,' he said.

He told her that despite the opposition she would go back to Pakistan to a tumultuous welcome from the people and it was then that I realised what a brave girl this was.

'Get the people behind you,' he kept saying. 'It's the people who count. You can pick any monkey out of the jungle and stick him in a uniform and he'll think he rules the world, but the people will know. You can't fool the people.'

He went on to give Benazir the names of the people she could trust and those she couldn't and he talked of papers locked away in a safe somewhere, that she might need.

It was a marvellous sitting and over and over he kept reminding her, 'I'll always stand by you. I promise.'

Afterwards as she rose to go a look of great determination came into her fine dark eyes. 'I'll do it, and I'll do it for my father,' said Benazir.

'No forget that, love,' I told her. 'Don't do it for your father. Do it for the people.'

Shortly afterwards I heard that Benazir, at great personal risk, had returned to Pakistan where thousands upon thousands of people had turned out to greet her. I marvelled at her courage; that slip of a girl hoping to rule a country and now I follow her career with fascination. I just hope her dad's taking good care of her.

Shortly after Benazir's visit, a family from Finland came to see me. As I said before, Laurie never tells me anything about my sitters in advance so their stories are always a complete surprise to me as they unfold. But in this case I sensed great tragedy as soon as the family walked in.

It turned out that their teenage son and their nephew had died in separate incidents, both of which could have been regarded as suicide.

The couple's son, Karri, soon put me right about his passing.

'It was an accident, I didn't mean to do it,' he assured me. 'I was cleaning the gun and looking down the barrel when I tripped and it went off.'

Pira, his poor mother, had found him. Apparently the boy was very interested in chemistry and he wanted to be a pharmacist. He liked to carry out experiments in his bedroom and when she heard the bang, she thought something had exploded. She raced upstairs expecting to have to put out a fire. Instead she found her son slumped back on the bed with shotgun wounds.

The other boy, Petri, was just as tragic. His father was rather strict and he was worried about some exams that were coming up. Anyway, one day he went along for the ride while his father visited a sick friend in hospital. While his father was at the bedside, Petri took the lift to the top of the building and jumped off. Another friend who was with him, Kolevi, also jumped.

'It was the drugs,' said Kolevi, 'I honestly thought I could fly.'

Petri was very sad about the pain he'd caused his family.

'We were in Dad's Landrover,' he said. 'The last time he saw me alive I was sitting in the Landrover – the next I was lying dead at the foot of the building. I'm so sorry. I was depressed.'

There were a great many family details as well as these harrowing accounts, but most of all both boys wanted to get through to Pira's other son, Nicholas, who'd come with her.

'Don't get involved in drugs or anything,' they kept saying over and over again. 'Be a good boy Nicholas.'

Nicholas kept protesting that nothing was further from his mind, but they seemed so worried about him that it made me wonder.

In direct contrast to the warning mood of the Finnish sitting was the little girl who came back to her parents shortly afterwards. They'd hardly sat down when a little girl danced into the room, there was no other word for it, and said:

'Gay by name and gay by nature.'

'Now what does she mean by that?' I asked. 'Was her name Gay?'

'No it's our surname,' said her mother.

And the next moment the little girl gave me her Christian name. I thought she said Leonie, but it was Lianne.

Lianne had great vitality and she bubbled on without inhibition.

'I was crossing the road,' she told me, 'and I was ever so careful. I was on the zebra crossing when the car hit me. But I didn't feel anything.'

She chatted about her mother's new flat and the new car.

'But she hasn't seen it,' said her father incredulously.

'I have you know,' said Lianne indignantly.

She even mentioned Brian, the disc jockey who lived next door who sometimes put records on for her.

'I loved dancing,' she said, 'and I had a boyfriend called Terry.'

'Yes, little Terry Williams,' said her mum.

She was so eager not to miss anything that sometimes I had difficulty catching up with her and when this happened she got cross with me.

'I *am* impatient,' she admitted when I appealed to her to slow down a bit, 'I'm like me dad. He gets impatient.'

By the end of the sitting both parents were almost speechless.

'I didn't think it would be like this,' admitted Lianne's father at last. 'It was so different to what I'd expected.'

Like a lot of people he feared to find me in long flowing robes, earrings down to the shoulders and maybe a crystal ball for good measure, but of course it's not like that at all. I smile to myself as I watch their faces when they see my sunny sitting room, the mugs of coffee and me wandering about in my carpet slippers. I often feel it must be a great disappointment to them!

Not all spirit people are as easy to talk to as Lianne however. Sometimes they are still so indignant about what they consider to be their untimely passing, that the sheer force of their resentment blocks everything else out.

I felt particularly badly about this when I came up against the problem with a sitter from America. He'd come such a long way to get a message from his mother and when we finally got started she was so stifled with bitterness that other spirit people kept popping in with good wishes for the friend who'd come with him.

All I could learn from the mother was that she'd passed away during an operation. She kept touching me behind the ears to indicate where she'd been cut until the end I realised that she'd been having a facelift.

'It needs looking into,' she said again and again. 'It shouldn't have happened. I shouldn't have come over here yet. I'm only sixty-one and I didn't even look sixty-one. They are saying my heart gave out. Nonsense. There was nothing the matter with my heart. It needs looking into. See a lawyer.'

She was a very forthright lady and she didn't mince her words but I couldn't get her to discuss anything else. She grudgingly showed me a brief picture of her house, a beautiful single storey place in a pale wash colour, set in a beautiful garden, but then she kept returning to the operation and the possible court case.

She was all for legal action, no doubt about that.

'I hate injustice,' she said, 'and this isn't right. It needs looking into.'

I could get practically nothing else from her and it was clear that I wouldn't for quite a while yet. Once she's accepted her fate and settled down on the other side the bitterness will clear, but until then there was nothing much I could do.

'I'm sorry love,' I told her poor son. 'She's making it so hard for me.'

And his friend was embarrassed too, about all the personal messages *he'd* received:

'I shouldn't have come, I've spoiled it for you,' he said apologetically.

'No, really, I don't mind,' the sitter told him gallantly. 'It's been fascinating to hear your messages.'

I felt dreadful but it couldn't be helped.

'Perhaps we can do better next time you come to England,' I promised.

But not all my sittings are conducted face to face with my sitters. Sometimes I have to work by telephone. Recently I even gave a radio interview, broadcast in Belfast, from the comfort of my own bed! This wasn't the height of laziness I hasten to add. I'd fully intended to go to the studios in London but unfortunately a tummy bug struck just as I was getting ready to leave.

I was up, washed and breakfasted. The car was waiting and I slipped upstairs to put my boots on because it was a cold morning. I bent over to pull on the right boot and suddenly my head swam, my breakfast came back and there was an intense pain in my stomach. Oh no, what's the matter now? I wondered. I went back, washed again, reapplied my makeup and ignoring my bendy legs, I went downstairs.

The driver was waiting in the hall.

'Come on Doris the traffic's building up,' he said. He helped me on with my coat, then he stopped.

'You can't go out like that, you're burning up.'

I put my hand to my cheek. Sweat was pouring down my face, yet I felt cold. John came out and felt my forehead.

'Yes, love, you've got a temperature. You can't go out like that. Go back to bed.'

So the electric blanket was switched on, I climbed thankfully back into bed and Laurie got the studios on the phone to break the news to them that I wouldn't be coming. They weren't pleased of course, but they managed to arrange a link-up with Belfast to my phone and I did the whole thing tucked up in bed!

But most of my phone work I'm happy to say is conducted from the armchair in my sitting room. A phone sitting can never take the place of a personal meeting of course, but sometimes the case is so urgent, I have to contact the people immediately. I can't give them much over the phone, but a few scraps at the right time can mean more than yards and yards of messages years after the event.

Not long ago I talked to a couple who'd written to me with a very distressing story. The previous Easter their little son had been given a small chocolate egg containing a model car. The egg was not recommended for children under three years of age, but their little boy was three and they couldn't imagine what danger could lurk in an innocent looking piece of confectionery.

The little boy tore off the foil wrapping, bit into the chocolate and then started to choke. The model car inside was in pieces, ready to be assembled, and the lad had swallowed a lump of plastic with his mouthful of chocolate. It lodged in his throat and no amount of slapping on the back would shift it.

The frantic parents rushed him to hospital but it was too late. Before the surgeon could operate, he was gone.

In fact at first, the parents didn't even want a sitting. They contacted me to ask if I could tell Esther Rantzen about the case. They were anxious to get the eggs banned from sale to prevent any more tragedies happening.

'We wouldn't want any other parents to have to go through what we've been through,' they said.

Laurie wrote to *That's Life* explaining what had happened and got a very nice letter back, thanking him for drawing the matter to their attention and saying that they were investigating the case. That was the last we heard and sadly it was too late to get the eggs banned for Easter 1986. But it wasn't the last we heard of the story. Not long afterwards Laurie had a phone call from the father of the little boy. It was now a year since his son's passing and his wife was taking it very badly. Could I possibly talk to her on the phone?

I couldn't refuse. Laurie gave me the number, which was in Ireland and I rang it immediately.

The poor couple were still very upset and a bit nervous but I was able to get their son quite quickly.

'Daddy's been painting,' he told me.

'Is he an artist, love?' I asked. 'Does he paint pictures?'

The boy laughed, 'No he's been painting the house.'

'Does it look nice?' I asked silently.

'Yep!' said the boy. Not yes, but yep.

His father was amazed. 'That's right. That's just what he used to say. It was always yep.'

The boy went on to talk a little more about his family and what they were doing. He also mentioned the new car they'd recently bought.

By the end of the call the parents sounded dazed but happier and I could only hope that my few words had been of help.

I had a similar request a few weeks after this. A man whose handicapped son had passed unexpectedly just two or three *hours* before, phoned Laurie with a desperate appeal. His wife was expecting a baby and she was so distraught at the loss of her first child, that he feared for her and the unborn baby.

Apparently their much loved first child, Mark, was a bit of a handful and they were persuaded to put him into a home for a few days to give his mum a break while she had the baby.

Mark was cutting his back teeth at the time so when the home phoned shortly afterwards to say that he had a slight temperature, they weren't worried. But Mark's temperature did not respond to junior aspirin. He was sent to hospital and by the time the family found out the next day, he was dead.

It was a terrible shock to them. They'd accepted that he wouldn't have a long life, but they'd hoped they might have him for five or six years at least. Worse still was the way they'd discovered the news. They'd telephoned the hospital to find out what ward their son was in and were told he wasn't in a ward. He was in the morgue – he was dead.

It was a shocking blow.

'Please could Doris just speak to my wife?' the husband begged. 'She's in such a state we don't know what to do with her.'

How could anyone refuse such a plea? I telephoned immediately. The poor girl was sobbing uncontrollably at the end of the phone but I did my best. In such circumstances you can't do a lot because the grief has to come out but I hoped that a little reassurance got through.

I saw the little boy within seconds of tuning in even though he'd passed such a short time before. He was a dear little chap standing straight and firm on his own two legs. I knew he was handicapped but I didn't know in what way, until Mark showed me. He kept drawing my attention to his head which he held with great pride and he tilted his chin and put his head right back, so that he could look at the ceiling. Then he grinned triumphantly at me. He was obviously showing off a new ability and I guessed that he'd had no control over his head before.

'That's right,' said his mother, 'he had cerebral palsy. He couldn't hold his head up. It used to flop.'

'Well he can now, love,' I told her. 'He wants to emphasise that. He's all right now.'

Mark was too young to hold a conversation himself, so the people who were looking after him, his great grandmother I think it was, came to give a few family details. It was all rather difficult and confused, the contact blurred by the tremendous emotions coming from Mark's mum, but at the end, just before the power went, Mark came and put a blue and white teddy bear on my knee. This was the toy he wanted to take with him.

'Yes he loves that bear,' said his mother. 'I'll put it in his coffin with him.'

It was all very sad, but they seemed to find a little comfort in the news of their son.

Afterwards I received a beautiful letter from them thanking me for my time. Those few minutes on the phone had made all the difference to them, they said. Now they were trying to pick up the pieces of their lives in the knowledge that their little boy could run and play like other children in his new life on the other side.

10

The other day I was reading through my morning mail when one particular letter which had started quite normally suddenly made me choke on my eleven o'clock coffee. I was so angry I could hardly finish the page. It was from a distressed young mother whose baby daughter was stillborn. The poor girl had gone to a local medium in Shoreham, Essex hoping for some comfort and instead had been given some news that nearly made her take an overdose.

'You're being punished,' the medium told her. 'In a past life you abused children and so now you have to pay for what you did.'

The poor girl was in a terrible state wondering what on earth she could have done and how long her 'punishment' was going to last. Did this mean she'd never bear a healthy child?

Without further ado I dumped a whole lapful of letters on the floor and reached for the phone. The spirit world were right behind me in this because the girl had printed her phone number on the letter and when I dialled it she was in.

'Of course you're not being punished love,' I told her when I'd explained who I was. 'I've never heard such nonsense.

God wouldn't do that. Your little girl is one of the special children who didn't need to stay on earth.'

I calmed her down and explained our philosophy as best I could.

'You go and have another baby, love, I'm sure it'll be all right this time,' I said. 'But listen, this is important. Have you got the number of that medium who told you such wicked things? We've got to put a stop to this.'

'No I didn't keep it. I didn't want anything else to do with her,' she said, 'but I can find it. She advertises in the local paper every week.'

She went off and I heard the crackle of newspaper. Then she was back.

'Yes, here it is Doris,' and she read me the number.

'I'm afraid she's not available,' said the man who answered the phone. 'Can I make an appointment for you?'

'No,' I said firmly. 'I'd just like to speak to her. My name is Doris Stokes.'

'Doris Stokes?' His voice changed, 'Well to be honest Doris she's in the bath at the moment. Just a minute I'll get her.'

It was 11.30 in the morning, an odd time to be having a bath but there you are. There was a long pause and then this 'medium' came to the phone.

'Did you tell a young woman who came to you after having a stillborn baby daughter that she was being punished?' I asked after introducing myself.

'Yes,' she said calmly.

The lack of remorse in her voice made me so angry I could hardly speak.

'Well I've lost four children, three before they were born. How d'you account for that?'

'You're being punished too,' she said. 'You both must have

abused children in a previous life and you're working out your Karma.'

'Where on earth d'you get such ideas from? I've never heard such rubbish,' I spluttered.

But the woman was unshakeable.

'It's true,' she insisted. 'I'm not a spiritualist, I've broken away from that and followed my own ideas.'

'But don't you realise that the woman was on the point of taking herself over because of what you told her?'

The 'medium' at the other end of the phone sighed unrepentantly.

'I look on myself as a surgeon,' she said, 'a surgeon has to cut out the bad parts to make the rest well, and the operation hurts. It does hurt when you come to realise the wrong you've done in previous lives, but once you understand it you can start to put it right.'

'Do you really think God would allow a tiny child to go back to the spirit world before it was born simply because of the mother?' I asked, in a last vain hope that she would see sense.

'Yes,' she said.

It was hopeless. I couldn't get through to her. Either she genuinely believed what she was saying or she simply didn't care about the grief she was causing.

'Well I think it's disgusting,' I said angrily, 'and I don't think you're worthy to call yourself a medium.'

And I put the phone down.

But I couldn't let it rest there. I invited the young mother to my next demonstration and at Question Time she raised the subject in the form of a question so that I could reassure the whole audience that people are not punished in this life for things they'd done in previous lives.

Better still, while I was answering the question I suddenly

heard one of the young woman's relatives speaking to me. Now normally I try not to go into sittings during Question Time because it's not fair to the rest of the audience who're waiting patiently for contacts, but on this occasion I broke my rule.

'They're telling me your child went back to the spirit world fifty minutes before she was born,' I said.

The young mother gasped.

'That's what they said at the hospital. They said she stopped breathing fifty minutes before she was stillborn.'

I went on to tell her who was looking after the baby and a few more family details and she seemed much happier.

Afterwards I had a letter from her husband saying, 'You don't know what peace of mind you've given us. My wife was going through hell thinking it was her fault we lost our daughter.'

I was very pleased to have been able to help and even more pleased that we could have got the point across to so many people. That's the marvellous thing about Question Time, it gives everybody a chance to talk about the things that have been bothering them and people who are too shy to come forward often hear answers to questions they were too nervous to ask.

I thought you might like to see a cross-section of the sort of points that come up at Question Time:

Q. *What happens if there's a nuclear war?*
A. We'll all go over together love. It would probably be the end of this world but not the spirit world.

Q. *Is there any reason why your loved ones can't get a message through, no matter how hard you try to receive it? Is it a judgement?*

A. You need to be a medium to pick up messages and sometimes even a medium is not successful with everyone. The sitter has to be on the same wavelength as the medium.

Q. *My husband died at forty-two. If I live to be eighty will he be eighty when we meet?*
A. No. He'll be just as you want to see him and you will look younger too.

Q. *When my mentally handicapped son dies, will he be like it still and will he remember his life with us?*
A. Of course he'll remember his time with you and he'll lose his handicap. He is a soul that has chosen to come back like this to make you learn. I'll lay odds everyone loves him and that you've learned lots from him.
Yes we have.
You must be a wonderful person to have one of these special children. God only chooses the best.

Q. *If someone didn't believe in life after death when they were alive, can they get a message through when they've passed?*
A. Oh yes. He'll have found out now, won't he!
Q. *Will he be treated the same as those who believed?*
A. Of course he will.

Q. *When I pass over will my husband come for me?*
A. Yes, love, you will see him before you leave the earth plane. Nurses who've seen patients 'die' will tell you that they start talking to people who're not there and this is often dismissed as 'rambling'. Not

so. The patient has seen his spirit people who've come to help him over to the other side.

Q. *When someone wants to get in touch with you can you tell by his smell?*

A. Yes. When a man is present you might smell his favourite tobacco, when a woman is there you might smell the perfume she loved on the earth plane. This doesn't mean they still use it. It's simply a means of identification.
I can smell my father's after-shave.
He's obviously trying to let you know that he's close.

Q. *If someone commits suicide, how long is it before they can make contact through a medium?*

A. I've had them back the same day.

Q. *How many different planes are there?*

A. I don't really know love. I know there are very low planes where people like Hitler go. I also know that I won't be able to go where my children are because they knew no sin so they will be higher up than me. But this doesn't mean I won't see them. They can come and see me whenever they like.

Q. *Do they still cook on the other side? My nan used to love cooking and she made delicious oxtail soup. Will she still be able to do it over there?*

A. Well I expect she will if she wants to love, though I don't suppose it'll be necessary.

Q. *When you sit in a developing circle can two people be helped by one guide?*

A. No. Each one of us has our own spirit guide or teacher and that person has voluntarily given up their progression in the spirit world to come back to the earth plane with us. Even before your body is conceived your guide is with your spirit in the spirit world and when you go back to the spirit world the guide goes back.

We had a little dabble with a board and it said two of us had the same guide.

I wouldn't think so, love. I know my guide couldn't cope with two like me. It takes him all his time to keep me in order!

Q. *Why do some people suffer so much in the world while others come through unscathed?*

A. I think it's all to do with what we have to learn. I have learned a lot through suffering. Before I lost my baby I could meet people in the street and say, hello so and so, you don't look very well, and she would say, 'No, I lost my mother yesterday.' I'd say how sorry I was and I'd mean it but then I'd walk around the corner, see a dress shop and forget all about it as I looked at the dresses in the window. Yet once I'd had tragedy myself, my attitude changed. Now I suffer with people because I understand what they're going through.

Q. *Some people seem to get away with doing such bad things.*

A. Yes I know they do but they don't get away with it on the other side. Hitler will have to start at the bottom in a cold desolate place over there and until he shows remorse he won't rise. There *is* evil in the world. All we can do is try to brighten our own little corner.

Q. *If you lose a baby through miscarriage does it meet up with your loved ones?*

A. Not immediately. They wait till they're full term and then they are born into the spirit world and go to your relatives. Did you lose your baby at four months?

Yes.

Did you know it was a boy?

Yes.

Well they've called him Simon over there!

Q. *I lost two children last year. Will they be together?*

A. Yes.

11

Practically every postbag these days brings me one or two beautiful poems along with the sad stories of tragedy and heartbreak. I save them up to enjoy when I've got a moment or two to spare and I must say the talent of perfectly ordinary people who've never written a poem before in their lives, never ceases to amaze me.

I can't possibly publish them all, there just isn't the space, but I thought you might like to see a selection of some of my favourites.

The first, 'So Now You Know' was sent to me by George Gordon from Tyne and Wear. George didn't actually write the poem himself, apparently the author is unknown, but it so accurately portrays the way I feel half the time that I couldn't stop laughing.

So Now You Know

There's nothing the matter with me
I'm as healthy as can be
I've got arthritis in both knees
And when I talk I talk with a wheeze

My pulse is weak, my blood is thin,
But I'M *AWFULLY WELL* for the state I'm in.

I've got arch supports for both my feet
Without them I couldn't go out in the street
Sleep is denied me night after night
But every morning I find I'm alright
My memory's failing, my head's in a spin
But I'M *AWFULLY WELL* for the state I'm in.

The moral is, as my tale I unfold
That for *You* and *Me* who are both growing old
It's better to say 'I'm fine' with a grin
Than to let other folk know the state we are in
How do I know that my youth is now spent?
Well my GET UP AND GO just got up and WENT.

Old age is golden I've heard it said
But sometimes I wonder as I get into bed
My ears in the drawer, my teeth in a cup
My eyes on the table until I wake up
As sleep overtakes me I say to myself
Is there anything else I should lay on the shelf?

When I was young my slippers were red
I could kick my heels right over my head!
As I grew older my slippers were blue
But still I could dance the whole night through
Now I'm older, my slippers are black
I dash to the shops, but puff my way back.
At last dear Doris my tale is told
So harken you all who are now growing old

Get up each morning, sharpen your wits
Pick up the paper and read the obits
If your name isn't in there, you'll know you're not dead
So have a good breakfast then go back to bed.

So when you've read this just say with a grin
Old so and so's not too bad
FOR THE STATE HE'S IN!!

Thank you George, I feel a lot better for that!

This next poem *Tribute to a Medium*, brought tears to my eyes when I read it. It's by Sylvia Mallett.

Tribute To A Medium

There she sat, centre stage, an ordinary woman like me,
Nothing special about her, well nothing that I could see.
Why had they come all of these folk, what did they
    think she could do?
Why had I come I asked myself when I don't believe in
    you.

Too much sorrow had touched my life, too many tears I'd
    shed
And now the hardest blow of all, my most dearly beloved
    was dead.

I will walk out now I thought, (I must have been out of
    my head),
When a voice came floating across the crowd, is Eileen
    here, she said.
Bert says to tell you he's OK and why did you cry today,

When you walked down the garden to his old shed and
    threw all his things away.
He was walking with you and felt your gloom and this
    made him ever so sad.
Because he is happy and wants you to know that on this
    side nothing is bad.
Wait for the flowers to bloom in the Spring, the ones
    that you both chose with care,
As they appear and make your heart dance, you'll know
    that I am there.

So many messages she gave out that night to people lost
    in grief,
So much love poured from her heart as she said sorry it's
    been so brief.
She was weary now, but still she tried to pass out comfort
    and hope.
Still she smiled that radiant smile as she begged us,
    please don't mope.
The door never closes, it's always ajar and you can step
    inside.
If you remember with love all those that you've lost they
    are always by your side.
An ordinary woman, was that what I'd thought as I
    scoffed and made up jokes.
She is no ordinary woman I say, she's special she's Doris
    Stokes.

I think I shall pin that poem up on my wall, and when
the critics get me down I'll recite it over and over again to
remind myself what my work's all about.

On a more serious note, Shirley Sutcliffe's poem, inspired

by the death of her mother, sums up the feelings often experienced by those who see someone die.

To Die

Wait! I was to hear her cry,
Not now, please wait a while
I want to see the flowers grow
Not have them when they're there for show
Had I known it would be so soon
I would have listened more in tune.
I didn't know, I couldn't guess
That time would be so much less
Than I had hoped and prayed
No! That's a lie
Perhaps that's why I know you're there
I feel your hand
Not cold but warm like sun kissed sand
I'm ready now let's go in haste
Before I lose this joyous taste.
At that her eyes were still, at peace,
A look of wonder, a smile in crease
I felt no sadness, How could I?
It made one think
Life is given to die.

Shirley's mother had obviously caught sight of her loved ones in the spirit world who had come to meet her, and her passing was so happy that it stopped those who witnessed it in their tracks.

It's surprising how common this is. Even people who've previously scoffed at the idea of life after death have found their views profoundly changed by watching someone 'die'.

And some psychic people are able to sense their own passing months in advance and are able to leave behind words of comfort.

I'm sure this must have been the case with Frank Walsh. He wrote my next poem *Passing Over* two years before his death, and the moving words were read out at his funeral.

Passing Over

Shed no tears when I am leaving,
They won't help me on my way;
Stop the sentimental grieving,
Let it be a normal day.
I am simply passing over,
To a better way of life,
From this testing-ground of living,
Strewn with trouble and with strife.
Help me to prepare with fervour,
My last moments by your side,
So that I may be the stronger,
When I cross the Great Divide.
We will meet in the hereafter,
I don't know exactly when,
There will be much joy and laughter,
But my darling until then—
Know that I am always with you,
Every moment every day;
Waking, sleeping, meditating,
I'll never be far away,
So take heart and be not lonely,
Let me feel your love in prayer,
And remember that I'm only,
Always, ever, waiting there.

No matter how comforting the words however, it's always painful for those of us who're left behind. Even the strongest believers in life after death can't escape grief. It's only natural because even though we know that the separation isn't permanent, we miss the physical presence of our loved one. We need them with us here, we think, and so we grieve. But grief is a healing process. The tears must be shed in order for us to get over the shock and pick up the pieces and start again.

The worst grief I believe comes with the loss of a child and I can hardly read this next poem sent to me by Mrs Jean Bayford without dissolving into tears. But don't be put off by that because it's so beautiful. It sums up everything I hoped for for my little John Michael when he was taken from me at five months old. Unfortunately Jean doesn't say who wrote it. Perhaps it is anonymous.

Farewell To A Little Boy

Honey there will be a hoop
And hill to roll it down . . .
(God wouldn't give a little boy the burden of a crown)
He'll show you lots of trees to climb
And where he keeps the swings.
(God let him have a bat and ball instead of shining
    wings).
And will he let you sail a kite up where the sky is clear
Without tall buildings stooping down?
Of course he will my dear!
Now close your eyes . . . I'll kiss them shut
The way I always do . . .
(I must not, *must not* cry dear God I know he's safe with
    you).

Some parents of course are devastated not by the loss of a child, but by the birth of a handicapped child. Andrew Hughes in his poem *Little Did We Know*, which is, I suspect autobiographical, puts this heartache into perspective and points out the joys these children bring with them.

Little Did We Know

Little did we know these few years ago
When we first began our days as man and wife
Little did we know all the heartache we'd go through
And the many different views we'd see of life.

We knew nothing of immobility, of handicaps or spasticity
We thought these things were far away from home
Oh, we'd heard in different places of some isolated cases
But we never dreamt we'd have one of our own.

When our daughter was born though in Swindon that
    morning
We knew that she could lose her life
But nothing could compare with the shock and despair
As the doctor confronted my wife.

They said she'd not walk, they said she'd not talk
She was blind and would never see
What they failed to impart was what she'd have in her
    heart
And what really good fun she could be.

We don't need sympathy cos we love her you see
And although her needs are really demanding

We'll give her our best, let the future do the rest
All we ask for is some understanding.

We're four now but hey there's another on the way
Should we worry, be frightened or what?
No we'll sit back and trust that our next child will just
Be as much fun as the ones that we've got.

If there's a message to say to all parents today
It's this, and I hope you take heed
For life with a spastic can be just as fantastic
Trust in God and that's all you need.

Finally I thought it would be nice to end with a little philosophy. John Pratt's poem *Nothing Comes Easy* is worth repeating aloud in all those impatient, frustrated moments we none of us escape. John was actually writing about his early days in spiritualism but I think his words apply just as well to life in general.

Nothing Comes Easy

Are you searching for something that's so hard to find?
In need of a friend, or just peace of mind,
There's an answer to all things, believe me, I know,
But remember that nothing comes easy.

Learning to walk before you can run,
Can take longer than expected I know I was one
Who wanted a miracle, an instant result,
But remember that nothing comes easy.

Practice makes perfect the old saying goes.
A man only reaps the seeds that he sows.

Go slowly and surely, absorb what you're told
And remember that nothing comes easy.

It's wrong to see others more learned than you
And envy them for the things they can do,
I'm sure they've been told many times before now
To remember that nothing comes easy.

So remember, whatever it is that you need
It has to be worth waiting for . . . Agreed?
Be patient my friend and keep one thing in mind,
You've been told that nothing comes easy.

12

Every day, as I've mentioned before, I get dozens and dozens of letters and although most of them contain requests for sittings, this isn't true of them all. Many are what I call my 'tonic letters'. Words of thanks and appreciation that do so much to make me feel that all the hard work is worthwhile. Others are simply accounts of interesting experiences that readers wanted to share with me.

They are such a fascinating and varied mixture that I thought you might like to see a few of them:

Dear Doris,

I have read all of your books and how I would love to meet you and talk to you.

I'm not asking for a sitting, for you help so many people already and you must get so desperately tired at times.

What I wanted to say is, I 'died' thirty years ago and it was an incredibly beautiful experience.

I was almost four months pregnant when I fell downstairs. This shock caused a miscarriage and I lost so much blood that I was admitted to hospital for a D & C. I was in dreadful pain but was told I would only be in the operating theatre for twenty minutes.

The anaesthetist put me out and suddenly I had no more pain. I was so warm it was like being wrapped in soft black velvet. I was holding a flower and was filled with such a deep sense of peace and happiness. At first I floated slowly through the black tunnel towards a light that seemed far away.

Then suddenly, came the LOVE. I was surrounded by it, filled with it, it was everywhere. I knew it was the most perfect and unselfish love and it was taking me faster and faster with it into the beautiful place that I knew was waiting for me in that gloriously brilliant light which grew stronger every moment. I wanted that LOVE, Doris, so very much and the being who was giving it to me, but suddenly I was looking at a clock and feeling not only icy coldness and pain but also utter despair for it had all been snatched away and I was back in the ward. It was two and a half hours after being taken to the theatre. The porters were just putting me back on the bed and the evening visitors were arriving.

Oh Doris to have had it all taken away like that seemed so cruel, even now I have to hold back the tears when I think of it.

I supposed I was sent back because of the children and yet I have the feeling there must have been more that I was meant to do.

When I try to tell people about it they look at me in a way that makes me believe they are very sceptical yet if they would only listen, they would never be afraid of death again. I know that when my time comes I will go gladly and with a prayer of thanks to that being who loved me so completely in spite of all my faults.

My love to you

Mrs H.

Harrogate,

Yorks

I would be very interested to hear of other readers' experiences of 'dying'.

Dear Doris,

I just had to drop this card to let you know what a laugh it was lining up for tickets this evening.

Of course everyone was saying they felt like a frozen *****s. But stood behind us were a couple of real naturals. They had the crowd in stitches.

They said, 'Well if they don't start selling the tickets soon, Doris won't have an audience – we'll all be over the other side!' You can imagine the laugh.

Thank you for the coffee. We waited for 3½ hours but were lucky to get tickets.

I am glad you love your lovely house. I used to clean it for the next to last owner.

We have lived close by you for twenty-nine years and I could not think of a nicer place to live.

I am on your last book and the photo of you and your hubby in your sitting room I can well imagine because I have cleaned it so many times.

Had to laugh about Freddie Starr wanting to park his helicopter in the garden! He could have landed over on the sports ground by my husband's allotment. What a grand person Freddie is.

Two views of Wembley Conference Centre, August 1986.
(*Above*) Enjoying a cup of tea in the interval backstage in the Green Room.
(*Below*) The audience I faced out front!

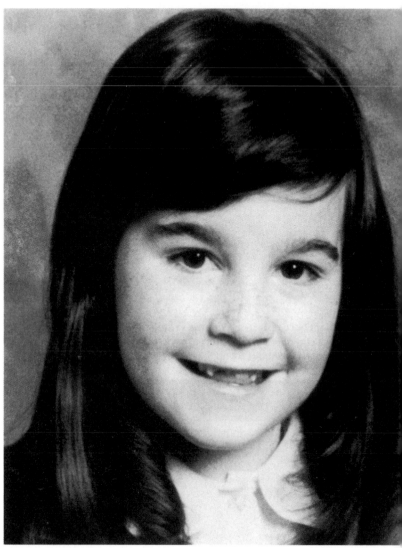

Six-year-old Collette Gallacher – 'A sunny, happy little soul arrived singing happy birthday in a sweet, childish voice.'

(*Above*) Giving little Ayse Danyal a cuddle on a cold January day.

(*Below*) Another cuddle, this time at a signing session in Birmingham. Mr Pugh brought his daughter along to see me after I had given him a spirit message from his wife at the Birmingham Odeon demonstration.

John, forty years to the day he came home from the war.

(*Above*) Jonathan Reynolds and his fiancée, Fiona Pinnells. Victims of the Zeebrugge ferry disaster, they are now happy together in the spirit world.

(*Below*) Stuart Harrison, also a victim of the ferry tragedy. At a sitting with his family he told me his sister was going to get engaged. And he was right!

Happy scenes from the magical trip on the Orient Express. *(Photographs courtesy of Steve Rapport)*
(Top left) Pete Murray was there.
(Bottom left) Opening one of the many gifts I received.
(Top right) Lillian Monger with John and me. Lillian's husband, John, made contact with her at the Wembley demonstration in August.
(Bottom right) The irrepressible Rusty Lee had John and me and Jenni Barnett from TV-am in stitches!

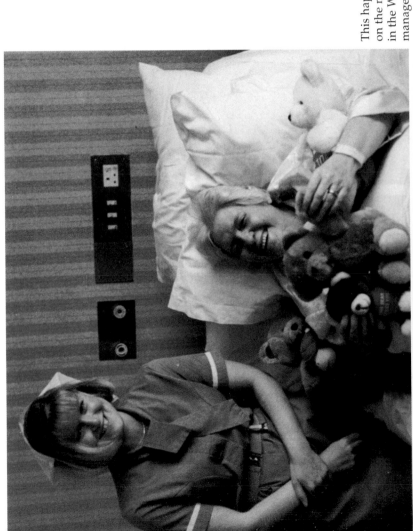

This happy photograph was taken on the morning of Doris' operation in the Wellington Hospital by her manager, Laurie O'Leary.

I'm not looking for a sitting. I am one of the lucky ones.

Hope your health is keeping well,

Mrs E.H.
London

Dear Mrs Stokes,

I must start off by apologising for the disgusting pen colour [it was bright turquoise!] but I couldn't find anything formal! I am thirteen years old and I have just read all of your excellent books.

I first saw you on telly and from that day I have been a dedicated fan. I hope you write more books as they are so intriguing and I just cannot put them down.

A few days ago we had a discussion on spiritualism, ouija boards, etc. in an RE lesson and I am lucky to have quite an open-minded RE teacher who didn't put down every suggestion of abnormal happenings. In fact I was very surprised and enjoyed the discussion. But near the end I asked him if he had ever heard of Doris Stokes. He then went on to talk about what you did and all that, telling us he'd read *Voices in My Ear* – then he said something that made my blood boil. He said you were a fake.

I went mad! He told us that he thought the spirits giving you information were bad and imitated friends and relatives etc. because God condemns contact with the dead.

I told him that the Bible also says to test the spirits to see if they are good – and he sort of mumbled something incomprehensible. I suppose he is entitled to his own opinion but I just had a heart attack.

I have lent my books to friends that asked about you

and we have agreed to go to one of your performances if you tour again.

Did you know that you helped me come top of the year in last year's English exam?! You see I had to write a story on 'A figure from the past' – So I wrote about a family who thought their dead baby boy was a figure from the past, but really he was alive and growing by their sides all the times. Now I am very average at most subjects so when I received my paper back I couldn't believe it! If I didn't know what I know from you – I would have come about 99th!!

Forget about Joan Collins and Lady Di – you are my heroine Doris,

Keep going cherub, love to everyone, lots and lots and lots of love,

Amy,
Sydenham

Dear Doris,

Last night my family and I watched you on Jimmy Young's TV programme. We could tell that you were utterly frustrated and not well yourself, we were so sad about it that I felt I must write and say thank you for all the comfort and hope that you give to so many, many people.

I've bought all your books and found them fascinating, so much so that when a young piano pupil lost her little sister I gave them to the family to read. She wrote to you and was overjoyed to receive an answer. The difference you have made to that child is remarkable – and her piano work is now back to normal!

Please don't trouble to reply, I know how much mail you will receive. Just accept my thanks and best wishes too for a speedy recovery so that you may continue God's work,

Yours
Mrs S.
Leeds

Dear Doris,

Please find enclosed a photograph of my precious little girl Mikaela.

Mikaela was a perfectly healthy little girl until October 25th, 1985 when she contracted a very rare virus called Reyes Syndrome and within 24 hours of her falling ill, she died.

My husband and daughter Kerry are absolutely devastated and feel so lost without her.

I have read all of your books and would be very honoured and grateful if you could put Mikaela's photograph with all the other children on your board. I know she would feel at home there and I would feel a little bit better knowing she was there.

I really hope this letter reaches you. Please look after Mikaela for us too, we love and miss her so much, it's so very hard to go on,

Yours in friendship,
Mrs W.
Cornwall

Dear Doris,

I just wanted to write to you and say 'thank you' for the peace of mind you have brought me. It was quite by chance that a friend at work gave me a copy of *Whispering Voices* to read. I found this so interesting I went out and bought your other books to read.

This year did not start out very well for my husband and myself. We have been married nine years and this September we were both delighted to find I was pregnant for the first time. At first I couldn't believe it, I was so afraid something would happen and we'd find it was a mistake. As time went by I eventually started to let myself start planning for the new baby. In the New Year we decided we'd start looking round for things for the baby.

Then things started to go wrong. I had opted to have the blood test to detect spina bifida, never thinking anything would be wrong. To our dismay it was. I had an amniocentesis and very detailed scans and our baby was diagnosed as having spina bifida and a build up of fluid on the brain. The doctors advised us that our baby could be crippled and may suffer brain damage. We were shattered. We learnt this just before Christmas and really didn't know what to do. The hospital suggested I have another scan in the New Year to see if any more information could be obtained.

Anyway in January and twenty weeks pregnant I had my scan. The diagnosis was confirmed, in fact the fluid in the brain had increased. My husband said he didn't want his child to suffer numerous operations as would probably be the case and perhaps not even then have a good chance of survival. I knew I didn't either but felt that termination still seemed an awful thing.

Anyway after much talking between ourselves with the family and doctors we decided to terminate the pregnancy. My husband was with me the whole time and we saw our daughter afterwards. She was so lovely and perfect looking even at twenty-one weeks apart from her back.

Since then even though I have told myself that it was for the best, still I have felt guilty and like a murderer until I read your books. Particularly in *More Voices in My Ear*, regarding your visit to the spirit world in the last chapter. When I came to the part where you visited the 'waiting area' where babies return before they are born on earth I burst into tears. Not because I was sad, but it made me happy to think our little girl would be there waiting to be born into the spirit world to be loved and looked after.

In reading your books, until then I wondered what would have happened to our baby, how she could have passed over into the spirit world if she had never actually 'lived' here on earth. Now I know it was right to end my pregnancy. Instead of having to have known pain and suffering here on earth in her life, now she will only know love and happiness.

Your books have given me a completely new outlook on life. I always thought there was something else but could never really imagine it. From reading all your experiences and how you have helped so many people, I now believe absolutely in the spiritual side of things and it has seemed to bring so much more hope and love into my life.

Anyway sorry this letter has been so long, I know you get so many, but I really wanted to write and say thank you so much for bringing new hope and happiness into my life at a time when I was feeling pretty awful about things.

With love,
Mrs A.
Chingford

Dear Doris,

I hope this letter finds you in good health, I'm just writing to thank you for the marvellous reading you gave to me and my family when we saw you at the London Palladium. We are all confirmed believers in the afterlife and have been for quite a while. But what you said, just made us even more sure that we don't die, but live on in another better life with God.

My father died when I was nine years old and my brothers were five and six. Mum had a hard job bringing us up but she was always there when we needed her, with lots of love and cuddles. She's always been the type of mum that we could talk to about anything and of course we were all so very happy for her when she remarried a very kind and caring man.

My dad was only thirty-six when he died but I knew even then that he hadn't really left us. I've always been aware of his presence around us. At night I used to feel the end of my bed go down as if someone had sat there to say 'Goodnight'. And I was never scared, after all it was only Dad. As I got older my interest in the Spiritualist Church and its beliefs grew, as did the interest of the rest of the family.

I've seen my dad a couple of times, not a crystal clear image, but all the same I knew it was him. Anyway after our visit to you I wrote an account of our reading. We were so surprised to get something, out of all those people there. But obviously Dad was keen to get through because he even came through on the previous reading. So from all the family, thank you and God bless,

Miss W.
Surrey

Dear Doris,

I lost my dear wife three days before our 43rd wedding anniversary whilst we were on holiday in Jersey.

I can't even begin to tell you the devastating effect this had on me. I was so in love with her. I had been so lucky to marry the prettiest girl in our small mining village where we were both born.

I prayed each time I took flowers to her grave that I could be given a sign that one day we would meet again.

God surely works in a mysterious way. One Sunday morning I went to the local newsagent to get my usual Sunday paper. They had sold out but the paper I did get showed on its book page the publication of *Whispering Voices*.

I had heard of you but I must admit only vaguely. I certainly didn't know that you had written any books. I read quite a lot.

I have now read all five.

I am so grateful to you for the comfort they have given me and to know that I shall meet my dearest wife again.

God bless you Doris and John too. I shall be ever grateful.

Mr T.
Wales

Dear Doris,

I am writing to say thank you for the relief I feel, having read your wonderful books. I no longer cry over my stillborn baby as much as I used to.

I still feel after ten years I would like to have seen her and held her for just a moment and in my circumstances, unmarried and penniless, I agreed for the hospital to make the funeral arrangements. It wasn't until I got home to my parents' house that the overwhelming grief really hit me.

I phoned the hospital to find out where she was either buried or cremated, but they didn't know. I was given the name of the funeral parlour but they didn't have a record of a baby girl so I was at a dead end. My Natalie Amy had just gone and I didn't know where.

Now dear Doris after ten years I know she is with all the other spirit children, with my two miscarried brothers and your own dear son John Michael.

Doris I have cried with you and laughed with you. Because of you I am now looking forward with happiness, not fear for my time to go over to come, so I may hold my Natalie Amy in my arms at last. But first I want to see my son grow and marry and even make us grandparents, but he's only four now so I am going to give him as much as I can before we come to that stage.

I have a lot to do before then and I want to make as much out of my life as I can.

Well we've made ourselves members of your Sod-It Club. When we feel nothing is going right anymore we think of what you say, and we say Sod It! and it all goes better after that. My son has even joined in, when his puzzles don't go right or he's not near enough to the loo and misses he says 'Mummy's sod it!'

Thanks to you for being a friend to us and millions like us,

May God bless you and yours
Mrs S.
Canterbury

13

I think it was the day the car came through our front garden wall that did it. There we were, minding our own business one Saturday morning, when suddenly there was a great screech of tyres across the road, followed by a tremendous bang.

Horrified, we ran outside to see an ancient and now much battered Triumph Herald in the garden and a gaping hole in the front wall six feet above it, (our house is set down from the road, consequently our garden is several feet below the pavement).

Shocked, I dashed inside to call an ambulance, but fortunately the driver wasn't hurt.

What a day we had. Police, ambulancemen, garage people to remove the car, builders to make the wall safe – it was like Piccadilly Circus and the kitchen was turned into a mini cafe to cope with all the cups of tea.

The driver must have been a bit dazed because all he could think about was his car.

'When will my car be back on the road?' he kept asking anyone who'd listen.

One of the policemen eyed the wreck with distaste. Even

before its argument with our brick wall it was clear that the only thing holding the car together was the rust.

'Never,' he said grimly. 'And have you got an MOT for that?'

But the aftermath of the accident was only phase I. Phase II was the rebuilding of the wall, a long and complicated job because the entire wall had to be removed and rebuilt with special reinforcing. There seemed to be no end to it.

For a long time I'd been feeling in need of a break but now it came to a head. If I didn't get away for some peace and quiet, I'd go mad I told myself.

It's funny, I always used to think that if you lived in a nice place you wouldn't need to go away for a holiday. A deckchair in the garden'll be good enough for me when I get my house I used to say, but now I've got it, I find that that's not true. Working from home means that you can never really stop working while you're there. You can't stop the phone ringing or the mail from dropping through the letter box, and despite your good intentions you soon find yourself being drawn back onto the merry-go-round.

It soon became obvious that a holiday was essential, but where? I'm lucky enough to have dozens of invitations to all sorts of exotic places. The other day someone even invited me to stay with them in Istanbul! But quite honestly I do so much travelling throughout the year, the last thing I want to do with my time off is climb on a plane. Neither do I want to stay in hotels. I see enough hotel rooms when I'm working to last me a lifetime, nice though most of them are.

Another problem about staying in public places is that these days people tend to recognise me and many of them don't seem to understand that when I'm on holiday I need to rest.

'I know you're very, very busy,' they say, 'but couldn't you just do a sitting for me?'

It's very difficult to say 'no' and sometimes I'd rather stay in my room than risk meeting someone like this.

The problem was still unresolved when one day I picked up the local paper and saw the solution staring me in the face. There was an advert for a number of holiday cottages for sale on a site near the coast. Apparently a former holiday camp had been taken over and the new owners were reno-vating the old chalets and selling them privately.

I'd never heard of the place so I asked Terry, who does a lot of driving about, where it was.

'Only about forty-five minutes from here in the car,' he said.

'That'll do me,' I said happily.

It was the ideal answer. Since the chalets were being sold privately the same people would use them all the time and if they recognised me, they'd soon get used to me and realise I didn't want to work on holiday. What's more, the place was close enough to keep travelling to a minimum, yet near enough to the sea to be a real tonic.

'Oh Terry, let's take a run over there and look at it!' I said.

So one bleak, windswept day we drove down to the chalet park. It was only five minutes' walk from the sea and the fresh, ozone smell caught in my throat as soon as I stepped out of the car. The site was open with a big grassy space in the middle and a number of neat little chalets around the edge.

We were shown to a semi-detached cottage near the park boundary. The decorating wasn't finished but you could see the place was going to be nice. There was a good sized living room with a fitted kitchen leading off it through an archway, and at the other side of the room, doors opened into two airy bedrooms and a modern bathroom. Outside there was a tiny lawn overlooking a little stream. What's more, the site contained an indoor swimming pool, and a takeaway restaurant in case you didn't feel like cooking.

It was ideal.

'We'll take it!' I said.

The people who run the park were marvellous. I was too busy to get down to the cottage to organise the furnishing and colour schemes, so the wife of the owner did it for me. And what a wonderful job she did. The sitting room was all in shades of pale green, the main bedroom pink, the kitchen beige and the bathroom, deep sea green. It was beautiful.

Our first week's holiday wasn't without its teething troubles however. Terry brought us down one Friday morning for a snatched week in the spring between theatre bookings. Everything was wonderful. John and I spent a happy afternoon unpacking and admiring the beautiful rooms. We weren't planning to do anything. I'd brought a stack of books and I was looking forward to peace, quiet, a good read and watching the seagulls drift by.

But Saturday didn't turn out quite as planned.

Everything went well until lunch time when without warning the electricity went off. The cottage was all electric so very soon we were shivering and we couldn't so much as make a cup of tea. All the other cottages in our part of the park were similarly affected, but undaunted, the family who ran the place raced up and down ferrying boiling kettles of water from cottage to cottage from their own house which still had electricity.

It was funny to watch all those hurrying kettles and the curious gliding run with which they were carried so as not to spill a drop, but after a while it got beyond a joke. Hours passed and there was still not a spark of electricity in the cottage.

John and I were frozen and we wondered if we should go home.

'This holiday won't do us much good if we both catch pneumonia,' I said. 'But if we go now I won't feel like coming back later in the week. I don't think I could face all that packing and unpacking twice.'

Terry offered to come and fetch us, but still we dithered. And it's just as well we did.

At five o'clock the owners took pity on us and invited us to sit by the fire in their house and there we stayed until 11.45, when the electricity finally came back on!

Well it was certainly an experience, and I must say I've never drunk so many cups of tea in my life!

I'm very glad we stayed. The weather was gloomy but it didn't matter. The air was very strong and we slept like dogs and by the end of the week I felt much more refreshed.

But we did have a bit of excitement. While we were at the cottage, John Inman from *Are You Being Served*, came to tea.

I adore John Inman as a comic. Most years Terry gives me theatre tickets to a good show for my birthday and once he managed to get me into *Mother Goose* with John Inman. Unknown to me, Terry had phoned John's manager and asked if John could wish me happy birthday from the stage.

Well I knew nothing about it and there I was watching the show and laughing my head off when John suddenly said, 'Oh I see the Duchess is here.' (Terry always calls me the Duchess, I don't know why.) 'Happy Birthday Doris,' John went on, 'and what would you like for your birthday?'

'You John!' I said. 'Are you free?'

'I'm free!' he said. 'And have you anything to tell me?'

'Yes, everything's going to be all right.'

'Thank goodness,' he said.

And that was my only encounter with John Inman, or so I thought. But then *Psychic News* phoned me as they do every year to see if I could get any of my show business friends to be guest of honour at the annual dinner dance, and make a funny speech.

Well I tried Freddie Starr, but he was working that day and I didn't know what to do.

'Can you think of anyone, Fay?' I asked Fay Hillier when she phoned one day. Fay was the girlfriend of my old friend Dick Emery. I'd met her through Dick and I'd been able to give her a few personal details in a sitting after he passed, which seemed to impress her and we've been close ever since.

'Well I'm appearing in a play with John Inman at the moment,' she said, 'I could ask him.'

To my delight, because I love John Inman, he agreed but he wanted to meet me first and hear more about *Psychic News* and what he would have to do.

'I'll bring him down to the cottage,' said Fay. 'He'll love it.'

So the Thursday of the visit we were bustling round polishing everything that stood still until the whole place sparkled. By an amazing stroke of luck, the daughter of the family which runs the site is a caterer and she offered to make some dainty sandwiches for me. But hours before John was due to arrive she staggered in with the most fantastic buffet you've ever seen. It was like the cold table at a wedding reception.

'Well if this doesn't impress them nothing will,' I said, as she laid it all out on the table and around the kitchen. 'You've gone mad, Kathy.'

Our visitors arrived just after 4.00. Fay, who's an ex-Bluebell Girl with legs that go on for ever, was wearing an off-white leather jacket, off-white boots and a pair of off-white pants with green stripes.

'She looks like a tube of toothpaste!' said John Inman.

John himself was conservatively dressed in a navy blue blazer and slacks, with a trilby complete with feather to top it off.

He looked just the same as he does on TV, but he's not at all camp and unlike his TV personality, he's a very shy boy. At one point Kathy put her head round the door and asked if her little daughter could just come and have a peep at John Inman. The child was only a schoolgirl, but John was so shy he blushed.

Like so many big stars he wasn't at all grand. I didn't have to fuss round him. He made himself at home and soon he was wandering round the kitchen supervising the tea-making because: 'I do like a good cup of tea.'

Generally he was quiet and fairly serious but when he told us his funny stories he had us in stitches.

'Shall I tell you how I first met Fay?' he asked. 'Well I was in New Zealand waiting for a plane to Australia and I had about three hours to wait.

'The man who was looking after me suggested I go and sit by the pool in a nice hotel nearby and he said he'd pick me up later in plenty of time for the flight. So I was sitting there on a sunlounger having a drink when all of a sudden I noticed this creature coming towards me. He was wearing a safari suit and dark glasses and he was mincing along the pool.

'My God, I thought, that creature is coming straight for me. And he was. "Hello Ducky," he said when he got to my sunbed, "are you lonely?"

'I was just going to tell him where to go when he suddenly started to laugh. It was Dick Emery. He had the most infectious laugh you ever heard.

'Apparently he'd been sitting on the other side of the pool with Fay and he said, "Won't be a minute, I've just spotted someone I know," and he put on his camp act and came mincing over. Of course he introduced me to Fay then and we've been friends ever since.'

It turned out that John had also been a friend of Diana Dors and we swopped stories about that lovely lady. John too had been impressed with her courage and kindness. Even Fay had reason to be grateful to her.

Apparently while Dick was seriously ill in hospital, Fay was marooned at his bedside, unable to pop out for meals because the press were hounding her. When Diana, also a friend of Dick's, got to hear about it, she had sandwiches sent in to Fay every day and arranged for a car to take her to and from the hospital.

All in all it was a very enjoyable afternoon and we were sorry to see them go when they left for the journey back to London at 8.00.

There was another enjoyable interlude around this time. About two months before, I'd been invited to a function at the Institute for the Blind in which a new machine called a moon writer was presented.

Apparently it was invented by three schoolboys and their science teacher, and it is a godsend for the blind.

The machine is like a typewriter but it produces big raised letters on the paper so that a blind person can read the letter by touch without having to learn braille. The machine can also produce raised letters on strips of metal to be attached to tins and cartons of food so that a blind person can go through his store cupboard and choose exactly what he wants to eat without fear of opening a tin of peaches instead of a tin of salmon.

I thought it was a marvellous idea and I enthused about

it to the other guests, most of them authors whose books had been translated into braille. There was Molly Weir, Hammond Innes, John le Carré and many others. Wouldn't it be wonderful if one day, every blind person in the country had their own moonwriter and learned how to use it, I thought. It could make such a difference to their lives.

'If I buy five for them, will you buy five?' I asked Sue Townsend, the author of the Adrian Mole books.

'Certainly,' said Sue.

So it was arranged. I don't know what Sue did with hers but a few weeks later I went to Linden Lodge, a special school in Wimbledon, to make my own presentation.

Linden Lodge was an inspiring place. A large old house at the end of a long drive, it was surrounded by the most beautiful gardens. Lawns sloped away to a tennis court, and there were sweetly scented flowers and great leafy trees all over the place. In the courtyard three rabbits frisked around on a patch of grass and a silky cat watched them without interest. They were quite safe with her.

Inside the house was comfortable and well laid out. We were led from classroom to recreation room and even, I was amazed to see, a fully equipped gymnasium where blind children leapt about fearlessly. Watching them jump and run without a second's hesitation, you'd never have guessed these children couldn't see.

Finally we came to the classroom where the presentation was to take place. The children waited patiently at their little tables, quiet and well-behaved although they must have been getting very bored. We were so interested in everything we were shown at Linden Lodge that we had taken far longer than expected to reach the classroom.

It wouldn't have been right to make a speech to these little mites, so I just wished them lots of fun with their new machines and presented the moonwriter to a slender little black boy. He took it back to his table and immediately most of the children clustered round to finger it wonderingly.

One little girl named Carol gravitated towards me however.

'Can I talk to you?' she asked. 'You smell like my mummy and I do miss my mummy.'

Poor little soul, I thought. It must be bad enough to be blind without having to be parted from your mother as well, even though it was for her own good.

'Yes you come and sit here, love,' I told her. 'But don't forget it's Friday tomorrow so you'll be going home.'

Her face lit up. 'Is it Friday tomorrow? Oh good.'

She chatted to me for a while then she asked, 'Can I feel your necklace?'

'Of course you can,' I told her and I bent down while her small fingers explored my necklace, my neck and then on to my face.

They were lovely children, calm, polite and obedient, yet some of them had been difficult when they first arrived, the teacher told us. There was one little boy in particular who had been uncontrollable when he came to the school a year before. He used to shout all the time at the top of his voice. Then they discovered he was deaf as well as blind but nobody had realised it until then and the poor lad was simply trying to make his presence known in the only way he could.

He was fitted with a special hearing aid and now he sits as quietly as the other children listening to the lessons.

By this time the teacher had become very interested in the moonwriter and he took out the instruction leaflet to find out how to operate it. The children became restless and out of the corner of my eye I noticed a pile of rolled-up towels on a table at the back of the room.

'Are you going swimming?' I asked the teacher.

'Yes,' he said glancing up from the instructions. 'When we've finished here they're going swimming.'

There was something about the expectant, impatient look in the children's faces that made me feel we were outstaying our welcome.

'I think we'd better leave, Laurie,' I said quietly. 'The kids are waiting to go swimming.'

But I'd forgotten the acute hearing of the blind and one of the girls caught my words.

'We don't want to appear rude and ask you to go,' she said earnestly, 'but we do want to go swimming.'

I thought that was hilarious. 'That's right, dear, you tell us to go,' I said patting her cheek and trying to keep the laughter out of my voice. 'Of course you want to go swimming.'

We said our goodbyes, and polite as ever, the children gathered gravely round to thank us for coming.

Returning home from Linden Lodge was just like coming back from a refreshing holiday. The presence of children always has a tonic effect on me. In their company I forget all my problems and worries, all my aches and pains fade away and I enter their innocent world.

These days I get asked to do all kinds of exciting things. I mentioned earlier about being approached to switch on the Christmas lights in Halifax. Well, not long ago I achieved another ambition – I opened a fete. The story started in fact some months before. Earlier in the year after our long, terrible winter I was feeling in need of a holiday. It was still so wet and cold that someone suggested John and I go on a cruise.

'It's expensive,' they warned, 'but it's so relaxing. You really unwind. It's worth every penny.'

They were so enthusiastic that by the end of the conversation John and I were convinced that a cruise was the only thing that would set us up for the rest of the year.

'I'll go down to the travel agents on Monday,' John said, 'and book us up.'

There was a gap in my bookings coming up and we were hoping to leave on the next available boat, so I started sorting through my wardrobe putting to one side the things I would take.

'We're going on a cruise!' I told everyone proudly.

And so we were. But then the next morning I opened the paper and read a particularly tragic story. A young mother had lost her unborn baby because her local hospital in Basildon didn't have enough foetal heart monitors. Apparently these machines can detect if anything is going wrong with the child, and if so the medical team can step in. Perhaps the baby would have passed over anyway, who knows, but the distressed girl was convinced that a monitor could have saved her child's life.

Having lost three unborn babies myself, I knew how she felt. If there had been a machine available in my day which might have saved my children's lives I would have wanted heaven and earth moved to provide it for them.

Impulsively I phoned the newspaper and asked how much the monitors cost. The price turned out to be near enough what we'd planned to spend on the cruise.

'All right, tell the hospital I'll buy them one,' I said to the astonished reporter.

As I put the phone down I turned round and saw that John had come quietly into the room and was grinning at me.

'Oh, John, I'm sorry,' I said. 'You didn't really want to go on the cruise did you? It's much better to save all those babies.'

'Of course it is, love. I don't really mind. There's always next year.'

The hospital wrote a beautiful thank you letter and that I thought was the end of the matter until a few months later they contacted me again. They were organising a summer fete to raise more funds and they wondered if I'd like to officially open it. While I was there perhaps I'd like to see the monitor I'd bought and have a conducted tour of the baby unit?

It sounded to me a lovely way to spend an afternoon and I accepted gladly. A few weeks later John, Laurie, Jean, who helps me with my cleaning, and I piled into the car on a hot, sunny morning and made our way to Basildon.

'There's going to be a baby born while we're there,' I said suddenly as we sped along. 'I'd better buy it a present.'

'You've been talking to them upstairs again,' said Laurie.

And I had to smile. I knew I was right because I'd heard a spirit voice say, 'The baby won't be long now. He'll be born while you're there.'

I'd not been to Basildon before and it struck me as an impressive place: spacious and new with wide airy streets and bright flower beds.

Our first stop was the hospital building itself and Laurie found it without difficulty. Outside was gathered a little welcoming committee headed by chairman Tom Swan, and after the introductions we were whisked away to maternity to inspect the first baby unit. There in pride of place stood our heart monitor, complete with a little plaque which read: 'Presented by spiritualist Doris Stokes.' But it was also covered by a cloth.

'I wouldn't let anyone use it until you'd been,' said the sister, who'd actually come in on her holiday to watch me officially hand over the machine. She removed the cloth and

I looked at the monitor with interest. It was rather like an ordinary heart machine with a print-out for the heart-beats, but it didn't mean a lot to me. Things have changed so much since I was a nurse.

'We've got a mother on a monitor now,' said sister, reading my thoughts. 'Would you like to see it working? She doesn't mind.'

The young mother was lying on a bed with sensors on her tummy and the machine by her side. It was quite extra-ordinary. The monitor picked up the sounds of the baby's heartbeat and magnified it right round the room. Boom – boom – boom – boom went the baby's heart, clearly strong and healthy.

I shook hands with the mother, then I bent down to her tummy and said, 'Are you all right in there?'

And to my amazement the noise changed, speeded up, and the heart went 'Boomboom boom boom boom.'

'You've got it excited now,' sister laughed.

'I'm sure it knows you're talking to it,' said the mother.

We chatted for a few minutes. She told me she'd got another three weeks to go and confessed that she was a bit frightened of the birth.

'Well it's no picnic, love,' I said, 'but when they lay your baby in your arms you forget all that. I'm sixty-seven and I still remember that wonderful moment when they laid my baby boy in my arms. It was the most wonderful moment of my life.'

Sister was keen to show us the rest of the maternity unit but just as we were leaving the mother and monitor, a thought struck me and I turned back.

'Will you do something for me?' I asked. 'If it's a girl will you call her Charity for her second name, because that means love.'

'Oh yes I will, Doris,' said the mother.

Back outside we toured the maternity ward where I stopped to admire a beautiful baby with the most gorgeous blue eyes. I put my finger down to him and his little fist curled round it and hung on with an amazing grip. Then we went to the special baby unit and stared in astonishment at these tiny little scraps in incubators. The babies were so small you felt you could lay them in the palm of your hand.

From there we went to intensive care where little Philippa, who was having trouble breathing, was on a ventilator.

'But she's doing extremely well now,' said sister.

By now time was getting on and although I could have spent all day with the babies I knew I had to go and open the fete. We retraced our steps and outside the maternity ward we found a young man sitting tensely on a bench.

'He's waiting for his wife to be delivered,' said sister.

'The baby will be born soon love, don't worry,' I told him.

He shrugged, his face pale. 'Oh I don't know. You never can tell,' he said.

I smiled to myself. The spirit world can, I thought, but I didn't say anything. Afterwards they told me he thought I was the mayor!

An hour or so later as I was going round the fete there came an announcement over the loudspeaker.

'Doris Stokes, the baby was born at ten past two, his name's Christopher and he weighs 6lbs.'

'You can always rely on the spirit world,' I told Laurie as I bought the biggest teddy bear I could find for little Christopher.

They had gone to a great deal of trouble with the fete. The field was bright with flags and bunting and the platform was decorated with flowers. There were seventy stalls, a giant rubber castle for the kids to jump on and the local Blue Eagles Band marched up and down playing rousing tunes. Unfortunately the sun had disappeared behind a bank of cloud and a bitter wind sprang up, but the people were determined to have a good time.

'It gives me great pleasure to open this fete,' I said from the platform, 'because I am speaking from both sides of the fence. I've lost four babies and also I'm an ex-nurse. I know what it's like for a mother to lose a baby and also what it's like to be a nurse. When a nurse loses a patient she goes off and has a cry in the bathroom . . .'

Once the fete was well and truly open we walked round looking at the stalls and as well as the teddy bear for Christopher I bought a big doll all dressed in pink with frilly underwear, for the first girl born after the visit.

Throughout the afternoon I was kept busy signing autographs, and a number of people came up to thank me for buying the monitor. One lady was particularly moving.

'Can I give you a hug,' said the young mother leading a small girl by the hand. 'I had two miscarriages before I had my little girl and if there'd been a monitor then I might not have lost them. Thank you so much.'

And I thought, 'What's a cruise, if you can do this?'

By now I'd been on my feet for hours it seemed, but there was still one more task to perform. I presented the Vic Mason memorial shield for the St John's Ambulance stretcher race, and then I was able to escape for a quick peep at baby Christopher before I left.

He'd been in this world just two hours when I saw him and his little face was still red, but he was gorgeous. Perfect in every minute detail.

'How can anyone not believe in God?' I wondered, as I stared down at him. 'Surely every new-born baby is a miracle.'

'Never again, never again!' the mother was groaning ruefully but her eyes were alight with joy.

It was a wonderful end to a wonderful day.

'Who cares about a cruise,' I said to Laurie later as we climbed thankfully back into the car. 'I expect I'd have been seasick anyway!'

I enjoy my work, even though it sometimes gets me down, but if in doing my work I can help little children like these, then my pleasure is doubled. Children are our future and we should guard them well.

At the moment strangers coming to my house think I must have a whole family of little ones staying there. There's a rag doll, a teddy bear and a Wurzel Gummidge scarecrow on the sofa, and the mantelpiece is crammed with children's pictures. In fact the toys, like the photographs, belong to children who've recently passed to the spirit world and whose parents want me to keep an eye on them.

The same goes for my board of spirit children which hangs out in the hall where it is the first thing that greets a visitor's eye.

The other day a telephone engineer came to the house to do some work on our phone.

'I'm intrigued by all these pictures of children,' he said, after passing the board for the umpteenth time and staring at it fixedly.

'They're my grandchildren,' I told him.

'Grandchildren?' he said. 'There must be 300 of them. Surely you can't have 300 grandchildren.'

'Well not exactly,' I said. This was going to be difficult. 'They're my spirit grandchildren. They are children who have passed over to the spirit world who have adopted me as their granny because I've brought them back to their parents. After the sittings their parents give me a picture for my wall and the kids can come and see me whenever they want.'

The young man's eyes bulged at that and he backed away rather warily I felt.

'I've just got to go and collect some more equipment,' he said quickly and the next thing I knew he was hurrying outside to his car as if he feared I might pin *him* to my board.

I shrugged to myself and went back to my letters. It's very awkward when people ask you a question but don't really want to hear a truthful answer.

But later on that afternoon the young man reappeared and his attitude had changed completely.

'All the girls in the office know you,' he told me eagerly, 'and they want to know if I could take your autograph back to prove that I've been here.'

I burst out laughing.

'Of course you can, love,' I said, and I scribbled out my name on a piece of paper for him.

This sort of thing tickles me to death because after all, I'm just an ordinary housewife like thousands of other housewifes, struggling to cope with a job and a family, and not always succeeding.

Right now though, fingers and toes crossed, everything seems to be going smoothly. John is pleased because his healing work is going well and he's just had a postcard from a woman who suffered from agoraphobia and had not been outside her front door for seven years. She wanted him to know that she was enjoying her first holiday for years thanks to his healing. It made John's day.

I'm pleased because I had a demonstration last week that

went particularly well and a TV director in the audience said he'd like to make a film about me.

Of course the chances are it won't come to anything, but you never know. Life is getting so exciting these days I just can't imagine what will happen next!

Joyful Voices

1

It must have been mid-afternoon when we saw him. John and I were having a sit-down after lunch and we lay back in our armchairs, staring out of the patio doors into the garden.

I was trying to tune in, in the hope of picking up a spirit contact to start me off at my demonstration that evening. I was appearing at Wembley Conference Centre. It was a big place and I was anxious in case I arrived there and nothing happened. If I could get just one little message to open the evening, I knew I would be all right.

John, who has been a healer ever since his spirit guide appeared in our bedroom and insisted that he start using his healing gift, had no such worries. He was relaxing and letting his lunch go down before tackling an after-noon's healing session. Terry was out taking Boots for a long walk.

So there we were, just the two of us, watching the birds squabbling over the crumbs on the bird-table when, suddenly, we both saw a man walk past the kitchen window towards the side door which leads into the sitting-room.

'Oh, Terry's back,' said John.

'He wasn't gone long,' I said, abandoning all hope of tuning in. I knew I wouldn't be able to concentrate with Terry and Boots jumping about all over the place. 'He said they were going to walk miles today.'

John shrugged and we waited for the side door to open, shattering our peace. But it didn't. Nothing happened.

'That's funny,' I said. 'Why haven't they come in?'

But even as I said it I realized that we'd heard no footsteps and there'd been no excited bark of greeting from Boots. In fact we hadn't even seen the man's face.

'John . . .' I began, but John was up and out the side door.

'There's no one here,' said John in bewilderment, staring up and down the empty patio.

'John . . .'

'Where can he have got to?'

'John – I think . . .'

But before I could stop him, John raced round to the back gate and then out into the front garden. There was no one to be seen there either. But he's nothing if not persistent, my John. The garage door was open so he searched the garage and then got down on his hands and knees on the ground to look under the car, though why he thought the man should have hidden underneath our car I can't imagine.

I was killing myself laughing by this time.

'John!' I called. 'You won't find him. You've just seen your first spirit person!'

I tuned in again and I was just able to pick up our visitor although I didn't see him again.

'I came to talk to you in the night,' said a man's voice.

'Oh, it was you, was it?' I'd woken up at ten past three that morning with the feeling that someone was mentally tugging my sleeve.

'Doris, this is John,' a man's voice had said out of the darkness. 'Pat's very poorly, you know. Tell them that we're with Pat.'

And then he was gone, leaving me to get back to sleep as best I could.

The actress Pat Phoenix, who was a personal friend of mine, was seriously ill with lung cancer at this time and at first I took the message to be a warning that she wasn't long for this world. I'd guessed as much myself but it made me very sad to think of it. But on this occasion, I now discovered, I'd got the wrong end of the stick. I always was a one for jumping to conclusions.

'So it's John again, is it?' I asked.

'Yes,' he agreed. 'They'll all be there tonight, you know, and Pat is very poorly. You will remember to tell them about Pat. We're with her.'

So it wasn't my Pat he was talking about. It was another Pat unknown to me.

'Yes of course I'll tell them,' I assured him.

Then he mumbled something about a football team, which I didn't catch, and part of an address. It sounded like '14 Orelia Gardens'. And then he faded out again.

Well, I thought, it's not much to go on but with a bit of luck it'll get me started tonight.

I did try to tune in again but it got me nowhere. In fact, I began to think that the spirit people were having a bit of a game with me because every time I tuned in, all I could hear was a chorus of voices singing: 'Here we go, here we go, here we go . . .'

'Look, I know I'm going to Wembley but I do wish you'd shut up about it,' I told them crossly after the umpteenth rendering, which was not even particularly tuneful to my mind.

It was no use. At the word 'Wembley', they launched enthusiastically into a fresh verse . . . 'Here we go, here we go, here we go . . .'

'Oh, I give up,' I cried. It was no use my trying to work. I might as well go and make a sandwich for tea.

If I'd been nervous before going to Wembley, I was petrified when I arrived and saw the size of the place. It was enormous.

John and I had left in plenty of time because we knew how difficult crossing London can be and consequently we arrived before Laurie (my friend and manager) and had to find our own way about. It was pretty daunting. The new building seemed to have several entrances and John and I trailed about, carrying my stage dress in its flapping polythene bag, looking for the right one.

Eventually we came to the stage-door where a kind man directed us.

'Now you want to go up those stairs,' he said, pointing to the flight behind him, 'turn right, then left and keep going.'

'Right, then left and keep going,' I reminded John as we climbed the stairs and admired the beautifully-polished brass handrail.

We followed the instructions to the letter and found ourselves in a long, silent corridor, studded with endless bright-red doors. On and on we walked, each scarlet door looking exactly like the last, until I felt thoroughly bewildered. It was like something out of *Alice in Wonderland*. Perhaps this corridor went on for ever.

Then, just as I was beginning to feel that we'd taken a wrong turning somewhere and might easily spend the whole night parading amongst eerie red doors, John stopped abruptly.

'Here we are, love. This must be it.'

Relief. At last he'd found a door that was different to the others. It said: 'Doris Stokes.'

Inside was a beautiful, modern dressing-room, complete with shower and bathroom, and there was also a comfortable Green Room for us to use. Green Rooms can sometimes be a bit scruffy, but this one was smartly decorated with what looked like green velvet on the walls. There was a bar and several small tables covered in spotless white cloths, just like a restaurant.

'Oh look, John – look at that photo on the wall,' I said, spotting a familiar face. 'That's Jack Jones.'

I'd met Jack when I was in Los Angeles. Then nearby I saw another photograph. It was Ernie Wise. I'd met Ernie too, at a Children of Courage carol service. Round the room I went, discovering more and more famous faces. I'd met this one, I knew that one, I'd always dreamed of meeting him! And so on until it was almost time for me to go on stage. I couldn't believe how quickly the minutes passed.

I didn't escape stage-fright entirely though. Interesting though the Green Room had been, there is no getting away from that terrible moment when you're standing in the wings waiting to go on and you feel so dreadfully alone.

Fortunately it soon passed. All at once the announcement was finished. My feet started walking with a will of their own and before I knew it I was standing on the stage at Wembley dressed in my finery and breathing in the sweet perfume of the flowers which, together with a comfortable chair, form my only props.

I was trembling inside, as usual, at the sight of all those people (two thousand, five hundred and twelve, they told us afterwards). But at least I had something to talk to them about, and with a bit of luck, someone out there in the audience would recognise the names, John and Pat, and the address: 14 Orelia Gardens.

'. . . And so you see, John saw his first spirit person today . . .' I said, as I finished the story of our mysterious visitor. But even as I was speaking the words were drowned out in my head by those infuriating, singing voices.

'Here we go, here we go, here we go . . .'

I was about to dismiss it impatiently when Ramanov, my spirit guide, who is always there when I need him, cut in.

'No. Listen, child. Don't be hasty. This means something.'

I paused. What on earth could it mean? It sounded like nonsense to me but you never know with the spirit world. Things that don't seem to make sense at all can often prove to be amazingly significant to other people. The only thing to do was try it on the audience.

'They're at it again! Here we go, here we go, here we go . . .' I said out loud, 'and I think it must mean something other than the fact that we're at Wembley. So can anybody place this contact . . . a man called John, something to do with a football team and the address: 14 Orelia Gardens?'

A movement out there in that sea of faces caught my eye and, as I watched, an attractive middle-aged woman detached herself from the seats and came hurrying down to the front.

'It's for me, Doris, I think,' she said, 'only the address is Aurelia Gardens – not Orelia.'

'Well at least we found you, love.' I knew she was the right contact because the moment she reached the microphone the football chant swelled deafeningly in my ear.

'And what does, "Here we go, here we go," mean?'

The woman burst out laughing. 'They've been singing that to me at work.'

'What – today?'

'Yes. All day. Every time my trip to Wembley was mentioned they started singing it.'

'I couldn't help laughing myself. I knew exactly how she must have felt.

'And who's John?'

'John's my husband.'

The moment she used his name, I felt my spirit visitor return. I couldn't see him this time but I could sense him standing right beside me. His presence jogged my memory.

'They're very concerned about Pat, you know,' I said, 'she's very poorly indeed.'

'Yes, she is,' the woman agreed.

And satisfied that I'd kept my word, John started joining in. He gave me the name Lillian.

'That's me!' said the woman, obviously thrilled. 'I'm Lillian.'

Then the name Dave came through and the fact that he wanted to wish Dave a happy birthday.

'That's right, Dave's his friend and his birthday's coming up,' Lillian confirmed.

John was really getting into his stride now. He was a wonderful communicator with a great sense of fun. He kept wandering over to give his wife a hug and then rushing back to speak to me. He started talking about the football team again and there was something about the cheeky way he said it that made me feel it was some kind of joke.

'He's mentioned this football team again,' I said, rather perplexed because I still hadn't been able to catch the whole message. 'It seems to have some special significance because he keeps going on about it.'

'Well, Dave's got a football team,' said Lillian. 'Dave's the treasurer.'

It seemed a likely explanation. I was prepared to accept it but John wasn't.

'No, no,' he said, just as frustrated as I was at my inability to get it right. 'That's not what I meant. It's a joke.'

'Well, I'm sorry, but I don't know what you mean, love.'

'It's a joke. There's eleven of them,' he said.

I passed this on and Lillian suddenly clapped her hand over her mouth and fell about laughing.

'I know what he means! There's eleven of them at work booked to come and see you at your appearance at Lewisham Theatre!'

'And that's a football team . . . ?' I said slowly, light dawning at last. 'John – you're a right old kidder.'

John was having a good laugh now and just to cap it, to prove we were on the right track, he gave me the name Mo.

'Yes. That's my boss at work,' explained Lillian.

'It was quite obvious that John kept a very close eye on his family indeed. He knew everything they were doing, including the costumes they wore to fancy-dress parties.

He mentioned the name of his son Grant and of Grant's girlfriend, Tracey, and then he said something about a policeman.

'No, he means a policewoman!' said Lillian, collapsing into giggles again. 'Tracey's just been to a fancy-dress party dressed as a policewoman.'

'That's right. I know what they get up to,' said John proudly. 'Just because they can't see me, it doesn't mean I'm not around.'

He gave me some more names and family news, including the fact that his sister-in-law, Betty, had been to the hospital – again.

'Nice woman,' he said, 'but she's never happier than when she's being examined or having something done.'

By this time Lillian couldn't speak for laughing and I gathered that John had given a pretty accurate picture of his sister-in-law. But he hadn't come simply to joke and lark about. Pat wasn't far from his thoughts and it wouldn't be long, he told me, before she would be joining him.

Now how do I say that? I thought. I don't want to upset anybody if they don't know.

'Pat is very poorly, love,' I said to Lillian, stressing the 'very'.

'Yes. We know she's terminal, Doris.'

I was relieved. I could pass John's message on without fear. 'They're waiting for her and preparing her a place,' I explained. 'John would like you to take her some flowers from him and to tell her to keep her chin up because there's nothing to it. He says he suffered very badly himself before he went over and he's so glad to feel well again now.'

Lillian nodded, taking it all in, and I knew that very soon Pat would be receiving those flowers. But by now I was beginning to feel a bit guilty about the amount of time John was taking up. He was such a good communicator it was a pleasure to talk to him and he successfully kept other spirit people from elbowing him aside with their own messages. Nevertheless, it was only fair to let other members of the audience have a turn.

'Well now, John . . .' I said, ready to thank him and move on.

'I know, I know,' said John, 'but just one more thing before I go.'

A deep sense of concern flooded through me and, at the same time, I found myself looking at a picture of an unusual building. At first I couldn't make out what it was. Then I saw a pigeon fly into it and I realised it was a pigeon loft.

A *pigeon loft*? I've been shown some strange things by spirit people in my time, but never a pigeon loft. Still, as Ramanov keeps telling me, mine is not to reason why. I stared at the little building a moment longer and, as I did so, I felt a deep ache down my right side.

'This sounds silly but you don't keep pigeons do you, love?' I asked Lillian, although she didn't look that sort of woman at all. 'Only he's showing me a pigeon loft now, and when I look at it I ache all down my right side.'

Lillian's eyes grew round with amazement. 'I don't. It's Dave. He's building a pigeon loft. He's just started building it in his garden.'

'And does he have a job to lift his arm?'

'Yes, he does,'

So that was the reason for John's concern. Dave got angry and fed up with his problem and sometimes he was reduced to swearing in frustration.

'John says he is going to get better, you know,' I told Lillian, 'but, in the meantime, tell him when things get tough to sit down and say, "Come on John, give us a hand."'

Lillian promised to pass this on to Dave, and John, pleased to have got through so well, finally moved off the vibration to let other spirit people have a turn.

I was sorry in a way to lose him. He'd given me such a marvellous start to the evening, but I had to be fair to the others, and by now there were quite a few spirit voices clamouring in the background.

Everything went well that night. At half-time there was a hot cup of tea waiting for us in the Green Room and when I emerged on to the stage afterwards, the voices were back, clear and strong. There was a father who wanted to reassure his grown-up daughter that he'd seen her new-born baby. There was a little boy called Jason who had been tragically killed in an accident, and there was a much-loved husband who had passed with leukaemia and who wanted his wife to know that she had nothing with which to reproach herself.

Apparently she was tormented with guilt because, during her husband's illness, her fear and grief had caused her to lose her temper with him at times. She's bitterly regretted it ever since and could find no peace until she knew she was forgiven.

And so it went on. Small messages of love and affection that meant so much to their recipients.

We even had one case which indirectly answered a question I'm asked many times. People who have been married more than once often want to know which partner they'll end up with in the spirit world. Well, the lady standing nervously at the microphone sorted that one out straight away. She had been married twice, lost both husbands through illness, and now they had come back together to speak to her.

I got the names Bill and Charlie. Apparently Charlie had passed first, some years before, and then Bill had gone over just over nine weeks ago. Poor Bill had suffered very badly with cancer of the stomach but he was glad to say that he was now free of pain and full of energy once more.

He talked of his funeral – because spirit people are usually fascinated to attend their own funerals – and he knew that there had been a mix-up over the flowers and the cars.

'She got a bit upset about that,' he confided, 'but she needn't have worried. It didn't matter a bit.'

Most important of all, they wanted their wife to know that they were together.

'Charlie came to meet me, you know, when I passed,' said Bill.

Charlie agreed that this was so. 'It was grand for me to be able to thank Bill for looking after her.' he said.

It was quite clear that they both loved their wife dearly and, when her time comes, they will both be there to lead her gently into the spirit world. Jealousy seems to fade away on the other side. All that counts is love.

The evening ended in a tremendous burst of applause and cheering – so much so that the manager came over to ask when I'd come back!

'D'you think she liked it here?' he asked Laurie. 'D'you think she'd like to come back?'

I certainly would. The theatre was clean and comfortable and the audience was marvellous. Once again, I was delighted to see that so many young people had bothered to turn out for an old girl like me!

'Look at those two cockatoos!' someone said afterwards, nodding towards two young punks who were making their way towards the exit, their hair standing up in stiff spikes on top of their heads for all the world as if they'd just seen a ghost.

But what did it matter what they looked like? They'd sat there quietly and politely throughout the demonstration and they were obviously interested. We couldn't ask for anything more. How they chose to dress was their business. I don't suppose they would have wanted my hairstyle any more than I would have wanted theirs!

I went back to the dressing-room as I always do, to flop, have a reviving cup of tea and a cigarette. Then, drained but happy, I collected up my things and stepped out into the night. Before I could reach the car a young lad pushed forward and thrust a potted plant into my arms.

He was only seventeen and he'd been waiting an hour and a half outside the stage-door to give it to me.

I was touched. How can you criticize young people when they do such lovely things? I thanked the boy, and clutching the plant and my dress I climbed awkwardly into the car.

Well, after all my nerves, Wembley had certainly made me feel welcome. And as we pulled away past the famous stadium, I found myself humming a familiar tune, 'Here we go, here we go, here we go . . .'

2

It was the laugh that did it. I'd gone into the bathroom to clean the sink and I was just taking off my new, 'good' wedding-ring, the way I always do so it doesn't get spoiled by scouring powder, when suddenly this rich, warm laughter spilled out behind me.

I almost dropped the ring in surprise. Automatically, I turned round but of course there was no-one there. The room was quite empty. In fact the whole house was empty except for me. John had taken Boots out for his morning walk and Terry was at work. Could Jean have popped in unheard, I wondered briefly, but then I dismissed the thought. No, she would have knocked first.

Besides, that wasn't Jean's laugh. There was only one person I knew who laughed like that and that was Pat Phoenix – kind, warm-hearted Pat Phoenix who had passed over the day before.

Quickly I put my ring on the top of the cistern for safety and this action brought a fresh chuckle from my unseen visitor.

'That's right, love,' said a friendly voice. 'you look after it.'

'Is that you, Pat?' I asked, rather unnecessarily because there was no mistaking that vibrant tone. 'Are you okay?'

'Yes, I'm okay, kid,' she said, 'I just wanted you to tell Tony to keep the ring, the one I married him with. I was very fond of that ring. I don't mind about the other things but I would like him to keep that. Tell him to put it on a chain.'

'Don't worry, Pat, I'll tell him,' I assured her.

And then all at once, that indefinable feeling of electricity went out of the air and I knew I was alone in the bathroom again.

'Pat?' I said experimentally just in case I'd made a mistake. But there was no answer. She'd gone.

It was so unexpected and so brief, I felt quite frustrated. If only I'd had a bit more warning I'd have been prepared for a longer chat. Still, that's the spirit world for you. You can't force spirit people to work to appointments. They pop in and out when they've got the time. And it was very good that Pat was able to get a message through so soon after her passing. It takes quite a bit of effort.

I abandoned the sink and went off to phone the Booth's home with the news. Pat's husband, Tony Booth, was in deep mourning of course. I didn't want to disturb him, so instead I passed the message on to Kitty, Pat's loyal friend and house-keeper.

'Just tell Tony we're thinking of him and that I hope the message will be of some comfort,' I said when I'd explained.

And Kitty, who was naturally very distressed herself because she'd loved Pat too, promised that she would.

It was a sad time. We'd been expecting the worst for some time, of course, but nevertheless it's always a blow when it comes.

Over the last few weeks I'd got into the habit of phoning the hospital now and then to see how Pat was, and just the day before she passed, about five o'clock in the afternoon,

I had a sudden impulse to ring the ward. When someone is as ill as poor Pat was it's wise not to ignore such impulses. I had a dreadful feeling that she'd taken a turn for the worse.

'Hello, nurse, it's Doris Stokes here,' I said when I was put through to the ward. 'I don't want to be put through to Pat's room, I'm just ringing to ask if you could give Pat and Tony my love.'

'Of course I will, Mrs Stokes,' said the nurse.

'And how is Pat today?'

There was a tiny pause and then came the professional nurse's trained response. 'There's no change,' she said, matter-of-factly.

But I wasn't going to be fobbed off like that. After all I'd been a nurse myself. 'She's not very well, is she, love?' I persisted.

There was another slight hesitation and then I got through to the real person underneath the professional exterior.

'Well, no, I'm afraid she's not, Mrs Stokes,' the nurse admitted.

'Oh dear. I thought as much,' I said. 'Well could you tell her that we're thinking of her and praying for her?'

'I'd be glad to, Mrs Stokes,' said the nurse.

The next morning chaos broke out in the Stokes household. It so happened that we'd arranged to have our carpets cleaned that day. They hadn't been down very long but they'd had to stand up to a growing puppy rushing around with muddy paws and having the odd 'accident', and they were looking distinctly grimy.

Anyway, just after breakfast three men and a van arrived with a great big hose affair. Boots, of course, had never seen anything like it and he started to charge about, barking his head off. John went to see if there was anything he could do, got tangled up with everyone and added to the confusion. Terry decided he'd better make a big pot of tea and then Jean arrived to help with the cleaning.

It seemed as if there were people and dogs everywhere. I bustled about trying to clear furniture out of the way without tripping over anyone and then, in the midst of it all, the phone rang.

'Hello, Doris,' said a voice, 'this is the . . .'

'I'm sorry,' I shouted, putting one hand over my free ear. 'Can you speak up a bit? I can't hear you, it's a bit noisy here.'

'. . . the *Manchester Evening News*,' repeated the man. 'We just wondered if you'd heard . . . Pat Phoenix passed away at 8.45 this morning.'

I sat down heavily in an armchair that had been pushed against the wall.

'No. No, I hadn't heard,' I said. 'I'm very sorry.'

I had been expecting it, of course, but I was shocked just the same. I felt a bit guilty too. It was terrible to think that Pat had slipped away while my back was turned, as it were, at a time when I was so preoccupied with the upheaval at home that I hadn't even given her a thought. I didn't even send up a prayer for her this morning, I realized in shame. Pat would forgive me, I knew that, but I still felt bad.

It got worse as the day went on. By mid-morning the phone was red hot and it didn't stop ringing until late in the evening. Newspaper after newspaper, knowing of my friendship with Pat, rang to ask for a 'tribute' to her. A few minutes' conversation, however, soon established that they didn't really want a tribute, they wanted to know if Pat had come back to talk to me.

The reporters turned the questions around and wheedled away, trying to get me to say that I'd had contact with Pat. But I couldn't say that because it wasn't true. I hadn't heard a word from Pat and I didn't expect to.

It's very difficult to get people to understand that I can't just ring the spirit world and have a chat to anybody I choose. When the time is right spirit people will make contact with their loved ones – except in a few unusual cases, love is the link that makes it work. Now Pat and I were very fond of each other but uppermost in her mind as she started her new life in the spirit world would be people like Tony, her husband, not me.

'I'm sorry, love,' I explained for the umpteenth time to a reporter, 'it doesn't work like that. I haven't heard from Pat and I don't suppose I will.'

Which just goes to show, as I've often said, how wrong a medium can be. Pat came to speak to me the very next day but only because she wanted to get a message through to Tony and she knew that I would be able to pass it on easily because I had their home telephone number.

I first met Pat some years ago when I was invited to appear on the Russell Harty Show. As I explained in one of my earlier books, the show proceeded quite normally until, towards the end, Russell sprang a little surprise on me.

'Now,' he said, with a merry glint in his eye, 'we have a surprise mystery guest here tonight. We thought it would be a bit of fun if Doris could discover her identity.'

I was rather taken aback, I must admit, because identifying mystery guests is not something I do. I had no idea if it would work or not. In fact I had a nasty suspicion that it wouldn't, but I've never been able to resist a challenge so I said I'd have a go.

The mystery guest was hidden away somewhere at the back of the studio and I was linked to her by telephone.

'Hello, Doris,' said an Irish voice, sweet as honey.

'Hello, love,' I replied calmly, but inside I was quaking. This was going to be impossible. I didn't have a clue. I'd been to Ireland a few times but I hadn't met this lady, I was sure. I didn't recognize her voice at all. What's more the clock was ticking away and I knew we only had a moment or two before the show ended.

'Be careful,' said Ramanov, my guide, breaking into my panic, 'the accent's not genuine.'

It had me fooled. Nevertheless, if Ramanov said it was a phoney accent then phoney it must be.

'I don't think that's your real voice,' I said slowly to the mystery lady.

'Oh, sure it is,' she insisted.

'No, I have a feeling you don't normally speak like that,' I said. 'In fact I think you're an actress.'

Every time she spoke, her spirit people came closer and I was suddenly aware of a lady in a wheelchair.

'Yes, I know who that is,' said the Irish voice when I told her.

'And I'm getting the name Minnie or Mimi.'

Again the mystery guest agreed that she knew who I meant.

'Pat,' whispered a voice close by.

'Who's Pat?' I asked, thinking it was someone the guest knew.

There was a tiny hesitation.

'Yes, I know a Pat,' the guest admitted.

Then I stopped. There was something wrong here. Surely Pat was the name of the guest herself, not a friend or relative. Time was running out. Should I risk a guess? Could it be Patti Coombs?

'Sorry,' said Russell Harty, stepping in quickly and cutting me off. 'That's all we've got time for, I'm afraid. And now here is our mystery guest.'

I craned forward eagerly, and out from behind the screen came, not Patti Coombs but Pat Phoenix.

Disappointment at having failed to identify the guest in the time available melted away. I was thrilled. *Coronation Street* was one of my favourite programmes and, at that time, Pat, who was in it every week playing Elsie Tanner, was the character I loved best.

'Never mind, Doris,' said Pat, 'if you'd had more time you would have got me. You were getting so close!'

We had a long chat after the show and we became friends from that moment.

Pat was a wonderful lady. She could be fiery-tempered and could blow up in a moment if something annoyed her but the next minute she was sorry and looking for a way to make amends. She always had time for the underdog and she was one of the most generous people I've ever known.

'God, it's only money,' she used to say as she bought yet another expensive present for someone.

She always had time to listen, too, and if she sensed you were feeling a bit depressed she did her best to buck you up.

'I get so embarrassed about my shaky leg,' I confided one night when she rang shortly before I was due to leave for a theatre appearance. For some reason, ever since my stroke, my leg has had a tendency to shake uncontrollably and to my chagrin it often decides to do it when I'm sitting on the stage talking to an audience.

'Forget about that, love,' said Pat 'You just go out there and slay 'em. You've got your work to do. Once you get going they'll be listening to you – not looking at your leg.'

She was always very kind. Soon after we met on the Russell

Harty Show she sent me a beautiful, signed photograph of herself and I put it proudly on my bookcase. You couldn't miss it when you walked into my sitting-room. Well, naturally, visitors noticed it and invariably they said: 'Oh do you know Pat Phoenix? I love her.'

And some were such great fans they begged for the chance just to say hello to her. It was very hard to resist and occasionally when I knew she wasn't too busy, I'd phone Pat and ask if she would help.

'Pat, I've got so-and-so here,' I'd explain, 'd'you think you could just say hello, it would mean so much to her.'

And Pat, bless her, never refused. 'Of course I will, Doris,' she would say and would patiently chat to whoever it was I put on the line.

She was generous in every way: with her money, her time and her genuine delight in the good fortune of others. When she heard I'd been able to buy my own house at last after a lifetime in rented accommodation, she was almost as thrilled as I was.

'Not before time, Doris,' she said. 'You enjoy it, love. You deserve it. I know what you do for people and what you give.'

Pat hadn't had an easy life, perhaps that's why she was able to be so compassionate to others, but at last things were going well for her. She had sorted out her career and was tackling all kinds of new and exciting roles. And at last, after years of being unlucky in love, she'd found happiness with Tony Booth. They had their fights, of course, but then doesn't any couple in love? Making up was all the sweeter.

Yes, things had come right for Pat. It seemed so unfair that at this time when she ought to have been enjoying herself, she should be struck down by lung cancer. I was very, very sad when I heard the news, particularly when the hospital announced that they wouldn't be giving her any treatment. That meant they didn't hold out much hope.

Yet despite the gravity of the situation, Pat still found time to think of others. I phoned her in hospital to try to cheer her up a bit and all she could think of was her friend Pauline, who'd popped in to see her.

'Doris, do me a favour, will you?' she asked.

'Of course I will if I can, Pat,' I assured her.

'Well I've got this friend here who's just arrived, her name's Pauline and I wondered if you'd have a word with her. She came to see you in Manchester – I was coming with her but then I had to go to London to rehearse – anyway, she thought you were marvellous and she'd love to say hello.'

What a small request, I thought, and how could I possibly refuse after the many times Pat had done the same for me.

'I'll talk to her with pleasure, Pat,' I said warmly.

I spoke to Pauline for a few minutes and then Pat came back on the line.

'Oh thank you, Doris,' she said. 'That's made her day.'

And I thought to myself, 'What a wonderful girl you are, Pat. In spite of all you've got to put up with you still think of your friends.'

Pat didn't ask for anything for herself, but the spirit world would let me know if there was any tiny way in which I could cheer her up. The first time I sent flowers to the hospital, I ordered them by phone, and half-way through my instructions to the florist, I stopped.

I'd been planning a gorgeous display of pink and white flowers but all I could think of was teddy bears.

'D'you think you could go out and buy a teddy bear and put it in the basket of flowers?' I asked slowly. I couldn't think what made me say it but suddenly it seemed very important that Pat should have a teddy bear.

The florist promised to do as I asked and I could only hope that Pat would be pleased.

Pat *was* pleased. I discovered afterwards that, that very afternoon, Pat had looked around her room which was overflowing with flowers because so many people loved her and said, 'There are so many flowers. I wish someone would send me a teddy bear.'

And ten minutes later my flowers arrived, complete with a pink teddy bear sitting in the basket. I didn't know it then, but apparently Pat used to collect teddy bears and one day she lent her collection to a charity and they got lost. She never saw them again.

Tony told me about this afterwards when he rang to thank me for the flowers, to save Pat tiring herself with too many phone calls. Through Tony I discovered that the bear Pat missed most was her beloved Paddington.

That did it. I was determined that Pat's Paddington should be replaced at all costs. I knew there wasn't much time left so Laurie, Terry and I started scouring London. There had been a run on Paddingtons, it seemed, and for a while it looked as if we were out of luck. Shop after shop declared themselves sold out. Then we found a place that had two Paddingtons left and Laurie raced over to claim one of them.

I had this terrible feeling that Pat wouldn't have long to enjoy her new bear and I wanted her to have it as soon as she possibly could, so Terry very kindly offered to fly up to Manchester and deliver it personally to the hospital.

I know Pat was pleased. I was very touched a few days later to see a photograph taken at Pat's last press conference in which she was holding a few teddy bears and there amongst them was Paddington.

I only spoke to her once more before she passed over and by then her illness was really taking its toll.

'Oh, Doris, what a thing,' she said wearily, 'I've been on oxygen today.'

'Never mind, darling,' I said, 'as long as it helps you breathe.'

I didn't keep her. I didn't want her to use up her strength talking to me.

That night I couldn't sleep for thinking about Pat. I was sure she was having a bad night and as I tossed and turned, a little poem about Paddington Bear came into my head.

It was only a silly little rhyme but I thought it might make her smile and so I got up and wrote it down. The next day I phoned Tony and read it to him.

'I haven't brought you flowers tied up with golden string,

'I haven't brought you perfume or a diamond ring,

'But here I come with my wellies on with a heart as big as a bucket,

'Filled to the brim with love for you and a message –
'Dear Pat, sock it!'

Tony roared with laughter when I'd finished. 'She'll love that, Doris,' he said.

And I can only hope that it brightened her day a little.

Pat's last wish came true, I'm glad to say, when she married Tony Booth in a moving and beautiful little ceremony at her bedside. She passed over peacefully soon afterwards as Mrs Booth.

It annoyed me rather when I read later that her priest had said, 'She turned to God in the end,' as if Pat had belatedly discovered religion. In fact, Pat had never turned away from God. She believed implicitly in life after death and she'd had several personal experiences of the spirit world.

Soon after I met her for the first time she gave a long interview to *Psychic News* in which she described how she saw a ghost in her own home.

Apparently, Pat had bought an old Georgian house in Sale, near Manchester, and she was busy restoring it to its former splendour.

One night she was sitting watching television when suddenly she heard a muffled thud from upstairs. She wasn't alarmed. Old houses are never silent and she thought something had probably fallen over in the bedroom.

Then about twenty minutes later she glanced up from the television screen and saw an old lady walk past the open door. For a moment she thought it must be her cleaner – then she realized it was far too late for any cleaner to be working. Something strange was obviously going on. Surely it couldn't be an elderly burglar?

Pat raced upstairs and searched every room. There was no one there. She ran down and searched the downstairs rooms. There was no one there either. Pat was alone in the house. She could only conclude that she'd seen a ghost.

The next evening at the same time, the same thing happened, only this time Pat noticed that her visitor seemed to be holding something in her arms.

From then on the old lady made regular appearances and Pat's mother, who often came to stay, grew so used to her that she regarded her as a friend.

Eventually, through a neighbour, they discovered the ghost's identity. Years before, an actress named Madame Muller had lived in the house. Her theatre days must have been behind her because she was reduced to giving drama and elocution lessons. She was a lonely woman. Her marriage had failed, and on warm afternoons she used to stand at the front-garden gate with her little dog in her arms, watching the world go by.

I believe that poor old Madame Muller felt a great empathy with Pat, an actress and dog-lover like herself and, what's more, a woman with a great feeling for the past who was trying to restore the house to the way it used to be. I expect she liked to drop in to see what Pat was up to and had they lived on earth at the same time, they might well have been friends.

Pat, of course, was very psychic, which is why spirit people were drawn to her and why she was able to see them.

We'll all miss Pat. She was a gutsy lady right to the end. Not for her any dreary, mournful hymns at her funeral. She arranged for a rousing rendering of 'When the Saints Come Marching In'.

I switched on the television to watch the ceremony and I was instantly reminded of a conversation we'd had months ago, long before she became ill.

Pat had phoned to ask if John and I would send out prayers to a friend of hers who needed spiritual help. I took down the details and then the conversation moved on to other things.

'Did you see that bit in the paper about the old-age pensioner who saved up for her funeral?' I asked Pat.

'No,' said Pat, 'what about her?'

'Well, I thought it was fantastic. She saved enough to hire a brass band and as the coffin was carried out of the house the band played, "Wish Me Luck as You Wave Me Goodbye". What a way to go. That old lady certainly did it in style. She must have been a marvellous character.'

Pat agreed that if you had to go, that was certainly the way to do it, and I think the conversation planted the idea in her mind. She too had a wonderful send-off.

At around this time I opened *The Sun* newspaper and came face to face with a marvellous cartoon. Chatting and sipping their drinks in a cosy pub were Ena Sharples, Albert Tatlock, Jack Walker and other members of the *Coronation Street* cast who've passed over. On the window was the name, The Spirits Return, and walking in through the open door was Pat Phoenix.

'I thought I'd find you lot in here,' Pat is saying.

And I had to smile. Pat would enjoy that no end, I thought. I bet she's laughing her head off up there.

3

It was a terrible moment. A few words, carelessly spoken on the telephone, suddenly pitched me into a nightmare.

'You know this case where the little girl's disappeared, Doris,' Laurie said casually, after bringing me up to date with my work for the coming week. 'Any idea what's happened to her?'

I hadn't. I'd heard the story on the news, of course. Six-year-old Collette Gallacher had left the house on Friday morning to catch the school bus at the stop just a few minutes from her home and she hadn't been seen since. She hadn't set foot on the bus and she didn't reach school that day.

I sympathized with the parents and, like most of us in these dreadful times, I feared the worst for the poor child because such awful things go on these days. But I didn't know. I'd had no eerie forebodings. I knew no more about the case than anyone else.

And then Laurie came out with that casual question.

'No, Laurie,' I started to say, 'I hope she's . . . Oh no!' The words choked in my throat and I let out a strangled cry of horror.

As we talked I'd been looking at a vase of flowers, placed

on the shelf only a few minutes before. Suddenly, as I started to talk of Collette, the beautiful pink carnation I'd been admiring turned into the face of a child. The face of a very dead child.

She had dark, almost black hair and huge dark eyes from which the life had already departed. I was looking at a body. The child, little Collette Gallacher, had made her journey into the spirit world.

Then there was a sort of jerk, the child's face disappeared, and I was looking at a street, a plain, small town street that could have been anywhere.

'She's only four doors away,' a voice said loudly.

Abruptly the street faded and I had the sensation of bumping up a lot of stairs, climbing high.

'She's in the top room,' the voice added, and at the same time I felt something over my face and I couldn't breathe, I was suffocating . . .

'Doris . . . are you still there? Hello? Hello?'

Mercifully, I could breathe again, the awful pictures melted and I was looking at nothing more alarming than a vase of carnations.

'Oh Laurie,' I gasped.

'Doris, are you all right?' he asked anxiously.

'Yes, yes I'm fine,' I said, collecting my wits. 'But the child. It's about the child. She's over, Laurie. I'm absolutely certain of it and she's not far away.'

I told him what I'd seen. 'And the poor child's got a sock or a gag or something in her mouth,' I added, 'because I felt something over my face and I couldn't breathe.'

There was a shocked silence.

'I don't know what to say,' said Laurie after a moment or two. 'You see, the reason I asked is that I've had Collette's aunt on the phone asking if you could help find her. They're obviously still hoping that she's alive somewhere. We can't tell them what you've just said.'

'No, of course not,' I agreed. I was quite certain I was right, but supposing I wasn't? Supposing there'd been some appalling mix-up? I couldn't possibly put the parents through that torture.

Once upon a time I might have gone straight to the police but, sadly, I've learned the hard way that this is not a good idea. These days, unless the police come to me and ask me to help, I know it's better not to interfere with their investigations.

'You'll just have to be very tactful, Laurie,' I said. 'Tell them that we are praying for them and will do everything we can and should there be any bad news and they want to see me, I'll willingly see them at any time.'

I hoped the tiny hint about bad news might go some way towards preparing them for the shock to come.

Laurie agreed to be as tactful as he knew how and he was, but shortly afterwards the aunt phoned him again.

'She's been found,' she said.

Laurie sighed, 'Just a minute then, love. I can tell you now what Doris said.' And he explained to the aunt what I'd seen and why I felt it would be too distressing to pass on to the parents until the body was found.

'Well, Doris was exactly right,' said the aunt, 'except for one thing. She didn't have a sock or a gag in her mouth. It was a plastic bag over her head.'

In fact, as we found out later, it wasn't even a plastic bag. The wicked man had wrapped cling-film round the child's head. No wonder I'd felt as if I couldn't breathe.

Poor Mrs Gallacher was devastated as any mother would be, but when the first terrible grief and shock had eased slightly, she came to see me.

She arrived at the house, a tiny little woman with huge, haunted eyes. She looked like a child herself, hardly old enough to be a mother, and she'd brought with her her friend Teresa because, like many people, she didn't know what to expect.

John and I got them settled with a cup of tea and as soon as I tuned in, the chilling, goosebumps-all-over feeling that I always get when a murder victim moves close swept over me. I shivered involuntarily. Then, to my relief, the sensation passed and a sunny, happy little soul arrived singing Happy Birthday in a sweet, childish voice.

'She's singing Happy Birthday,' I said. 'Is there a birthday in the family?'

'It's her nan's birthday today,' said Karen Gallacher.

A warm feeling of love filled the room and Collette gave me the name Anne.

'That's my mum,' said Karen.

As she talked I glanced over at Karen and briefly I saw a pretty dark head close to hers and two dark eyes beaming up at her. Whatever the poor child had gone through she was now bright as a button and chattering excitedly.

'What your mummy really wants to know is if you're all right now, darling,' I explained to her after she'd mentioned a few family members and friends. 'Are you happy?'

'I wasn't happy when I first came but now I'm all right,' said Collette.

She spent a lot of time drawing and painting, she told me, and had got ever so good at it. She also liked helping with the babies and she'd achieved a long-held ambition.

'I always wanted to go and see the Queen with her crown on,' said Collette. 'Well now I just go and see her whenever I like, but she doesn't wear her crown, you know.' She sounded rather disappointed.

'No, well I think she only wears it on special occasions, love.'

'Oh, and tell Mum I've got Mrs Mac here,' Collette added, as an older person joined her and no doubt jogged her memory.

'That's my nan,' said Karen. 'She was Mrs McAlpine but everyone called her Mrs Mac.'

The child's main concern was to cheer her mother up and she avoided the subject of the murder, but after a while she couldn't help blurting out the thing that was worrying her most.

'Is Mummy angry?' she whispered.' She always told me not to go anywhere with strangers. Well, I didn't really. I went on an errand for him. But is Mummy very angry because I went into the house?'

'No one's angry with you, love,' I told her. 'No one blames you.'

'He said he wanted to give me something for going. I wouldn't have gone in otherwise.'

'No, of course you wouldn't love,' I told her. 'But let's not talk about that. What else can you tell me?'

'Mummy's moved since then,' she offered.

'Yes, I have,' said Karen.

Then she said something about hospital.

'I'm going into hospital soon,' Karen explained.

'Well, don't worry, Mum, cos I'll be there,' said Collette. 'I always used to cheer Mummy up when she was crying, you know.'

'She certainly did,' Karen agreed.

But now the subject of the murder had been mentioned, Collette wanted to talk about it. Once again I felt that dreadful suffocating feeling and she told me various things that had happened which I felt I couldn't pass on to her mother.

'No, darling, I can't tell your mummy that,' I explained, 'it will only upset her and it doesn't matter now, does it? You're all right now.'

'But why did he have to kill me?' asked Collette in genuine bewilderment.

'He was a wicked man, darling,' I explained. 'Don't dwell on it. Tell me what else is going on now.'

'There's going to be a baby,' she said more cheerfully.

'My brother's wife is having a baby,' said Karen.

So I knew that Collette would be taking a great interest in her little cousin when he or she was born.

There were more family details and then eventually Collette ended on a happy note.

'Mummy's going to meet someone,' she confided. 'In fact she's already met him and she's going to start a new life. There's going to be a wedding.'

'Well I don't know about that,' said Karen.

'If Collette says so, it must be true,' I told her. 'You write and let me know. In fact you can send me a piece of wedding-cake!'

I was glad to see the laughter come back into her care-worn face.

'I'll do that, Doris,' Karen promised, 'I won't forget.'

A few weeks afterwards I heard that the sitting had made a dramatic difference to her life. Apparently all her friends commented on how much better she looked, as if a great weight had been lifted from her shoulders, and she was able to piece together the tragic story of Collette's last day.

On 26 February 1986 Collette had left home as usual in plenty of time to catch the school bus. She was six years old, a pretty child with shoulder-length hair and gaps in her teeth where her baby teeth had fallen out and her second teeth had yet to grow.

Not far from the bus-stop a neighbour, whom Collette probably knew by sight, put his head out of the front door to ask if she would buy a packet of crisps for him from the corner shop. Collette was the sort of child who would do anything for anybody and the shop was only yards away so she probably thought she had time to buy the crisps and still get back for her bus.

All the police know is that when she returned to the man's house, he took her inside, assaulted and murdered her. They found her body four days later and only then because the man, overcome with remorse, had tried to slash his wrists and left a suicide note.

The suicide attempt failed and he was sentenced to life imprisonment with a recommendation that he serve no less than twenty-five years.

'And I hope he never comes out,' said Karen Gallacher.

And who can blame her?

It took me quite a while to recover from that sitting. It's very important to help parents in cases like these but I must admit that I hate doing them. It tears my insides out. After Karen had gone I sat there looking at the photograph she'd left me of her daughter. Collette was such a beautiful child with her big, wide smile and her two front teeth missing, and I thought, you poor little darling. How frightened you must have been . . . What makes men do these terrible things? What's the matter with them?

I do get rather depressed with it all at times, I'm afraid, and to make matters worse, not long after I met Karen I did a demonstration at Canterbury where I came across another particularly sad case.

There was nothing wrong with Canterbury, of course. Although we didn't have time to look around you could see from the car that it was a lovely place. We passed higgledy-piggledy old timbered houses that leant drunkenly out over narrow little streets. There were picturesque shops selling all kinds of fascinating things and tiny lanes that wound tantalizingly away allowing snatched glimpses of yet more beautiful buildings. And the cathedral, of course, is legendary.

Surprisingly enough in such an old place, the theatre was quite new. Backstage it even had an unfinished air about it. I nearly had a fit when I was shown into the 'star' dressing-room. It was a long, narrow room complete with washing machine, spin-dryer and mops and buckets for decoration. It quite reminded me of the old days going round to church halls.

The main body of the theatre was beautiful, however, and the people were warm and friendly. We had a very good night but one case in particular stood out in my mind.

A young girl called Tracey came to talk to me. She even gave me part of her address: Bramley Cottage. Apparently, she'd left home to live with her boyfriend who turned out to be a bit of a swine.

'It didn't work out, Doris,' she said, 'but I was too stubborn and too proud to go back home.'

There was something peculiar about her passing and a verdict of misadventure had been reached at the inquest. I thought it best not to delve too deeply into that at a public meeting so I asked Tracey to tell me what her parents were doing now.

'They feel guilty,' Tracey said at once. 'They keep feeling guilty and they shouldn't. Tell Mum not to feel guilty because of what they can do now.'

I found this rather puzzling but I passed it on to the mother just as I'd heard it.

'Does this mean anything to you, love?' I asked. 'Because she seems to be quite worried about it.'

The little woman at the microphone nodded her head vigorously. 'I know exactly what she means,' she said. 'When Tracey was a little girl we didn't have very much. Life was always a struggle. But now my husband has his own business and we could give Tracey everything she wanted. We have plenty of money, but what good is money to us now when we don't have a daughter?'

Her poignant words seemed to tug at my heart and they haunted me for weeks afterwards. I gave her the big floral centrepiece from the stage; a magnificent arrangement of pink and white carnations, gladioli and white chrysanthemums, as a tribute from her daughter, but I couldn't get her out of my mind.

Then a few days later a strange thing happened. I went to bed feeling depressed, thinking about Collette and Tracey and wondering for the umpteenth time why these things have to happen. As I undressed I noticed with mild surprise that the fancy pillows that I move from the bed to the armchair at night, had been taken from the chair where I left them and placed on the blanket box.

Now what are they doing there? I wondered. But I was too tired to care much and certainly too tired to move them back again. Well, you can stay there till the morning, I told them wearily as I climbed between the sheets.

I stretched out my hand, turned off the lamp and I was just settling down to sleep when a shape made me gasp. There was someone sitting in the armchair.

My eyes flew open properly and by the light from the street lamps outside I saw that it was my father. He was sitting in the chair with his hands on his knees and he was smiling at me.

Strangely enough I could even see his reflection in the mirror doors of my wardrobe.

'Dad!' I cried. 'What are you doing here?'

He didn't answer, he just nodded reassuringly, as if to say, 'Everything's all right, Dol. I'm here. Go to sleep now.'

Suddenly I remembered that in addition to my depression, it was the anniversary of my long-ago, stillborn little girl. No wonder I felt down.

Yet as I looked at Dad's kind smile, the grey cloud seemed to melt away, my eyes felt unbearably heavy and I drifted off into sleep.

That night I had the best night's sleep I'd had for months and when I woke the next morning the bed looked as if it hadn't been slept in. I'd lain so still I'd hardly rumpled the sheets.

And when I looked down at the bottom of the bed I saw that the pillows had moved back from the top of the blanket box and were in their normal place in the armchair.

I felt cheerful and full of energy for the first time in weeks. 'Thank you, Dad,' I said out loud, 'I needed that.'

And I went off with a light step to start the chores.

4

It was one of the prettiest displays I'd ever seen: a miniature crib trimmed with pink and white frills and crammed to over-flowing with pastel-coloured flowers and little ornamental storks.

It was absolutely beautiful but there was surely some mistake.

'But this is for someone who's just had a baby,' I protested as the receptionist tried to hand it to me.

'Well, it definitely says Doris Stokes,' she insisted.

I laughed. 'Impossibilities I'll have a try at, love,' I said, 'but miracles I leave to God!'

Nevertheless, I took the little card that was pinned to the flowers and peered at it. Sure enough it was addressed to Doris Stokes and it came with love from my new friends, Erdal and Filiz Danyal and most particularly, from their new-born daughter, Ayse.

It was such a shame. I'd been looking forward to seeing the baby and the visit was all arranged, when I managed to land myself in hospital again.

It was nothing serious, I'm glad to say. I caught a nasty flu bug while travelling round the country in November and somehow I couldn't seem to shake it off. By December I had pleurisy and, despite the fact that the doctor had given me enough pills to stock a small pharmacist's, I seemed to get worse instead of better. Then one morning I was standing in the kitchen, stirring the porridge, when suddenly I collapsed.

I gave Terry a terrible fright I must say. I'm not the fainting type so he's not exactly used to me keeling over all over the place but I'm glad he was there even though it was a nasty shock for him. It was most peculiar. One minute I was concentrating on bubbling porridge, the next the room was fading away and I was falling backwards.

'Terry help me, I'm going!' I cried, meaning that I thought I was going to faint.

Terry, unfortunately, thought I meant that I was passing over and it shook him rigid. Somehow he half carried me into the sitting-room, propped me up in a chair and then frantically phoned the doctor.

I've mentioned our marvellous doctor before in previous books. Well, he was good as ever. He only lives round the corner and he arrived at the house within ten minutes of Terry's call. By this time, of course, I was groggy but conscious, and more worried about the burnt porridge than anything else. I don't like the boys starting the day without a hot meal in their stomachs.

'Never mind the porridge,' said Dr David sternly. 'What's all this? I think this bad chest of yours has gone on long enough. We'd better get you into hospital and find out what's wrong.'

It was only a couple of weeks before Christmas and there was stacks to be done. The letters were piling up, I had a public demonstration arranged, not a single Christmas card had gone out and I hadn't even started the Christmas shopping. I couldn't have picked a more inconvenient time.

'I can't go into hospital. I'm much too busy,' I explained.

'Oh yes, you can and you must,' said Dr David.

He was backed up by John and Terry and of course I was outnumbered. While I lay back weakly drinking tea, the doctor phoned around to organize a bed, John and Terry packed a few things into a case and before I'd fully recovered my senses I was on my way to the local hospital.

I didn't realize it at the time but the doctor feared there might be something seriously wrong with my heart or my lungs. He couldn't understand why I should have passed out so unexpectedly and why my illness was not responding to treatment.

The hospital doctors were puzzled too. They gave me oxygen to help me breathe and then conducted test after test. Thankfully my heart and lungs showed no signs of serious damage. In the end they came to the conclusion that I'd fainted because my chest was so congested that when I bent over the cooker to stir the porridge, the oxygen supply to my brain was momentarily cut off. As for my illness, it was hanging around because I was exhausted.

'Oh, that's all right then,' I said in relief when they told me, 'I can go home.' And I started collecting up the things on my bedside table and searching about for my case.

'Oh no you don't,' they said. 'You're to stay here.'

They couldn't hold me against my will of course, a hospital is not a prison, but they made it quite clear that I would be mad to leave just then. If I carried on the way I'd been going I would end up with double pneumonia.

Put that way there didn't seem to be a lot of choice. There was nothing to be done but resign myself to another stay in hospital. It was such a shame Laurie had to ring round cancelling all my appointments. The letters piled up unread and the Christmas shopping had to be left to John and Terry.

Goodness knows what we'll end up having for Christmas dinner with those two in charge, I thought. Still, it'll be a surprise!

Most disappointing of all was the fact that I wouldn't now be able to visit little Ayse in hospital and hold her in my arms when she was just a few hours old. I telephoned Erdal Danyal to apologize and he was most understanding.

'Never mind, Doris,' he said. 'As soon as you are better you must come and see us at home instead.'

And the next day the beautiful crib of flowers arrived to cheer me up. Actually I think the fact that I got a crib and storks was a bit of a misunderstanding on the part of the florist. I believe Erdal ordered flowers to be sent to me 'from the baby' and somewhere along the line the message got changed to 'for the baby'. But it didn't matter at all. The crib was exquisite, it gave us much more fun than a conventional bunch of flowers would have done and I shall keep it to remind me of the day Ayse was born.

I met the Danyals, as I do so many of my new friends, through a sitting. These days, I'm sorry to say, I can do very few private sittings and Erdal Danyal had been waiting a long time to see me.

Laurie arranges all the bookings from his office so I never know who's coming to see me until they arrive, but it turned out that Erdal Danyal was from Turkey and he had been given three of my books following the death of his father. He had been waiting for a sitting ever since.

I always enjoy working with overseas people because it's such a challenge. I don't speak a word of any language other than English, I'm afraid, so Ramanov (my guide) always translates the messages for me. Names, however, come in their original form as a means of identification for the sitter and it's quite a job, I can tell you, getting my tongue round some of them.

It was Erdal's mother I remember chiefly from the sitting. She had passed a few years before his father, and although I don't often see spirit people (these days I tend only to see spirit children) she communicated so strongly that I was able to catch a brief glimpse of her face. She was very much like her son with straight black hair worn in a plain style, and lively dark eyes.

Mrs Danyal senior had quite a lot to say for herself I recall, and in particular she was irritated because one of her other sons had not been able to name his boat after her.

She put into my mind a picture of a beautiful, blue sea and an island sparkling in the sun. Then she showed me a boat bobbing about on the water.

'That is my son's boat,' she said indignantly, 'and my son wanted to name it after me but his wife wouldn't let him.'

Erdal, somewhat surprised, I think, confirmed that this was true. Apparently, the family spent their holidays on this island and Erdal's brother had had a boat specially built. He had intended to name it in memory of his mother but at the last minute his wife had prevented him from doing so.

Mrs Danyal and some other members of the family chatted away for nearly two hours but since I can't remember all the details myself, I'll let Erdal explain what happened:

'I went along to see Doris with a friend,' said Erdal. 'She took us into the house and we sat down and I was expecting that she would concentrate and call something down. In fact it wasn't like that at all.

'I thought nothing was happening. Doris was just chatting to us and then suddenly she seemed to get onto the right frequency. She said she could hear a woman talking about a policeman.

'I couldn't think of any policeman in the family but

Doris said the woman insisted that this particular policeman was a family member. I couldn't place him so we left it and she moved on, but about half an hour later when she was talking to my father the policeman was mentioned again. He was definitely in the family she said, and he was now on the other side. And then I remembered that my uncle, who died seven or eight years ago, had been a policeman!

'It was an extraordinary experience. Doris gave me my mother's name – an 'a' sound, she said, Ayse – the fact that she had died in her sleep and hadn't been able to say goodbye and that she had five children and six grandchildren. All correct.

'She said my mother told her that four of her five children had got married and were happy but for a while she was worried about me because I hadn't settled down. I was the last of her children to marry but she was pleased now because I'd married a good wife and we were having a baby.

'She told me that I had my mother's wedding-ring. Not the ring she was given when she married but a more expensive ring my father had given her years later when he'd made his money. (This was true. I kept it at the time in my safe.) She said my mother wanted me to give the ring to my wife when she'd had the baby.

'She also gave me my father's name and the fact that he'd died suddenly of a heart attack. All correct. Then she·turned to my friend and said, "There is someone interrupting. It's your father. He died of cancer and he suffered for three months. You weren't there when he died. His name is Abba."

'My companion was very shocked indeed. He hadn't

been expecting any messages for himself but, once again, Doris was absolutely right.

'She went on to talk about the boat and the island – incidentally I've since bought the boat from my brother and I've changed the name to Ayse so I hope my mother is happy now! – and my brother Nail who deals with money and book-keeping (correct) and my sister who is having problems with her nerves at the moment (also correct). She also said that my sister moved house just after my mother passed away. I thought she moved before my mother passed away but when I discussed it with my wife later she reminded me that it was in fact after, so Doris was correct again!

'Finally, she said she could see a long bay with a very nice beach and a beautiful sea. This is where we have bought some land and at the moment we are building a hotel there.

'There were many other family details, including a brother who died twenty-two years ago when he was only twenty-one, but these were the things that most stand out in my mind. I was amazed by the whole experience. I do believe in life after death but I felt very nervous at the beginning of the sitting.

'The night before, I prayed to God and asked that it would work because I badly wanted to know if my parents and my brother had met and were together. I know that my prayers were accepted because Doris gave me the details I needed. Afterwards I felt much better. It was a very great relief.'

Erdal was pleased with his sitting, that was clear, and he has kept in touch ever since. I was the first person he telephoned when his little daughter was born.

'Has my mother said anything about the baby?' he asked me.

I tuned in and immediately I heard Mrs Danyal's voice. 'It's a girl and they've named her for me,' she said proudly.

'You've named her Ayse after your mother,' I told Erdal and he confirmed that this was true. His mother was thrilled and I expect she'll watch over her little granddaughter with special care.

Obviously, as I explained, I was unable to see baby Ayse in hospital, but Erdal and his wife Filiz invited John and I to tea a few weeks later. We had a lovely afternoon.

It was the first day of the big freeze of January '87, but Erdal sent a car to collect us and we were driven in comfort through a shivering London to a luxury apartment block in Kensington. There we sat on the ninth floor looking out over the snowfields of Kensington Gardens, eating delicious Turkish pastries made by Filiz, and drinking tea.

Ayse was asleep when we arrived but by the time we'd finished our first cup, she was awake and ready for inspection. Filiz put her into my arms, a warm little bundle in a deep blue babygrow, with velvety brown eyes and a cap of dark hair. She was absolutely gorgeous.

John, who'd rather overdone it that morning shovelling snow off the path and had consequently been feeling groggy ever since, perked up tremendously at the sight of the baby and insisted that he had a cuddle too.

All in all it was a special afternoon. It brought back memories, too. Erdal had employed a nanny to help Filiz with the baby while they were in England and watching her bob about in her dark dress and black stockings I was instantly reminded of my own nannying career. I was also fascinated to learn how things have changed since my day.

Ayse was suffering a little from wind.

'Oh, you'd better give her a drop of gripe-water,' I remarked automatically to the nanny.

'We haven't got any,' she said.

'Haven't got any? Oh, I suppose you've run out.'

'No, we don't use it,' said the nanny. 'There's no point. The doctor says it doesn't do any good at all.'

I was amazed. When I was a nanny we used to swear by gripe-water. No nursery was complete without it.

'No good?' I said. 'But in my day we used it all the time.'

The girl shook her head. 'Well we don't any more. The doctor says you might just as well give the baby plain water.'

I could hardly believe it. The doctor must know what he's talking about of course but to think of the gallons of gripe-water we must have poured down our babies for nothing! Surely it wasn't just our imagination that the little mites felt better after their 'medicine'.

I was also surprised at the way modern nannies swing a baby on to their shoulder. The girl was very careful of course, but in my day we never moved a child without cradling its head in one hand. It's much more casual now.

'This is how they teach us to do it now, Doris,' said the nanny with a smile as she patted Ayse's back and carried her away.

I don't know, I thought to myself, if I was trying to be a nanny in this day and age they'd think I was dreadfully old-fashioned. I'd better stick to being a medium.

Mind you, I don't regret my nannying years. I enjoyed them tremendously at the time and it certainly opened my eyes to the very different ideas of motherhood held by some women.

Loving children as I have always done, I couldn't imagine anything more wonderful than having a baby of my own and spending every possible moment with it. What's more, I believed that every woman naturally felt the same way – until I became a nanny myself and came across many different sorts of mother.

Some were busy women who didn't have the time to be with their children every minute of the day. Some were in poor health and couldn't cope with a boisterous child; others just needed a bit of help, but a few it must be said, simply weren't cut out to be mothers at all.

These were the women who would hand the baby over to the nanny on every possible occasion and appeared to take very little interest in it at all.

I remember one woman I worked for who asked me to do her a special favour and work on Sunday, my day off. It was the baby's christening, she said, and she couldn't manage without help.

Well, John wasn't very pleased because we valued the one day a week we could spend together as a family, but I couldn't refuse.

'Well, all right,' I said reluctantly, 'but I can't stay late.'

'No, of course not, Mrs Stokes. I quite understand, and my husband will run you home afterwards.'

It was a grand affair. Guests arrived from miles around in large shiny cars, the women resplendent in bright hats and matching coats, the men smart in well-cut suits. I felt quite shabby beside them and I kept in the background while the service was conducted and the proud mother posed for photographs.

Then to my surprise, when the last camera was put away, the baby was thrust into my arms.

'We'll see you back at the house then, Mrs Stokes,' said my employer and off she went with her friends, leaving me to change the baby, settle him back in his pram and wheel him slowly home.

Soon a magnificent garden party was under way and baby was forgotten. I fed him, changed him again and put him down in his cot for a nap, just as I did every other day. Perhaps I was wrong, but I got the impression that his mother was more interested in her guests than in her son.

It seemed strange to me at the time but it was good experience. Quickly I learned that we're all different and those early lessons helped me understand the plight of the penniless young girls you get nowadays, stranded alone in a tower block with a baby. I expect some of them are temperamentally unsuited to motherhood but, unable to afford a nanny, they have to struggle along as best they can. Is it any wonder that sometimes they can't cope?

The cold days of winter brought another delightful meeting. At around the time of our afternoon with the Danyals, John and I were invited to tea with our Indian friend, Sam.

For years Sam had only been a voice on the phone. As I think I explained in one of my earlier books, Sam first became interested in spiritualism when he was working for the Indian Embassy in Germany. Waiting for a telephone call in the office one day he found himself listening to the radio which was tuned to the World Service, and as luck would have it the programme was about my book.

As the interview went on, Sam grew so interested that, afterwards, he telephoned the publishers and asked them to send him a copy. Then tragedy struck. Three weeks after receiving the book his little daughter passed over. It was a terrible, terrible blow, but later when he got over the shock Sam contacted me to let me know how much my book had helped him in his grief. He has been phoning ever since.

On one occasion I happened to say: 'And how's your wife? Is she feeling a little better now?'

'Well, yes, I think so,' said Sam, 'though she still misses our daughter very badly of course.'

But before he'd even finished speaking I heard another voice telling me the good news.

'Don't worry, Sam,' I said firmly, 'your little boy is on his way.'

Sam was astonished. He wanted to believe me but he found it very difficult.

'Really, Doris?'

'That's what they've just told me,' I assured him. 'And they're never wrong. I make mistakes sometimes but they don't.'

Sam went away cheered but incredulous. Unknown to him however, his wife had an appointment with the doctor the next day and that day it was confirmed that she was pregnant. Their son, Manfred, was born several months later.

In recent years Sam has been able to visit me a couple of times when he's been posted to Britain, but 1987 was special. Not only was Sam himself in Britain, but his parents were visiting him here too.

'Do you think you and John could come over for a cup of tea?' asked Sam. 'My parents would love to meet you before they go back to India. They've read all your books.'

So once again, John and I found ourselves driving across London on a cold afternoon for a warm welcome and an exotic tea.

Oddly enough, we discovered that Sam was renting a house in Dulwich on the very same estate where Margaret Thatcher has bought a retirement home. It made me smile to think that having grown up with Margaret Roberts, as she then was, in Grantham, and having seen the corner shop where she started, I should now get the chance to see the place where she was planning to end her career.

The car brought us to an elegant estate where large mock-Georgian houses looked out over wide, open-plan lawns. There wasn't a wall or a hedge to be seen until we turned into a private side-street and suddenly came upon a place that positively bristled with fences. It was the future Thatcher home.

Very nice inside, I'm sure, although I was surprised at how close together the houses had been built.

Once again we had a lovely afternoon. Sam's wife served us with tea Indian-style, made with hot milk, accompanied by delicious apple pancakes, apple flan and yoghurt sweets.

Afterwards, Manfred, now grown into a quiet, beautifully-mannered little boy, played happily with the belated Christmas present we'd brought him – a radio-controlled car, while we adults chatted about every subject under the sun including reincarnation.

The time raced by and I think we were all sorry when it was time for John and I to go home.

I must say, moan though I sometimes do about overwork, I'd hate to have to give up my job. You really do meet the nicest people when you're a medium.

5

It was Christmas Day. The tree was glowing softly in the corner, the radio was playing carols and the house was filled with the smell of roasting turkey.

Happily, I started picking up discarded wrapping-paper before Boots could chew it to bits. Boots, of course, thought it was a marvellous game and trotted after me making little darts at the screwed-up sheets.

'Don't you dare!' I said, pretending to scold, as we had a fierce tug of war over one holly-strewn piece. 'I'll have your guts for garters if you get that all over the place.'

It was quite a tussle but Boots eventually conceded defeat, and just as I straightened up, the phone rang.

'Hello! Merry Christmas!' I said, stuffing the paper under one arm.

'Hello,' whispered a shy little voice, 'I'm going to sing.'

And she did: 'We wish you a merry Christmas, we wish you a merry Christmas, we wish you a merry Christmas and a . . .'

The paper fell from my arms and I stood there listening to the song with tears stinging my eyes. Little Beverley George was no Aled Jones but that carol was the most beautiful sound I heard all Christmas.

They'd said there was no hope for Beverley. At just a few weeks old she had suffered such a savage beating she was left blind, crippled and brain-damaged. She was a cabbage, her foster-mother, Wendy, was told and unlikely to live beyond a year.

Yet thanks to Wendy's faith, courage and devotion, Beverley, now nine years old, could see, talk and enjoy life.

'Thank you for my walking-frame,' said Beverley when she'd finished the song. 'I love you.'

'It's a pleasure, darling,' I croaked round the lump in my throat. 'You're worth it.'

We'd never met Beverley in person but John and I have known about her for a long time. She is a very special little girl. When she was about eighteen months old her foster-mother had written to us in despair. An orthopaedic surgeon had just told her:

'We don't waste our time on handicapped children.'

Now I'm not suggesting for one minute that this is the general attitude of orthopaedic surgeons, but this particular man was obviously tactless to say the least and he upset Wendy very much.

'I've got no one else to turn to,' she wrote to us. 'The surgeon says there's nothing that can be done, but I can't just give up on Beverley. I'd be very grateful if John would put her on his healing list.'

At this stage the child couldn't lift her head or move her legs and the medical profession held out no hope.

It seemed terrible to us to write off a poor little mite like that, and besides, John turns no one away. Beverley went on his absent healing list that very day.

Absent healing can't guarantee a cure, I must stress. If it's your time to pass over there's nothing that will hold you back. But healing will ease suffering, smooth a passing and in some cases, result in a dramatic improvement or even a cure.

What's more, in Beverley's case, contrary to what the doctors said, I felt that there was a lot of hope. Not for any medical reason (I'm not a doctor after all) but because quite clearly, the spirit world was hard at work on the child's behalf.

Already a couple of strange things had happened. On Christmas Day, when she was just one year old, Beverley had suddenly and quite unexpectedly got her sight back. Wendy had been warned that the little girl would probably never see again, yet on Christmas morning, she looked directly at the bright glass balls on the Christmas tree and reached out for them.

Tests revealed that the action wasn't just a coincidence. Beverley could definitely see.

It was like a miracle for the Georges but there were still serious problems. Beverley also suffered from terrible fits, sometimes undergoing ten or fifteen a day. In order to minimize the damage they caused and keep them under control, she was prescribed a number of powerful drugs. There was no alternative to medication, Wendy was told.

Mrs George struggled on somehow and that year she even managed to take Beverley away on holiday to Wales. One afternoon, as they were sitting on the promenade enjoying the sunshine, a strange thing happened.

'A woman suddenly approached us,' said Wendy. 'I'd never seen her before in my life. She could have known nothing about Beverley or what was wrong with her and yet she came up to us and said: "You are killing that little blossom bud. The more you give her those drugs, the more she will shrivel up and die." As she spoke, she cupped her hands into a bud shape and crumpled them. "But the more you take her off the drugs," she continued, "the more she will blossom and bloom," and she opened her hands like a flower unfurling. Then she walked away and I never saw her again.'

Wendy was naturally taken aback. There was something about the woman's manner that impressed her. She could not just dismiss her words and yet she felt confused and unsure. After all, the woman had not mentioned any kind of medical background that might lead her to give this advice and what she was suggesting could be very dangerous indeed.

What's more, Wendy, who was devoted to Beverley and had done everything in her power to help her, rather resented being told that she was killing her foster-daughter, albeit with kindness.

And yet, and yet . . . How had the woman known that Beverley was on drugs in the first place? It seemed very odd. And there was something about her manner . . . Wendy couldn't put her finger on it but she had the strangest feeling that she ought to take the woman's advice.

I believe that the woman was sent with a message from the spirit world. She might even have been a spirit person. But Wendy, of course, who knew nothing of such things at this time, simply found the incident oddly disturbing.

Nevertheless, by the time she got back to her room she had decided that she would be mad to do anything but stick to her doctor's conventional advice. And who can blame her? But that night Beverley suffered a terrible fit.

Wendy was badly shaken. She had given the child the correct dose of the prescribed medicine and yet it had done nothing to prevent the fit. If the drugs were not doing her any good and might possibly be doing her harm, then Wendy decided she didn't want anything more to do with them.

'But when I suggested this to the doctor she was furious,' Wendy recalled. 'She wanted to know why I was doubting her advice. After all, I had no medical training and she had spent years learning about such things.'

It was a difficult situation but the more Wendy thought about it the more convinced she became that the strange woman was right and the doctor was wrong. The next day she stopped Beverley's drugs.

'And she hasn't had a fit since,' said Wendy.

The years passed, Beverley slowly improved and Wendy kept us in touch with her progress. From being a helpless little rag doll, unable even to lift her head, Beverley changed into a cheerful, chattering child who could crawl about the house by dragging herself along with her arms. She was able to go to a special school in a wheelchair and she could enjoy the company of other children. No one could call her a cabbage and the experts were amazed.

We hadn't heard from Wendy for a while and so one day, when we were leaving for Birmingham where I was to appear at the Odeon, I must admit that I didn't give her a thought. It didn't even cross my mind that Wendy lived in a little village not too far from the city.

Still, when we arrived at the hotel there was a letter waiting for me in Wendy's hand-writing and as I read it, I could have kicked myself.

'Oh, John, what a shame,' I said. 'If only we'd thought. Wendy says that she tried to get tickets for herself and Beverley to come to the Odeon but they were sold out. If only we'd realized we could have asked Laurie to save her some.'

It was too late to organize anything now. It's very difficult for Wendy to do things at a moment's notice. Instead, we had to be content with a phone call.

'Oh, what a shame,' I said again as I unpacked my case. 'I would have loved to meet Beverley.'

John dialled the Georges' number and had a good old chat with Wendy. Then when he was fully up to date with Beverley's progress, he passed the phone to me.

'What a pity, love,' I said. 'If only we'd known before. We would have loved to see you.'

'Never mind, Doris,' said Wendy. 'Maybe next time.'

I didn't answer. She must have thought me strange, but at that precise moment someone from the other side butted in. Oh no, that can't be right, I thought, but I had to blurt it out just the same.

'You haven't had a baby today have you, love?' I asked, though I felt sure she wouldn't be talking to me on the phone like this if she had.

'No!' squeaked Wendy in amazement.

'Well, someone in your family has,' I persisted.

I think it was the grandmother who'd arrived to tell me the good news. She didn't stay long but she was quite definite.

'Actually my sister has,' said Wendy slowly.

'That's it,' I said relieved. I wasn't going barmy after all. 'A little girl.'

'Yes, that's right,' said Wendy.

'And she's got the name the wrong way round!' said the grandmother, but not crossly.

'Got the name the wrong way round?' I queried silently. 'What d'you mean, love?'

But grandmother was hurrying off somewhere, probably back to the baby and she didn't have time to chat.

'Just tell her. She'll know,' she said, as she moved away. 'She's got the name the wrong way round.'

And then she was gone.

'Well I don't understand this,' I said to Wendy, 'but I'm sure your nan just said that your sister's got the name round the wrong way.'

Wendy gasped. Then she started to laugh. 'Yes! Yes, she would. The baby's called Charlotte Elizabeth and Nan's name was Elizabeth Charlotte!'

Good old Nan, I thought. She doesn't miss a thing. Still, I'm sure she appreciated the fact that the baby was given her name even if it was in reverse order.

I hadn't intended to get into a sitting and it was only a tiny scrap of information, yet I hoped it would make up to Wendy for missing the demonstration. I started to 'switch off' but before I did so I picked up an agitated vibration from Wendy. She was worried about something.

'Is anything wrong, love?' I asked. 'You seem a bit bothered about something.'

'Well, yes, I suppose I am, Doris,' Wendy admitted reluctantly. 'Not bothered so much as angry, really.'

It turned out that she'd heard about a wonderful invention that could mean a lot to Beverley. It was a special sort of walking-frame in which a child like Beverley could be strapped upright, her feet on a swivelling platform which would move when she moved her shoulders. A twitch to the right would swivel the feet to the right, a twitch to the left would turn the feet in that direction and gradually the child would 'walk' across the room.

'Beverley's never been able to stand upright,' said Wendy, 'and it's her dearest wish to help me with the washing-up. This frame would allow her to do that. It would make her feel she was walking and it would strengthen her legs which are like matchsticks.'

There was only one problem. The frame cost much more than the Georges could manage and the council wouldn't help. Apparently they lived in one area but Beverley went to school in another and each authority said the other should pay. Wendy was left feeling that she was asking for some unreasonable luxury.

'Well, John,' I said, when Wendy had finished pouring out the sad tale. 'What shall we do about this? I think we'd better help. All right, Wendy. Don't worry about it. The money will be in the post.'

Wendy was flabbergasted. She had had no thought in her mind of asking for financial help from us – she'd simply poured out her troubles to a friendly ear.

'Oh, Doris . . . I don't know what to say,' she stammered, 'I wasn't hinting . . . I mean . . .'

'I know, love,' I said, 'but it will be a great pleasure for us to help. After all, a girl of nine should be able to stand up and walk if she possibly can. It's not a luxury.'

Wendy was thrilled. I couldn't stand chatting for long because I had to get ready to go to the theatre but I think our short conversation made her day.

It turned out to be a marvellous day for me, too. Readers of my earlier books will remember the time when I worked as a nanny for Wyn, the lady who lived in the big house near us in Grantham and who taught me how to lay a table properly, which fork to use and all manner of useful things. Well, Wyn has long since passed over, but her husband, Stan, now a fine old gentleman of eighty-six, is still going strong and he was coming to see me on stage for the first time, that night.

I had another special guest too. Rusty Lee, the irrepressible TV cook, had agreed to come on stage and introduce me. I'd met Rusty a few years earlier when we were both invited to be in the audience of Dame Edna Everidge's Celebrity Night Out on the South Bank.

Rusty walked into the room, a bouncing bundle of undiluted energy with a 100 kilowatt smile. She took one look at me, rushed over and threw her arms round my neck in a great big hug.

'Oh, I've been longing to meet you,' she cried and she chattered away and roared with uninhibited laughter for the rest of the evening. She was truly a sunny personality. She brightened a room just by walking into it.

Rusty moved to Birmingham shortly after this and one day, while driving past the Odeon, she saw my name on a poster outside. When she got home she phoned to see if she could get a ticket but they were sold out. Undaunted she asked to speak to the manager.

'Well, Rusty,' said the manager when she explained the problem, 'come down and we'll see if we can fix you up.'

Rusty duly arrived with a great big bouquet of flowers and the manager squeezed her into the theatre somehow.

'Oh, Rusty,' I said, when I saw her later in the dressing-room,' I don't suppose you've been very comfortable.'

'I've been fine,' she insisted, 'I'm having a wonderful time.'

'Well, I'll tell you what,' I said. 'Next time I'm at the Odeon why don't you come up on stage with me? We'll definitely find you a chair – you can be chairman for the evening!'

'I'll hold you to that, Doris,' grinned Rusty. 'I'd love to.'

She was as good as her word. And that night when I arrived at the Odeon, there she was, smile as wide as ever, eager to begin.

Stan arrived shortly afterwards. It was a bitterly cold night for anyone to turn out and Stan, who had to walk with the aid of two sticks, must have found it more difficult than most, but he came beaming into the dressing-room with the lady who'd brought him.

'I'm so proud of you, Nanny, 'he said. 'You do Grantham proud.'

Then he stopped. 'Oh dear. I must remember to call you Doris, but somehow it just comes out as Nanny. I know. Supposing I called you Poll?'

Long before I worked as a nanny, my nickname as a child had been Polly, or Poll for short.

'That's all right, Stan,' I said. 'As long as it's polite I don't mind what you call me!'

And I sat him down and gave him a cup of tea and a sandwich to warm him up before the demonstration began.

I didn't know whether I was coming or going that night with the excitement of my visitors and the crowded dressing-room. Hardly had we got Stan settled in his place of honour in the theatre than it was time for Rusty and I to go on stage. I just about managed to pat my hair into place and straighten my dress and I was on.

Rusty didn't seem a bit nervous. She strode out and chatted to the crowd as if it was composed of one or two old friends and not a theatre full of strangers. She was a great asset to the atmosphere. When there was an amusing moment she roared with laughter and set the entire audience off. When there was a touching moment I looked round and saw that there were tears pouring down her face.

Stan had his moment of glory too. I explained to members of the audience who hadn't read my books, about Wyn and all the things she'd taught me.

'That was a very long time ago, of course,' I said, 'but tonight I'm very thrilled because her husband is here in the audience. Come on, Stan. Stand up.'

And Stan, still an elegant man despite his age, stood up proudly and took a bow. The audience gave him a wonderful round of applause and he sat down again almost scarlet with pleasure.

It was pretty hectic during the intermission in my dressing-room. Rusty was in fine form, handing round cups of tea and making everybody weak with laughter at her jokes. It was great fun, but after a while, I realized I needed to tune in in order to sort out some contacts for the second half and I couldn't do it with all this noise.

Quietly I slipped into the bathroom to escape the hilarity. I stood there at the mirror fiddling with my hair and trying to concentrate.

'Poo!' said a spirit voice.

Slightly offended, I sniffed the air. 'There's no smell in here,' I told my unseen critic indignantly. 'Not unless you mean my perfume, and I think it's rather nice.'

There was a merry laugh.

'Not poo. Pugh!' she repeated. 'My name is Pugh and my husband is here. He was the last but one contact.'

Quickly I replayed the first half in my mind and I remembered an extremely thin man with dark hair and very intense dark eyes. He'd come up to the microphone because I'd made a contact for him but unfortunately I lost it almost immediately and most of the messages turned out to be for other people.

I do my best but this often happens, I'm sorry to say. Spirit people frequently think that because I can hear them, their loved ones can suddenly hear them too, and so almost as soon as they get through to me, they go darting over to their relatives or friends to talk to them and I lose them. They move off the vibration and another spirit person comes forward to take their place.

'I would like to speak to my husband,' said Mrs Pugh. 'Will you try again?'

'I'll do my best, love,' I promised her, 'but we always start the second half with question time. Will you wait around till that's over?'

'Of course,' said Mrs Pugh.

Sure enough, this time we got it right. Mr Pugh came back to the microphone and his wife talked to him at length about the children and how much she missed them. Poor girl, she'd suffered very badly and she'd left behind her a beautiful baby.

As she talked about it, Mrs Pugh showed me a mental picture of her bedroom. Her husband was in bed and he was cuddling something in his arms.

'Do you cuddle a pillow in bed at night?' I asked him.

'No,' said Mr Pugh.

'Well, she's giving me an impression of being in bed and I've got something in my arms and I'm cuddling it,' I said.

'That's the baby,' said Mr Pugh. 'Ever since my wife went, I've slept with the baby. I go to sleep with my arms round her.'

He had been devastated by his wife's tragic passing but now he felt a tremendous sense of relief to know that she wasn't totally lost.

All in all, I had a very happy time in Birmingham and though it was hard work I knew that the effort wasn't in vain. Come Christmas I received a beautiful letter from Mr Pugh, enclosing a photograph of the baby.

'Becky has quite taken to you, Doris,' he wrote, 'and calls you her new granny.'

I also heard from Beverley in the nicest possible way. Apparently these days she's getting on wonderfully with her walking-frame. She scoots about the house and classroom, she's learning to read, she's about to start learning to write and, best of all as far as she's concerned, she's helped her mum with the washing-up.

'The first time, she got water everywhere,' said Wendy 'The kitchen was flooded. But I wouldn't have cared if the whole house was awash. I just stood there and watched her with tears in my eyes. I never thought it would be possible. It was like a miracle.'

And just to round off a very special Christmas, we went to a pantomime.

Apparently Lewisham Theatre, where I do so many demonstrations I'm almost part of the family, was putting on *Snow White and the Seven Dwarfs* starring Gary Wilmott, that year. We hadn't been planning to go but Chris Hare, the manager, phoned and invited us.

'It's a good show, Doris,' he said. 'You'll love it.'

Now I must confess to a weakness for pantomimes. I know they're not everyone's cup of tea but then maybe I'm a child at heart. Anyway, I knew I'd love it too and I wasn't disappointed.

Chris met us at the door and made a great fuss of us. He took our coats and put them in his office for safe keeping, then he escorted us to our seats. It was the first time I'd seen the theatre from that side of the stage and I was impressed.

The seats were a pretty pink and very comfortable and there was plenty of leg-room. Even better still, though it's not a service everyone gets, I realize, as soon as the curtain came down for the intermission, Chris arrived with two cups of tea for us. We felt thoroughly spoiled.

Almost as soon as we arrived a hand tapped me on the shoulder and a woman said: 'Excuse me. It's Doris Stokes, isn't it?'

'Yes love.'

'Don't you want anyone to know you're here?'

'I'm not bothered, love,' I told her.

She began rummaging about in her handbag. 'In that case,' she said, 'would you mind signing an autograph? It's a new book and you'll be the first one.'

Naturally, people saw what was going on and a few minutes later I had a little stack of programmes and odds and ends to sign. But people were very good. They didn't pester us and we were able to enjoy the show in peace.

And it was just as well I hadn't been hoping to make a visit incognito because even before the curtain rose, a voice announced:

'Tonight, ladies and gentlemen, we've got Doris Stokes in the audience, so if you want to know how the story ends, you'll have to ask her.'

Marvellous though Gary Wilmott, who played a page called Muddles, was, I think it's children who make a show like that and the kids were hilarious that night.

When Snow White collapsed after eating the fatal apple, the dwarfs came home unsuspecting from their work and stomped about the cottage saying: 'Why isn't our supper ready?'

Then they discovered Snow White's body.

'She won't wake up, what's the matter with her?' they cried in distress.

'She's bloody well dead!' answered a boy behind me.

A bit later on, the Dame accidentally lost his wig and another small boy in the front row leapt to the stage, shouting in glee: 'You're a man! You're a man!'

The wig wasn't the only mishap that occurred that night. For reasons that escape me now, there was a camel involved in the plot – a pantomime camel, that is, played by two men, one at each end – and at one point the creature's udders fell off and you could see this man's arm groping around the floor for them.

'They're over there! They're over there!' yelled the lad in the front row.

He was so excited that at every point in the story he rushed to the edge of the stage to join in the conversation with the characters.

'You're mad,' he told Gary Wilmott after Muddles the page did something particularly daft. And without warning, Gary leaned down from the stage, picked him up and swung him high in the air.

'If I have any more trouble from you . . . !' he threatened jokingly.

The boy loved it. He was giggling so much he could hardly stand upright when Gary put him back on his feet again.

Naturally, when volunteers for a children's band were requested, our little friend from the front row was there first.

'What's your name?' Gary asked him.

'Richard,' said the boy.

'I might have known,' said Gary. 'Tricky Dicky.'

The instruments were handed out and surprise, surprise, there was an instrument for every child but Richard. One had a tambourine, one had a horn and one had a recorder but there was nothing for Richard.

'Oh. We haven't got anything for you,' Gary told him.

But the audience was sighing, 'Ahhhh.'

So, reluctantly, Gary went into the wings and came back with an enormous drum.

Well, Richard had a field-day. He really went to town on this drum. He boomed round and round the stage until Gary said, 'All right, all right. Don't take over the show.'

It was hilarious and by the end of the evening I was hoarse from shouting: 'Oh no, it isn't!' 'Oh yes, it is!' and all the rest of the daft things you do when you're at a pantomime.

Afterwards Chris brought us our coats and led us back-stage to meet Gary.

What a nice boy he was. There was no sitting about drinking in his dressing-room for him. He'd changed into his street clothes ready to go straight home to his family.

'I saw you on *This Is Your Life*, Gary,' I said when we were introduced. 'What a lovely little girl you've got.'

'Yes. That's Katie,' he said proudly. 'She's two now and we're having another one in two weeks' time!'

This was his first pantomime, he explained, and he'd been very nervous about it, but the rest of the cast had been a great help to him. He was enjoying it immensely.

'And of course the kids in the audience make the show,' he added.

Well, they'd certainly done him proud that night.

John and I went home with sore throats from shouting and aching faces and sides from laughing so much. Just the result you'd expect from a thoroughly good pantomime!

6

It was the moment millions of us had been waiting for. The glittering carriage stopped outside Westminster Abbey and Sarah Ferguson climbed elegantly onto the pavement, taking care not to crumple the foaming ivory skirts of her dress.

She looked beautiful and the wedding dress, about which there had been so much speculation, was truly magnificent.

'Oh, John,' I said, wallowing happily in sentiment. 'I think that's the loveliest dress I've ever seen.'

Sarah Ferguson and the newly-created Duke of York made a handsome couple and I felt sure they were well suited. Sarah seemed a brave, bright girl, able to cope sensibly with the pressures of royal life and she was old enough to know her own mind. As for Prince Andrew, I'm sure he had been much in love with his former girlfriend Koo Stark but he would never have married her. Sarah was different. Sarah was his friend. Andrew and Sarah were clearly mates in every sense of the word and that's an excellent basis for marriage.

I don't think I moved from the television set all day. The real life events were more fascinating than any soap opera as far as I was concerned. But then perhaps that was because I had a special reason to be interested. I felt almost personally involved, because just the night before I'd been celebrating the happy event at the Cafe Royal at a glamorous pre-wedding charity ball packed with celebrities and beautiful people.

Now, I'm not much of a one for going out. I don't drink, I can't dance much with my shaky leg and I'm getting on a bit after all, but the Royal Wedding Ball was different. This was a really special occasion and I wouldn't have missed it for the world.

I was having a little holiday at our chalet on the coast when the invitation arrived. Funnily enough I woke up that morning with an old song going round in my head:

'Give yourself a pat on the back, a pat on the back and say to yourself, jolly good health, you've had a good day today. Yesterday was full of trouble and sorrow, nobody knows what's going to happen tomorrow, but give yourself a pat on the back, a pat on the back and say to yourself, jolly good health, you've had a good day today.'

I hadn't heard that song for years and yet, as I stood there putting on my dressing-gown, I realized that someone from the spirit world was singing it to me.

I wonder why I'm being serenaded this morning, I thought, somewhat puzzled, as I went off to run my bath. And they weren't just sending me a song. Along with the music came a great feeling of anticipation, almost as if some nice little treat to cheer me up was on its way. Yet we weren't expecting any visitors or exciting events. The day ahead promised to be quiet, uneventful and relaxing.

'Well I don't know, John,' I said, over breakfast. 'They're still singing this song and yet we've got nothing planned at all.'

A moment later the phone rang. It was Terry. He'd stayed at home to look after Boots and the house and he tended to ring with daily bulletins on his progress.

Mentally I ran through the meals I'd left in the freezer for him.

'Hello, love,' I said, when John handed me the phone. 'Now there's a bit of chicken you could have for your dinner tonight, but you'd better get it out now to defrost . . . Or if you prefer, you could have . . .'

'Hang on a minute,' Terry interrupted. 'I didn't ring to talk about my supper. I've just been looking through the mail. Would you like to go to a charity do?'

'Not right now, Terry, we're on holiday.'

He laughed. 'So you don't want to go to the Royal Ball, then?'

'Royal Ball?' I asked. 'What Royal Ball?'

'They're having a pre-wedding ball at the Cafe Royal and you've been invited. If you'd like some complimentary tickets you have to fill in a form and send it off.'

I was thrilled. There would be no need to interrupt our holiday and it sounded like a tremendously exciting affair. I'd never been to a ball before.

'Of course I'd like to go, Terry!' I shrieked. 'Could you send off the form for us?'

'I've already done it!' he chuckled. 'I knew you wouldn't want to miss this.'

Well, I spent the next few weeks agonizing over a dress to wear. Since I'm not in the habit of going to balls, my wardrobe isn't exactly overflowing with ball-gowns and in any case I wasn't even sure what they wore to do's like that. Still, after much asking of advice and hunting round, I found a smart, pretty dress which I was assured was just the thing. And after all, I told myself as I hung it in the wardrobe, even if it's not quite right, with all those celebrities around, no one will be looking at me.

The night before the wedding, John, Laurie, his wife Iris and I all presented ourselves at the Cafe Royal in good time. We put our coats in the cloakroom and walked into the ballroom where the sight made me gasp. The whole place was decorated to look like a summer garden and the girls, the beautiful girls in their ball-gowns, took my breath away. They were just like flowers blooming.

One of the girls on our table was really glamorous in an off-the-shoulder dress of gold lamé that went down into a train and swept the floor behind her. Another had tiny white roses in her hair, a white lace bow hanging down at the back and an exquisite white dress with a boned bodice smothered in little pink roses.

It was all terribly grand but everyone was very friendly and we had a wonderful time. There was a delicious meal with the most marvellous dessert which had been specially created for the wedding. It looked like a flower on the plate and when you dug your spoon into it, it was filled with strawberries.

After dinner the waiter brought round little carrier bags containing perfumes and soaps, party poppers and streamers and small Union Jacks. Then the band of the Coldstream Guards marched in and played a truly rousing selection of tunes: 'I'm Getting Married in the Morning', 'Congratulations', 'Rule Britannia', 'Land of Hope and Glory' . . . and by the end of the performance we were standing up and waving our flags and singing along like mad. It was a marvellous experience.

Later on Leslie Crowther conducted a session of bingo and then there was a raffle for all sorts of gorgeous prizes from a holiday at the Hilton Hotel in New York, to a £150 necklace.

It was all in aid of country holidays for deprived children and the prizes had been donated by the guests.

John and I had given a cheque and a camera. We didn't win anything but then we didn't expect to. We had a wonderful time. Leslie Crowther came up and personally thanked us for our gifts, as did Lord and Lady Arran, and we chatted to quite a few celebrities. Lenny Fenton, who plays Dr Legg in *EastEnders*, brought his wife over to our table to say hello. June Whitfield, who was looking very young and lovely, passed by close enough to touch. We saw Tony Blackburn and Paul Daniels and as we were leaving at about 1.30 in the morning we met Ray Allen standing outside the door.

'Hello, Doris,' he said. 'Have you come out to get away from the noise?' Because by now the place was vibrating to loud pop music, the young things were dancing away and to be honest you couldn't hear a thing anyone was saying.

'No, we're off home now. We're not night birds,' I told him. 'Mind you, it is a bit loud, isn't it!'

The young people looked set to go on all night but John and I were very glad to get back to our beds. Besides, we wanted to see the wedding the next day and if we stayed out much longer I knew we'd be good for nothing in the morning.

As it turned out, we were yawning quite a bit but we arrived at our stations in front of the television bright and early for the royal wedding. Somehow, having attended the ball made it all seem more personal. The fact that we'd been drinking the young couple's health the night before made us feel almost like invited guests.

I love weddings at the best of times but royal weddings are something special. All that colour and pageantry – even the most cynical of men can't help getting drawn into it.

'Oh, I'm sure they'll be happy,' I said to John as we toasted Andrew and Sarah once more in tea. But this was just an emotional wish, not a prediction. As I've explained before, I'm not a fortune teller. Very occasionally a spirit person will give me a tiny glimpse ahead in the life of a sitter, but most of the time I know about as much of what's in store in the future as the next person – that is, nothing.

And sadly for many people, the marriage that starts off so full of hope and happiness in a wonderful wedding, ends not long afterwards in tragedy.

This was brought home to me very forcibly around royal wedding time by two quite unexpected occurrences.

The first happened one afternoon when I was alone in the house. John had popped out to the shops, Terry was off seeing to something and I was struggling round with my shaky leg trying to do all the housework because Jean was on holiday.

I was half-way through the dusting when the doorbell rang.

'Oh dear, I suppose John's forgotten his key again,' I said to myself as I went to answer it.

But it wasn't John. I found myself looking into the wide, tragic eyes of a very young girl.

'I'm awfully sorry. You'll think I've got a terrible cheek ringing your bell,' she blurted out before I could say a word, 'but I wrote you a letter last week and I hadn't heard and . . .'

'Well dear, all my letters go to the office first,' I explained, 'and quite often it's a few weeks before I even see them. I'll give you the office number, shall I . . .'

I stopped. There was something in her face, such a deep despair that I knew I couldn't send her away without talking to her.

'You're in great trouble, love, aren't you?'

Tears welled up immediately in her eyes.

'Yes,' she whispered, swallowing hard. 'But I didn't mean

to come. I don't know what made me. I was on my way to my sister's but I found myself outside your door.'

'Well, come on in and have a cup of tea,' I said. 'But you must understand I can't do a sitting for you. There are so many people waiting now that I get into terrible trouble if someone jumps the queue.'

'Yes, of course. I quite understand.' said the girl. 'But I'd better get my baby. I've left her in the car.'

She ran up the garden path and came back with the most adorable little girl, no more than eighteen months old, in her arms.

'This is Hayley,' she said.

We went inside and Hayley sat quietly while her mother and I had a cup of tea. It turned out that the poor girl had lost her husband just a month before and she didn't know which way to turn.

'I queued up for two and a half hours to get tickets for your demonstration at Lewisham,' she explained, 'but somehow I couldn't wait. I don't know what to do with myself . . . I didn't mean to come, I really didn't but I just sort of ended up here . . .'

I did my best to comfort her with the hope that her husband would be first in the queue at Lewisham but even as I was speaking I realized that her husband had arrived. He was in the room with us and it would have been cruel to ignore him.

I couldn't do a proper sitting because it would have caused such problems (life isn't simple any more) but I was able to give the girl a few little scraps that cheered her up. Her husband told me the whole sad story.

Apparently they had been on holiday in Spain with his two little boys from a previous marriage. Everything had been fine. They were having a very happy time and one morning the husband got up to make breakfast for them all. He had seemed perfectly fit and well but without warning he just collapsed and died as he was preparing the meal.

Unknown to them all he must have had something wrong with his heart and it chose that moment to give out.

The poor girl, still reeling with shock, had to get herself, the children and the body back to England and see to all the arrangements.

It was a terrible, terrible thing to happen.

The husband who was still quite upset to have been so suddenly parted from his family and his earthly life, wanted his wife to know that he still loved them all and was still looking after them from the other side.

'You will tell her,' he begged me.

'Of course I will, love,' I promised.

'He says he still loves you all very much,' I repeated out loud to the girl, 'and he's watching over you. If ever you need him just put out your hand and he'll be there.'

It wasn't a proper sitting, of course, but by the time she'd finished her tea, my unexpected visitor had dried her eyes and declared herself much better.

I thought at first that she was merely being polite, but not long afterwards she was back on my doorstep, bright and smiling, with a huge bunch of flowers. She looked a different girl.

'You don't know what you did for me, Doris,' she said, giving me a big hug. 'I was desperate but now the pain is easier . . . I can sleep at nights now . . .'

A few weeks later there was another desperate appeal. Laurie had a telephone call from one of the administrators at University College Hospital. Apparently they had a very sick young man on a life-support machine and all they could get out of his distraught wife was that she wanted to speak to Doris Stokes.

'I know Mrs Stokes is very busy,' said the administrator, 'but is there any chance that she could speak to this young woman?'

Laurie promised to ask me right away, which he did.

'Of course I'll talk to her,' I said when he explained the situation. 'I don't know whether it'll help but I'll do what I can.'

So Laurie called the administrator back and shortly afterwards the kind lady had got the whole family assembled in her office to talk to me on the phone.

It was very difficult. The poor family were extremely distressed and they were hoping against hope that the boy, whose name was Graham Monroe, could be saved. Yet when I tuned in I realized that he was half over already and that it wouldn't be long before he was completely in the spirit world.

In my mind's eye I saw a picture of a good-looking young man with red-streaked brown hair.

'Has he got auburn hair?' I asked. 'Or, at least, brown hair with reddish streaks?'

'His hair's brown,' sobbed his wife, 'the red is the blood. They haven't washed the blood out yet.'

I comforted her as best I could and promised that we would pray for Graham.

'John will put him on his healing list and we'll do everything we can,' I assured them. But privately I knew that no earthly power would keep that boy here because he already had one foot in the spirit world. The best we could hope for was that he would slip gently over without trouble or pain.

My heart went out to that grieving family and it was very difficult to sleep that night. I could imagine them gathered anxiously round the life-support machine trying to will their strength into a body from which the life had all but departed.

The next day, Pat, Mrs Monroe's mother, phoned to tell me they were leaving Graham on the life-support machine for one more day. But as I expected, there was no change. Graham showed no signs of life and on the third day she phoned again to tell me that they were going to switch the machine off.

I was very sorry for them but I knew they had made the right decision. Later that day I popped up to fetch something from my bedroom and half-way up the stairs I suddenly felt a tremendous sense of relief. It was as if a great weight had been lifted from me and I was floating light and free. I knew at once what had happened.

'Graham's safely over,' I called down to John who was busy at his absent healing. 'He won't need healing any more. He's fine now.'

Not long afterwards the Monroe family came to see me at the Palladium and when the show ended Graham's wife and her mother came backstage to say hello.

Graham was with us in an instant. He was a strong, athletic young man, full of health and vigour.

'Doris, I wouldn't have wanted to be a vegetable,' he said. 'Do tell them it was for the best. I couldn't have stood being a cabbage. I was always so active.'

And he poured out the whole story. Apparently he was a scaffolder and on this particular day he'd climbed up the ladder and stepped onto a board that wasn't secured properly. The plank tipped and he crashed down head first. He didn't stand a chance.

'I didn't want to come over,' he said bitterly. 'We'd only been married a year, the baby was only five weeks old and we'd just bought a bungalow to do up. I was so looking forward to it . . . But if the accident had to happen I'm glad I came over here. I would have hated being in a wheelchair . . .'

He sent a great deal of love to his wife and said that he wanted her to live a full and happy life. If she met someone else she could love, she wasn't to hesitate.

'I'd like her to marry again,' he said, 'I want her to be happy and I don't like to think of her on her own the rest of her life.'

Finally he asked her to give the baby a big hug for him.

It was another sad story and I must admit that I said goodbye to the Monroes with a heavy heart.

I don't know, I thought to myself, it's all brides and young widows at the moment. From the joy of the royal wedding to the grief of a young wife and mother left alone to fend for her family.

Why do these things have to happen? I wish I had the answers. They say it's God's will but it seems a very harsh will to leave a young girl alone with a baby to bring up. No doubt the poor widows learn a great deal from their experience but it seems a terrible way to learn a lesson. Sometimes I get very confused with it all and I don't know what to say to the kids when they ask me why.

All I can say for certain is that I know a little of how they feel. During the war, John, who was a paratrooper, went missing at Arnhem and I was told that he was presumed dead. As far as the War Office was concerned, I was a widow.

Later (as I explained in my first book, *Voices in My Ear*), the spirit world told me that John was in fact alive and would be coming home, but for a time I, too, believed I'd lost him. It was a dreadful blow and I've never forgotten it.

When you see the tragedy all around it makes you wonder why husbands and wives don't appreciate each other more and why we don't work harder at our marriages. I'm sure that far too many couples throw their marriages away, when in fact if only they'd tried, they could have saved them. It's a great shame.

These days I'm a bit old-fashioned and I believe that if you're married, you're married. Obviously if you've been unfortunate enough to marry a man who beats you or is cruel to the children, then of course you must get out as soon as possible. But in most other cases I believe that you should stick it out.

Marriage is like any other job. You have to work at it and it's not easy, as even Sarah Ferguson and Prince Andrew will find out in time. The trouble is, these days, with divorce being so easy, far too many people seem to give up when the problems begin.

I don't blame them. I know just what it's like because I walked out on John once and if it hadn't been for the good sense of my mother, who knows, I might be a divorcee by now. But thank goodness I listened to her, because if I hadn't I would have missed years of laughter and tears, years of sharing and loving – a whole lifetime of precious memories. What a waste that would have been.

It seems so long ago now, but the trouble began when John came back from the war. I knew he had been wounded but I had no idea of the extent of his wounds, and neither had he. He had suffered severe head injuries and was left with a hole in the back of his head, but the hair had grown over it and no one would have realized it was there.

When he was sent back from the prison camp an army doctor gave him a quick examination and pronounced him unfit for further service. The head injuries weren't even noticed and John was too confused and disorientated to point them out.

All I knew when he came home was that he seemed a

different person. The man I married had been a big, strong, athletic type with medals for boxing and football. The man who came back was quiet and withdrawn and couldn't even walk around the house without bumping into things, let alone play football.

I didn't understand what was wrong so I nagged. John was frightened because he himself couldn't understand what was wrong, so he lost his temper. All in all, after the initial euphoria of his homecoming had worn off, we had a miserable time.

Then one day after a row, I decided I'd had enough. I packed my things, slammed out of the house and went round to my mother's.

'I've come home,' I said, dumping my suitcase on the doorstep.

Mum stood in the doorway eyeing the case sourly. She didn't move aside to let me pass.

'Well you can just get yourself back again,' she said, blocking up the doorway even though she was a tiny little creature.

She was nothing if not blunt, my mum. She hadn't approved of my marrying John, but now I was married, then married I should stay.

'You've made your bed, now you must lie on it. You just get yourself back and cook that man's tea.'

I was pretty put out I can tell you. 'You would have thought you could expect some sympathy from your own mother,' I muttered angrily as I trudged away, my case getting heavier and heavier with every step.

I didn't want to go back but I had too much pride to go round to a friend's house and risk the possibility of being turned away again. There was nothing for it but to go home and make up the quarrel.

And make it up we did. There were more quarrels of course but knowing that I couldn't run home to my mother made me stand my ground and gave me added incentive to make the marriage work. It wasn't easy, but after two years we finally got some proper medical treatment for John and discovered what was wrong.

John was sent to Stoke Mandeville Hospital for a while. The treatment helped him and gradually he came to terms with his disabilities. I'm not saying there was an overnight miracle, but after that things grew easier and easier and I knew that our marriage was safe.

We've been together now for well over forty years – living proof that you can make a marriage work if you try hard enough!

7

Friday, March 6th was a dreary day. The weather was cold and dull and by evening a steady rain had set in. Outside, the crocuses were flowering well but the day belonged more to winter than to spring.

And so it was on that wet, gloomy evening that we first heard the news of a disaster that shocked the world.

John and I, supper over, had just settled down with a pot of tea to watch television. But the set had hardly warmed up when our programme was suddenly interrupted by a news-flash.

The teacups froze in our hands as we listened in horror. A Townsend Thoresen ferry, the *Herald of Free Enterprise*, had capsized just outside Zeebrugge. Hundreds of passengers were on board and every boat in the area was racing to the rescue.

Like most people, I think, our first reaction was one of total disbelief. I'd never been on one of those ferries but I'd seen pictures of them often enough. Huge and solid, seemingly crammed to overflowing with cars and excited holiday-makers, they looked stable, well-made and indestructible. How could one of these giants possibly turn over in a calm sea before it had even properly left the harbour? It just didn't make sense.

Yet, believe it or not, as that tense evening went on, it became clear that if anything the tragedy had at first been underplayed. Hundreds of people were saved, of course, but as we discovered later, close on 200 were killed.

Those poor souls, I thought. I've always been a bit claustrophobic and the idea of being trapped in a ship as it rolled over in the water made me shudder. How did they bear it? Even the ones who returned safely must have gone through an appalling ordeal.

What a way to end a holiday. My mind went back to my last stay in hospital. While I was there a number of nurses were collecting coupons for just such a trip. Apparently, a national newspaper was offering shopping-trips on the continent for £1 plus a number of special coupons printed in the paper. Every morning when I'd finished reading the news, I shared my coupons amongst the eager nurses.

I could only pray that I hadn't unwittingly sent some poor young girl to a watery grave by my choice of reading material.

For days afterwards, accounts of the disaster and the complicated business of recovering bodies went on and the newspapers were full of harrowing tales. Then in the midst of it all, Laurie rang. A desperate couple who'd lost their son in the tragedy had contacted him. Naturally, they were distraught and they wondered if I could help.

'What d'you think, Doris?' asked Laurie. 'I know you're very busy.'

I didn't hesitate. There was no question in my mind. I knew I had to see them. 'Fit them in somehow, Laurie,' I said. 'I'll see them as soon as I possibly can. In the meantime, I'll give them a ring.'

Mrs Reynolds had been in quite a state, as any mother would have been. Her son, Jonathan, and his fiancée, Fiona, had set off for a day's shopping-trip to Belgium, planning to return aboard the ill-fated *Herald of Free Enterprise*. They never came back. Since then Fiona's body had been recovered but Jonathan's was still missing.

There was no doubt in my mind. Jonathan was definitely on the other side. As I talked to his parents on the phone a young man's voice suddenly chimed in on the conversation. I had Mrs Reynolds in one ear and Jonathan in the other. He gave me a few family names. His mother was called Joan, he said, his father was Alan and his sister was Sonya.

'They feel bad because my body is still trapped down there,' he said, 'but tell them not to grieve. It doesn't matter at all because I'm not under the water. I'm here and I'm safe.'

I passed this on to Alan and Joan and I tried to explain that a body is just a coat we put on when we come to this earth and that once our time here is done, we don't need it any more. It really doesn't matter what happens to our old clothes. A funeral is just a comfort for the living – it serves no useful purpose to the loved one who's gone on, although he may well attend because it's a big family gathering, just as he'll attend future weddings, christenings and celebrations, because he's part of the family.

By the end of the conversation they seemed calmer and I think the chat brought them a little comfort.

Shortly afterwards they came down from their home near Oxford for a full-scale sitting. I'm sorry to say that when they arrived at midday I was still in my dressing-gown and not at all sure that I could go through with it. Once again I seemed to have been struck down by some mysterious complaint. My head ached. I felt dizzy every time I tried to stand and I kept going hot and cold. To make matters worse, we had a blocked drain that day and workmen were bustling backwards and forwards and the phone kept ringing.

Laurie called early that morning to drop in some papers and he found me weak and ready to panic.

'I don't think I'm going to be able to manage, Laurie,' I said anxiously. 'I feel so rotten I think we'd better change it to another day.'

But when Laurie rang the Reynolds' number there was no reply. They'd already left.

'Oh well,' I said as philosophically as I could, 'we can't turn them away. I'll just have to hope the spirit world doesn't let me down,' and I swallowed a couple of Disprin and crossed my fingers.

I'm so glad now that I did. The three Reynolds arrived dressed in black. They were smart and composed but the tension around their eyes belied the calm exterior. Inside they were suffering badly.

Laurie showed them into the front room and brought them coffee while I apologized for my dishevelled appearance.

'I'm so sorry,' I explained, 'I haven't been at all well and it was all I could do to get out of bed this morning. I don't know if I'm going to be any good to you.'

'That's all right, Doris,' said Mrs Reynolds sympathetically 'We quite understand. We're just glad you could see us at all.'

'Well, I can't promise anything,' I warned, 'I'll do the very best I can but quite honestly I don't know if it's going to work.'

'Well, if it doesn't, it doesn't,' said Mrs Reynolds reassuringly.

We sipped our coffee and chatted about the weather and the journey and the problems with the drains and all the time I prodded with my mind at the spirit world. At first there was a great deal of confusion. Hardly surprising really, when you consider how many poor souls found themselves ejected without warning into the spirit world in such an unforeseen tragedy.

Then, through the confusion there came a great sense of urgency. There was some important news on the way. In fact the news should be arriving that very day.

'I think we're ready now,' I said at last to the Reynolds. 'I'm getting a feeling of confusion and then this urgency. Something about some news. Have you had some news today?'

The family shook their heads.

'No,' they said.

'Well, there's some news on its way and it could come today,' I said.

They shrugged. There was, after all, no way of telling if I was right or wrong. Yet later that evening when I turned on the television, I was just in time to catch an announcement that the date for the attempted refloating of the *Herald of Free Enterprise* had been fixed that very day. The refloating was an important event because without it the remaining bodies could not be recovered.

This was the news the spirit world had been preparing us for. As it turned out, the intended date came and went and the ship stayed where it was, due to bad weather, but, nevertheless, the message had been correct. There was news that day.

That out of the way, two bright young people stepped boldly into the picture. I could hear them laughing and chattering together for several moments before they moved close enough to speak to me. What a happy pair they sounded. I've never heard a couple laugh so much as these two.

'Shush a minute, Fee,' said Jonathan, 'I just want to tell them we're together. They've been worrying about that. They think we got separated but we didn't. We came over together and we're going to go on together from now on.'

All three Reynolds were visibly relieved when I told them this.

'Thank goodness,' whispered Joan Reynolds almost silently, eyes half closed.

And suddenly I understood her fears. Fiona's body and the body of her thirteen-year-old sister, Heidi, had been found while Jonathan's had not, and she was worried that because they had not been 'laid to rest' together they might be separated for all time.

Of course, it doesn't work like that at all. People who both want to be together, can be together. They meet up as soon as they pass over if they wish to, it's as simple as that, but Joan, Alan and Sonya weren't to know.

'Now, I know we don't want to dwell on it,' I said silently to Jonathan, 'but can you tell us what happened?'

'There were seven of us,' he explained.

Later the Reynolds confirmed that Jonathan, Fiona and Heidi had indeed been part of a party of seven who'd set off on a day's shopping-trip in Belgium – just for the fun of it.

'Fiona and I went to the bar to get a drink,' Jonathan went on, 'and we got separated from the others. We never saw them again . . .'

As his words died away I felt the dreadful sensation of icy water all around me and a terrible dark, confined space. The water crept higher and higher and I could hear people screaming.

Quickly I closed my mind to the impression. With my claustrophobic tendencies I couldn't take much of scenes like that.

'It's okay, Jonathan, I get the picture,' I told him silently, 'Don't dwell on it, love.'

'I could swim and I was trying to help people . . .' Jonathan went on, 'but there was no way out.'

A bit later, he came in too close to me and I could feel my lungs filling up with water. I began choking and gasping for air.

'Jonathan!' I called out mentally. I didn't have enough breath to say it aloud. 'You've come in too close. Move back a bit, love.'

This sometimes happens with inexperienced spirit communicators, especially if the medium is tired or below par generally. The medium loses concentration and unintentionally fails to remind the spirit person to keep a safe distance between them. When this happens the spirit person's last impressions come across so strongly that the medium starts to live them, with potentially dangerous results.

Once I'd finished coughing I felt it was wiser to stick to more mundane subjects. I asked Jonathan if he'd had anything of value on him which his family could keep when the body was eventually found.

'A watch or something,' I suggested.

I felt him shake his head. 'Not really. My watch wasn't very safe,' he said.

'That's right, he was talking to me about it not long ago,' said Joan. 'The metal bracelet was dodgy.'

Jonathan gave some more family names and details and then I got a number. Someone lived at twenty-something. It was very fuzzy. Could have been twenty-two.

'Fiona lived at twenty-seven,' said Joan.

And at the mention of her name, Fiona made Jonathan stand aside for a moment to let her speak.

'All my things are still there at number twenty-seven, just the way they were,' she said. 'Tell them not to grieve. You see, my parents were separated and for a while it was difficult for me. Jonathan was my life. I wasn't very happy before I met him but then we met and he was everything to me. I looked on his parents as my parents and I loved them very much.'

'You'd better!' interrupted Jonathan, teasingly.

And then they were laughing again.

'Come on, you two!' I said, pretending to be irritated as the giggles went on. 'Let's give your mum and dad a bit more to go on. What did you do for a living, Jonathan?'

Instantly I was given a picture of a table piled high with books and papers and sheets of writing. It looked very much like a student's untidy desk.

'Was he studying?' I asked the Reynolds. 'Because he's showing me lots of books and papers. Was he still at college?'

'Yes, he was,' said Alan.

It turned out that Jonathan was only nineteen years old and he was taking a course in surveying and land management at a polytechnic.

Jonathan's rich, dark brown voice came back. He really did have a beautiful voice. Call it fanciful, if you like, but some voices sound light blue to me, yap, yap, yapping gratingly on the ear. But Jonathan's voice was warm and deep. A real dark brown, and a pleasure to listen to.

'I really got down to my studying when I met Fee,' he said. 'I was determined to make a good life for her. And I would have passed my exams, you know.'

But sadly, he wasn't given the opportunity to prove himself. Nevertheless he was a talented boy and his talents weren't going to waste. Now and again I could hear piano and guitar music in the background and this was Jonathan's way of telling me that he played those instruments on the other side.

'Very likely,' said Joan, when I told her what I could hear. 'He used to play the piano years ago and recently he started playing the guitar.'

We hadn't heard much about Alan during all this and I

felt it was time to bring Mr Reynolds into the conversation.

'What does your dad do, love?' I asked Jonathan.

Immediately, a picture of ladders leapt into my mind.

'He's always up and down ladders,' said Jonathan. 'Buildings and things.'

'Yes, that's right,' said Joan, 'Alan's a builder.'

Then I heard the name Laurence.

'That's our accountant,' said Joan. 'He was sorting out Jonathan's account.'

'Then there's Julie.'

'That's my friend,' said Joan.

'And now he's talking about Spain,' I went on. 'Are you going to Spain?'

'They had a holiday in Spain a couple of years ago,' said Joan.

'No, what I'm trying to say is that I don't want them to think that their life has got to come to a stop,' said Jonathan. 'I want them to have a holiday, to go to Spain or wherever. Don't you agree, Fee?'

Fiona agreed.

I was getting tired by now but Jonathan hadn't quite finished. He turned towards his sister, Sonya, a quiet girl with blonde hair, wearing an elegant black dress, and said something about a new car or a blue car. It was difficult to tell which.

'Both are right!' said Sonya in delight. 'I've got a new blue car.'

'And who's Trish?'

'Oh God,' said Sonya, laughing nervously, 'she's a friend I should have picked up today but I forgot!'

'See, I know what she's up to!' laughed Jonathan.

Before he went, Jonathan even found time to remember the dog.

'She's got a growth, you know and it's time she came over here with us. Don't let her suffer,' he said.

'Yes, she has. She'll be with him soon,' said Joan.

The power was rapidly draining now and the young people began to move away but before he went, Jonathan said impishly:

'Oh, one thing more before I go. My mother,' – I thought he said mother but it turned out to be his father – 'didn't like my name abbreviated. It always had to be Jonathan, but everyone else called me Jon and that's how I signed my name. So I want to say, Jon and Fee send their love!'

That set them giggling again and the last I heard was the sound of merry laughter as the couple returned to their life in the spirit world.

But that wasn't the last I heard of Jon and Fee. Shortly afterwards I spoke to the Reynolds on the phone and they told me that many of the names they'd been unable to place during the sitting had since made sense to them.

'For instance,' said Joan, 'there was a Harold or Harry. Well, we couldn't think of anyone of that name at the time, but afterwards we remembered a Salvation Army Major we'd met in Zeebrugge who was very kind to us. His name was Harold.

'Then, when you were talking to Fiona you mentioned Barbara and Carol and also something about a photo album. It didn't mean anything at the time but when we got home we looked through the photo album and there was a picture of Fiona with her friends Barbara and Carol.'

This often happens so I wasn't surprised. People attend sittings in an emotional state and it's very difficult to remember every relative, friend and acquaintance at a time like that. It's only afterwards that the significance dawns. So no, I wasn't surprised, but I was glad that the Reynolds were pleased with that morning's work.

The weeks went by and the *Herald of Free Enterprise* continued to make the headlines. The operation to right the ship was hampered at every turn by the weather and the date seemed to be changed and changed again. Then one morning while Laurie and I were discussing some office work and the ferry disaster was far from our minds, I suddenly heard Jonathan's voice. The letter I was reading slipped from my hand, so great was my surprise.

'Sorry to interrupt,' said Jonathan, 'but I just wanted you to tell Mum and Dad that my body's been found . . . Oh, and there's a service at Canterbury Cathedral for all of us who came over . . . I'll let you get on now.' And he was gone.

'Laurie,' I said slowly, 'Have you got the Reynolds' number? Could you give them a ring? There's been a message from Jonathan.'

Laurie spoke to Alan who was polite but puzzled. So far they'd heard nothing. Then a few hours later, he called back. They'd just heard. Jonathan's body had been found that day.

The service at Canterbury Cathedral took place shortly afterwards.

There's another little postscript to this story. A few days after Jonathan's funeral Mrs Reynolds was taken ill. It was during the night and there was a bit of a commotion but, surprisingly, their only grandchild, Nicola, normally a light sleeper, did not stir.

The next morning Alan remarked on her nice long sleep.

'Oh no, I wasn't asleep,' said Nicola. 'Jon and Fee came to play and cuddle me. They were with me for ages. It was lovely.'

Some people would have said it was a dream, but the child was so convinced the visit had really happened that Alan found himself believing it.

There's no question in my mind. Of course it happened.

Knowing that their mother needed a bit of help, Jon and Fee kept the little one occupied until the drama was over. Any loving son and daughter-in-law would have done the same.

But I wasn't quite finished with the *Herald of Free Enterprise*. Not long after the Reynolds' sitting, another anguished couple, the Harrisons from Somerset, got in touch. They too had lost a son in the disaster.

Young Stuart, only seventeen years old, had been one of the token-collectors. He had saved up his coupons for a cheap day in Zeebrugge and it had cost him very dear.

Like the Reynolds, the Harrisons also had a grown-up daughter, and Karen accompanied them to the sitting.

Stuart was a lovely boy with sandy, fair hair which kept falling across his nose. When the ship turned over, he said, he'd tried to hold up a drowning child but they got separated and he was swept away. He remembered nothing more until he found himself in the spirit world.

It was another very sad story. Throughout the sitting Stuart kept going to Mr Harrison as if to try to comfort him, but this made it rather difficult to catch what he was saying.

I heard the name Andy.

'That's me,' said Mr Harrison.

'That's funny,' I said, 'I thought I heard him call you John.'

Mr Harrison laughed. 'Well, yes. My name is John but everyone calls me Andy.'

Like Jonathan, Stuart gave the names of family and friends and many other details. One point in particular stands out in my mind.

'Karen's going to get engaged, you know,' Stuart confided.

But when I passed this on, Karen blushed and shrugged her shoulders.

'Oh, I don't know about that,' she said.

'Well, Stuart seems pretty certain about it.'

Karen giggled and the matter dropped.

That night however, when she got home, her boyfriend proposed to her and she accepted. So now she's engaged just as her brother predicted.

I breathed a sigh of relief when I heard the news. How nice to have one happy ending to such a tragic story.

8

I could see the similarity as soon as I opened the door. The woman was svelte and beautifully groomed with immaculate hair and rich, dark eyes, but when she smiled, her face lit up and I saw her daughter, Benazir Bhutto, the brave child of the late Prime Minister of Pakistan.

In my last book, *Voices of Love*, I described how Benazir came to see me because she badly needed the advice of her father. He, poor man, had been hanged by the military regime and his son had died in mysterious circumstances. Nevertheless, despite the decimation of her family, Benazir was determined to go into politics and take over where her father had left off.

She knew, of course, that this was a dangerous mission, but her father promised that he would stand by her. The people would be on her side, he predicted, and she would return to Pakistan to a tumultuous welcome.

Well, everything he said came to pass. A few weeks after the sitting I turned on the television to see some incredible pictures of little Benazir, hardly more than a child to me, moving through the streets of Pakistan surrounded by a quarter of a million cheering people.

It was an extraordinary sight and I had to admire the girl's courage. During the sitting, I could hardly believe it when ex-Prime Minister Bhutto told me that his daughter, this quiet, self-possessed child, intended to rule Pakistan one day. Now, watching her triumphant return, I could not only believe it, I felt sure she'd eventually pull it off.

But Benazir's plans did not go smoothly. As the weeks passed, President Zia grew more and more alarmed by her popularity and at last he could stand it no longer. He had her arrested and thrown into gaol.

It was at this point that Benazir's frantic mother got in touch. She had already lost half her family in the cause of Pakistan and she was terrified that she was about to lose her daughter the same way. After all, if Zia could execute the Prime Minister without any serious repercussions, what wouldn't he do to a slip of a girl? She was desperate to know what advice her husband would give, and whether he had any message for Benazir.

'She'll listen to you, Doris,' she assured me, 'and I think I can get a message through.'

It seemed that Benazir was being treated reasonably well in prison, although for two days and two nights after she was arrested she was given no bed or bedding and had to sleep on the floor. She was more comfortable now but her mother feared what might happen next.

'Well, you must come at once, love,' I told Mrs Bhutto. 'This is a very urgent case.'

She arrived, outwardly as calm and self-possessed as her daughter but inside I knew she was shaking.

'Come in and sit down, love, and we'll see what we can do,' I said.

In fact, I had no difficulty contacting her husband. He

knew me already, of course, and having communicated before he found it easier the second time. What's more, he had a particular reason for wanting to speak to his wife at that moment. He, too, was very anxious about Benazir.

'Eleven days,' he said in the beautiful English that I remembered from our last chat. 'She will be freed in eleven days.'

'I don't know about that,' said Mrs Bhutto doubtfully. 'We haven't heard anything.'

I checked that I hadn't misheard but Bhutto was adamant.

'Well he seems to think it will be eleven days,' I assured his wife, 'but he's anxious.'

'She will go straight to Lahore when she gets out and this she must not do,' said Benazir's father. 'Tell her to lie quiet for a while. Let things cool down. She must go softly softly now.

'You see, at first Zia laughed. He thought she was just a woman and he didn't take her seriously. He takes her seriously now.'

Mrs Bhutto nodded unhappily. You could tell that she was heartily sick of politics and would like nothing better than to have her daughter return to Europe, get married and settle down to rearing a family like other women. She would sooner have grandchildren round her knee than a country at her daughter's feet.

Her husband obviously read her thoughts. 'The trouble is, Benazir's a lot like me,' he said. 'I would never climb down from a decision even if it meant my death. And my wife, whom I love dearly, understood this. I could have run away. They would have given me anything I wanted, but I could not do that.'

'Yes, I know,' sighed Mrs Bhutto, 'I would rather he had resigned and left everything, but he wouldn't.

The ex-Prime Minister moved closer to her so that it was difficult to catch his next words.

'I wonder now whether it was worth my family's happiness,' he said heavily, 'but much as I loved them all, I could not have done any different.'

Mrs Bhutto nodded again, 'Yes, that's true. He believed so much in what he was doing.'

Her husband was silent for a while, possibly regretting this sad state of affairs, but then his anxiety for Benazir forced him to speak out again.

'I'm afraid for my daughter because she is like me,' he went on. 'People are very fickle. At the time I was killed, the people were for Zia. Now they are for my daughter. I ask myself, is it worth the agony? Inside she is weeping but nothing will change her.'

He gave his wife the names of people she could trust – necessary advice at such a treacherous time for Benazir. Then he couldn't help harping back on his own abrupt execution. He was still bitter about that and refused to call it an execution at all. He would only say that he was killed.

'I never expected to be killed, you know,' he said. 'And it was at night. That is the way this man fights. Not in the daylight where people can see. I thought God would see me through but, looking back now, I wonder if I had gone into exile whether things would have been different.'

He was silent again for a moment, and then there came a great wave of love for his wife.

'I was so proud of her,' he said. 'She had carried this great burden yet she walked out with her head held high. My wife could have crawled, but she didn't. She walked out like a queen.'

He remembered their forthcoming wedding anniversary

and then went on to talk of family matters and his grand-children.

By the end of the sitting I must say I'd grown heartily sick of the turbulent politics of Pakistan and I couldn't resist putting in my own two-pennyworth.

'Speaking as an ordinary person, love,' I said. 'I'd be tempted to say to hell with Pakistan, after all you've been through.'

Mrs Bhutto fished a crisp handkerchief from her bag. 'I know, I know,' she sighed. 'It's not as if Benazir couldn't do anything else. She could get a wonderful job anywhere with all her degrees. She's such a clever girl, but . . .'

I nodded, 'I know. You can't change them. People like Benazir have something burning in them and there's nothing you can do.'

As we walked to the door, where Mrs Bhutto's car was waiting, her husband's voice came back like an echo . . . 'Eleven days . . .' but I didn't repeat it again. It seemed too good to be true and this woman had been through enough. I didn't want to raise her hopes only to have them dashed once again.

Yet, as usual, I should have trusted the spirit world. Eleven days later came the surprise news that Benazir had been released at 8.45 that day. Her mother of course was elated and I'm quite sure she passed my messages on.

Whether Benazir heeds her father's warning of course is another matter. I haven't heard much about her for a while now, so I can only hope that she's treading softly as her father advised. In the meantime I'm keeping my fingers crossed.

A few months after Mrs Bhutto's visit, I had another famous guest trying out the sofa in my front room. Eddie Large, that hilarious funny man from the *Little and Large*

Show drove all the way from Bristol and back, just to spend the afternoon with us.

What a nice man he is. Like Freddie Starr, there was no side to him. He was natural and friendly, no airs and graces at all.

The visit came about through a newspaper article. I'm a bit of a newspaper addict, I must admit. Every day I look through most of the papers and the stories often prod me into spur-of-the-moment action. I've sent money to needy children, given a home to an abandoned dog (Boots) and taken an occasional editor to task, all because of stories I've read in the paper. So one day when I came across a sad article about Eddie Large, I found my hand straying automatically to the telephone.

Apparently, Eddie had been feeling very bad because he wasn't able to be with his parents when they died. He was torturing himself with guilt and in an attempt to find some comfort he had bought two of my books to see if they would help.

Now an awful lot of people who don't know about the spirit world suffer in the same way and it's such a shame because there's no need. Our parents know we love them. They understand the problems we face and it doesn't matter a bit to them who's standing around the bed as they pass over because they are concentrating on the people who've come to meet them from the spirit world.

These are long-lost loved ones whose sudden appearance fills them with wonder and joy. Once the parents are safely over they can come back and visit their children whenever they wish and they know what the grieving family is going through.

It's all very simple. There's no need to say goodbye and no need to feel guilty. Yet people who don't understand this get themselves into a dreadful knot. I've seen the suffering it causes, and it made me particularly sad to think that Eddie Large was going through such agony, because he's given me so much pleasure over the years.

The times I've laughed till the tears ran down my face at his antics with Sid Little! If I could help him at all it would be the least I could do to repay him for all the fun.

I picked up the phone.

'Laurie,' I said when my manager answered. 'Have you seen this article about Eddie Large? It says he's bought a couple of my books because he's so distressed over the loss of his parents. Do you know his manager? I was wondering if you could tell him that if Eddie would like to talk to me, if there's any way I can help, I'd be glad to.'

'Okay, Doris,' said Laurie. 'I'll give him a ring.'

Not long afterwards the phone rang. I picked it up, thinking it was Laurie calling me back.

'Hello, Doris,' said a familiar voice. 'This is Eddie Large. I was wondering if I could come and see you.'

'Of course you can, love,' I told him. 'Any time you like.'

So a week or two later, John and I were running around with plates and sandwiches and bowls of salad and trying to make the table look pretty.

'What on earth are you doing all that for? You're daft,' said Terry, as he passed on his way to take Boots for a walk. 'You don't even know if Eddie'll be hungry. He's only coming for a chat.'

'Well, you never know,' I said, squeezing a dish of tomatoes between a quiche and a plate of ham rolls. 'He's coming a long way. I expect the poor man will be worn out. He'll need something to eat.'

Terry raised his eyes in his 'the-old-girl's-barmy-but-it's-no-use-telling-her' expression.

'Come on, Boots. Let's get out of here,' he called, and he hurried away before he could be press-ganged into helping with the preparations.

I was still swopping plates around and wondering if there was enough food when there was a knock at the door and Eddie Large arrived. He was casually dressed in a leather jacket and woolly scarf and he looked exactly as he looks on television. I don't know why, but that's always a surprise.

'Come in, Eddie, you must be dying for a cup of tea after that journey,' I said, leading him into the sitting-room where the buffet was laid out.

His eyes opened wide at the sight of the food, 'Oh, Doris, I wasn't expecting all this.'

'Well, just help yourself, love. It's open house here.'

It took a bit of coaxing but Eddie loaded his plate, accepted a cup of tea and settled down for a chat. Like many comedians he was basically a quiet, thoughtful man and probably shy, deep down. The bubbly, extrovert nature only comes out when the spotlights are turned on.

I did my best to explain about the spirit world and what happens when you pass over.

'You see, you are never alone, Eddie,' I said, 'Someone always comes to meet you. That's why, if you've ever sat with people who're dying you often hear them talking to someone you can't see and who passed over years before. People say they're delirious. Not at all. They are seeing the spirit people who've come to meet them.'

Eddie listened attentively. He had just opened his mouth to ask a question, when suddenly I heard a woman's voice. 'That's right, Doris, you tell him,' she said encouragingly.

It was Eddie's mother – Jessie, I think her name was – and she was there in the room with us. After that, of course, the visit turned rapidly into a sitting. Both Eddie's parents came to talk to him and they were able to assure him that they understood why he couldn't be with them when they passed and that it didn't matter. When Jessie moved close I got an impression of glorious, red-gold auburn hair.

'Did your mother have auburn hair when she was younger, love?' I asked Eddie.

'Yes, she did,' said Eddie.

'Well, she's got it back again now. It's beautiful.'

What's more, Jessie told me that a child Eddie and his wife had lost through miscarriage was being cared for by herself and Eddie's dad.

'It's a little girl and she's got auburn hair, just like your mother's,' I went on. 'Oh, and your mother tells me February's important.'

'That's when the child should have been born,' said Eddie.

The sitting didn't go on all that long but, afterwards, Eddie assured me that he had found the visit comforting and that it was well worth the long journey.

'Where are you off to now?' I asked later, as Eddie, full of tea and salad and every other delicacy I could press on him, wound the woolly scarf round his neck once more.

'Oh, I'm going back to Bristol,' he said.

I was horrified. 'There and back in one day? It's too far, Eddie. Why don't you stay in London overnight?'

Eddie grinned. 'There's nothing to it, Doris. I do it all the time. I'm used to it. It doesn't bother me at all.'

And with a jaunty wave, he was away up the garden path, ready to tackle the long drive for the second time that day.

Not long afterwards, on Valentine's Day, I received a beautiful bouquet from Eddie. Inside was a little card: 'Thanks, Doris, for all the comfort you've given me.'

I was touched. I'd done so little. Just given a few hours of my time in return for so much entertainment.

The weeks passed, the weather grew warmer and all at once the bulbs in the garden were shooting into flower.

'Goodness, John,' I said one morning, as I turned over another page of the calendar. 'It's nearly April.'

Whenever I see April looming I think of my half-sister, Edna, whose birthday falls in that month, and this year I couldn't get her out of my mind.

'Edna will be sixty-nine this year,' I reminded John. 'Sixty-nine, nearly seventy. We really must get in touch.'

It's such a shame that we've drifted so much apart. We were never really close because our personalities are so different, but in recent years there has been no contact between us. I don't even have Edna's address. There hasn't been an argument, just a series of events that put greater and greater distance between us.

First Edna married a Catholic who disapproved of spiritualism, and then they moved to Canada.

Well, neither of us has ever been much of a letter-writer and so out of touch did we become, that when I visited Canada a few years ago, Edna couldn't think who I was. I got her phone number from Directory Enquiries and as soon as I had a few minutes to myself, I rang her from my hotel room.

'Hello, Edna,' I said when she answered.

'Who is this?' asked Edna doubtfully. She didn't recognize my voice, that was for sure.

'It's Doris!' I explained. Well, after all these years I couldn't expect anything else. It was so long since Edna had heard my voice on the telephone.

But the name didn't seem to help.

'Doris?' said Edna, obviously doing a mental run-through of her friends and acquaintances. 'Doris who?'

I was taken aback.

'Your sister Doris. Have you forgotten you've got a half-sister?'

I shouldn't have been surprised. After all, as far as Edna knew, I was still tucked away in Lincolnshire. The last thing she expected was to pick up the phone and find her provincial little sister talking to her from the next city.

Once Edna got over the shock, we had a nice chat on the phone, but my schedule was too tight to allow a personal visit. Sadly, I left for England without meeting my sister.

We've always been chalk and cheese, Edna and I. She was small and blonde, while I was well built and dark haired. She was inclined to be squeamish whereas I tended to blunder in and get on with things.

When our mum passed over, poor old Edna couldn't face the funeral. She helped me prepare the food and cut any number of sandwiches, but when it actually came to the service, she couldn't bear it. She sat in the car round the corner until it was over.

Yes, we're as different as it's possible for two people to be, but we're sisters, and I think it's a shame that at our time of life we're not closer.

'You know what, John,' I said, as I went into the kitchen to put the kettle on, 'I really must write to Edna one of these days. It's daft to be so far apart when you get to our age.'

I'm sorry to say that I didn't get down to writing to Edna. I didn't have her new address, it would have taken a few phone calls to get it and, as usual, my attention was diverted by urgent matters which had to be attended to at once. Life is always like that, isn't it? There never seems to be enough time and, somehow, important but not pressing matters tend to get pushed aside.

I'm not complaining, though. I know I grumble at times but I enjoy my work. People often say to me:

'Doris, isn't it about time you retired? You're sixty-seven after all.'

But, you know, if you're a medium I don't think you can retire. Being a medium is not just a job. It really is a way of life. Several of my colleagues have passed over recently and though, like me, they were getting on a bit, every one of them was working till she dropped. That's the way it is with us mediums. We can't stop.

Actually, far from retiring, I took on another job this year – one that has given me enormous pleasure. I joined the staff of *Chat* magazine as a kind of spiritual agony aunt with my very own column. I was thrilled when the editor wrote to welcome me to the staff and apparently, within a day of the announcement being made, the letters came pouring in.

I even made a commercial for the magazine. *Chat* had employed an agency called Doxat, Chapman and Partners to make a television advert about my new column. The only trouble was, advertising regulations wouldn't allow them to mention it on screen. Apparently, advertisers aren't permitted to promote what is termed as 'superstitious activity'.

I'm not a bit superstitious myself and I certainly wouldn't call my work a superstitious activity, but there you are. It was no use arguing. Rules are rules after all and Mike Chapman from the agency had dreamed up a way round the problem. An actress was to run through the major features in the magazine for that week and then she was to turn to me:

'What else have we got, Doris?'

'This might take a long time, lovey . . .' I was to reply, as if I could see into the future.

'You see, we can't mention the column, Doris,' said Mike, 'but we're associating you with *Chat* in the minds of the readers, which is the next best thing.'

It sounded fair enough to me and he obviously knew what he was doing.

'Okay, love,' I said. 'It doesn't seem too difficult to remember.'

The actress and I went to our positions, the lights blazed and the cameras started to roll.

'What else have we got, Doris?' asked the actress right on cue after the list of features had been read out.

'This might take some time, lovey . . .' I replied obediently.

'Smashing, Doris,' said the director, but I was too old a hand at television by now to imagine that I'd finished work for the day.

Sure enough:

'Could we just try that again?' he added, and off we went again and again and again. It's always like that with television. You need to be patient because you have to do everything about twenty times over.

After a few minutes, though, my concentration started to break up. The actress was saying her lines but suddenly I wasn't listening. Behind me I could sense the presence of a spirit person.

'I'm Tom,' said a man's voice. 'Tell her Tom's here.'

'Shhhh!' I said in my mind, 'I can't talk to you now. I'm making a commercial.'

The man ignored me 'But I must speak to her. Tell her it's Tom.'

'Look, Tom, I can't. You'll have to wait. They'll be furious with me here. Commercials cost a fortune to make. Every minute costs money.'

But Tom couldn't be bothered with such mundane matters as money. 'This is important,' he insisted.

'Later!' I hissed.

Quickly I glanced round to see if any of the crew had noticed my inattention and, to my horror, I realized they were all staring at me. I must have missed a cue.

'Everything all right, love?' said Mike, coming over ready to smooth out any problem. 'Getting tired?'

'No. No, I'm sorry,' I said, uncomfortably conscious that I was holding things up. 'It's just that someone keeps coming in from the other side.'

'It's that chippy!' said the director angrily. 'I knew it. Right, I want everyone out from the back of the set. Now!'

There was the sound of footsteps and then a couple of bewildered young men appeared, unsure what they'd done wrong.

I couldn't help smiling. 'No, love, not the other side of the set,' I said, trying not to laugh. 'I meant the other side. The spirit world.'

There was an uncomfortable silence. Mike and the director exchanged looks. They obviously thought I was a nut-case. Oh well, in for a penny in for a pound, I thought.

'Does anyone here know someone called Tom?' I asked.

The silence continued. Then there was a scuffle in the shadows and a woman emerged, rather shyly.

'Tom's my uncle,' she said.

It turned out that she was the tea-lady and she'd been hanging round the studio ever since she'd heard that I was coming. She must have known intuitively that there would be a message for her.

'Well, he's come along wanting to talk to you, love,' I explained. 'Perhaps we can get together when I've finished here.'

The woman agreed to wait until the end of filming and,

fortunately, this seemed to satisfy Tom too because once he heard what I said, he moved away and let me concentrate on my lines.

Things went smoothly from then on and the commercial was completed. Mike explained that they would have a lot of fun with special effects when they put the finishing touches to it and my voice would sound all echoey. I might even vanish at the end.

'You don't mind, do you, Doris?' he asked anxiously.

I think he was a bit afraid that I'd be all po-faced and silly about it. As it was, I just thought it was a great joke.

'Not at all,' I told him, 'I think it'll be hilarious. I can't wait to see it.'

Out of the corner of my eye I could see the tea-lady still hovering on the fringe of things.

'Come on then, love,' I called to her. 'Let's go and get a cup of tea and see if we can find out what Tom wants.'

Tom was back in an instant, of course, and there in the dressing-room I launched into a mini-sitting as I took off my make-up. It turned out that he was anxious to reassure his niece about some personal problems and once he'd done that he was happy to leave us all in peace.

It was great fun making the commercial, of course, but there's much more to being an agony aunt than larking around a television studio. I've always enjoyed reading the agony columns. Like many people, I turn to them first when I open a magazine. But I hadn't realized before what a responsible job it is. It suddenly hits you that people might actually follow the advice you suggest and for this reason the advice mustn't be lightly given.

I made up my mind to work very hard at each and every reply and I'm glad to say I've always stuck to that decision. Every week a very nice young writer called Nora McGrath arrives with a pile of letters and a tape-recorder, and then we sit down in front of the fire and work our way through them.

I read the letters and dictate a reply into the tape-recorder and then Nora sorts it all out afterwards at the office. The system seems to work well and there's never a shortage of correspondence.

Sometimes the readers confess to the most dreadful problems and when the subject is very complicated I often tune into the spirit world for guidance. Ramanov never fails me with his wisdom.

At other times the tone of the letters is so desperate that I feel compelled to phone the writer immediately and put his mind at rest. The answer still appears in the magazine a week or two later, but at least I know I've done my best. There are times when a week's delay can mean the difference between life and death.

There are many tragic letters, of course. Unless you do a job like mine you don't realize how much sadness there is in the world. But there are letters that make me laugh, too.

Not long ago a little girl from Nottingham wrote to me on the subject of reincarnation. She wanted to know if her granny had returned to her in the form of the family dog.

Well I roared with laughter when I read that letter, and in the spirit world I could hear her granny chuckling too. Nevertheless the child seriously wanted to know so, although I had to confess that the idea had made me smile, I explained that while I believed in reincarnation I didn't think her granny had come back as a dog.

'Animals have souls and they live on in the spirit world,' I said, 'but they're different from us. I don't believe for one moment that they can come back. They run free in the spirit world.'

The bulk of my letters, I suppose, concern worries that have grown out of all proportion in the minds of the writers. We find so many things to torture ourselves with, don't we?

Not long ago, two highly-distressed ladies wrote to me. One had been caught shop-lifting a few years before and was terrified that her husband in spirit knew about it and was so ashamed of her action that he'd ceased to love her.

The other, seriously ill with cancer, was desperate with guilt because after losing her husband she had launched into a couple of affairs, simply for the comfort of human contact. Now, facing the possibility of going to the spirit world herself, she was afraid that her husband would not be there to meet her because of her 'unfaithfulness'.

It's such a shame that these thoughts even have to cross our minds. I was able to reassure both ladies that they were still loved and respected as much as ever. Spirit people have a much better view of our problems than we do. They understand the pressures and strains we face and they don't condemn our actions.

Finally, now and again I get a really special letter. A letter so inspiring, so full of love and so unselfish, that it moves me to tears and I just have to share it with everybody. This next letter, reprinted with the kind permission of *Chat*, is just such a letter:

Dear Doris,

After ten years of longing for a baby my sister finally found she was pregnant. Her husband and she were thrilled beyond words. But tragically, their unborn son was lost at twenty-six weeks. From that cruel day on my husband and I couldn't stand to see their pain any longer. We decided to have a baby for them.

Don't misunderstand, Doris, because there is so much controversy about surrogate mothers, you may do. We gave her and her husband joy, we feel they deserve the baby I gave birth to this year.

I don't care what anyone on this earth says but I have to know; Doris, does my Nan approve? And does my sister's son know he has a little brother here?

We have two lovely boys who mean the world to us and we just wanted my sister and her husband to be as happy as we are.

Name and address withheld.

The tears trickled down my face when I read those words. How could she possibly think that anyone would disapprove of such a loving action? I could imagine so well the agony her poor sister must have gone through after losing her baby. It happened to me, after all, and how different my life might have been if a surrogate mother had been around to give me a child.

Of course, I know that there are all sorts of complicated problems surrounding surrogacy, particularly when it's done for money, but in a case like this I thought it was wonderful.

'My dear, what a wonderful, wonderful letter,' I wrote back, 'I'm in tears here. So much unselfish love that you had for your sister. You and your husband gave your sister the greatest gift that anyone in the world can give.

'Of course her son knows that he has a brother, and he'll understand more when he's older. He's growing up in the spirit world.

'Your Nanna is over the moon that your sister has her own baby to cradle in her arms.

'Your gift of love has made everyone so happy. God bless

you and your husband. I know you're all going to have very happy lives.'

I felt set up for the day after completing that case.

Yes, there's more to this agony-aunting than meets the eye, but I wouldn't miss it for the world. Long may the column continue!

9

Sadly, no matter how hard mediums work, there will always be sceptics; people who simply don't believe in life after death no matter what you say or do.

They dismiss my work and the work of people like me as trickery, telepathy or some kind of wicked spell.

Well, obviously, it hurts to be called a fraud, or worse still, in league with the Devil, especially when you work so hard to do good and to do your job well, but as I've said before, everyone's entitled to their own opinion. I don't try to force my beliefs on anyone and the doubters will eventually discover the truth for themselves on the day when, to their utter amazement, they wake up in the spirit world!

There is one area in the debate however where the sceptics are on shaky ground and that is the peculiar (to the doubters, not to me) phenomenon known as 'out-of-body experience'.

In recent years medical science has progressed so much that there are hundreds of people walking around today who have literally 'come back from the dead'. They have technically 'died' for a short time and then been resuscitated thanks to the efforts of hard-working doctors.

Now most of these people remember nothing of the episode, but a striking number do, and although rather embarrassed because they fear no one will believe them, when pressed, tell of an extraordinary experience in which they felt they stepped outside their body and embarked on the start of a wonderful journey.

Often they can repeat word for word the conversation going on in the room when medical staff thought them unconscious or even dead.

But what has amazed and baffled doctors and scientists is that although the accounts they collected have come from all over the world and from people from all walks of life who have never met each other, the stories of the wonderful journey are almost identical. The details may differ, some may describe a river that formed the boundary with the spirit world, others a gate, but in practically every case the essential elements are the same – some sort of tunnel and a very bright light.

I know what these people are talking about because I, too, have shared this marvellous experience. Over thirty years ago I almost died after a fallopian pregnancy. Suddenly, in the midst of my pain, I saw my father and my son John Michael, now grown from a baby into a handsome little boy, standing hand in hand at the foot of my bed.

As I stared at them, the pain melted away and they started to move backwards. Somehow I followed them feet first into a glorious tunnel of bright, whirling colours, and at the end of the tunnel I could see a bright, bright light. Once I reached that light I knew I'd be in the spirit world and all my troubles would be over.

I was filled with a wonderful sense of peace and love but it was not to be. Suddenly there was a great jolt, the tunnel, my father and son disappeared and I was back on the bed in hospital. The pain and the harsh, raw light of earth flooded over me and I was not at all happy to be back.

In common with all the other people who are privileged to undergo this experience, I have never been afraid of death since. I don't find it baffling. It makes perfect sense to me. You can't travel from one place to another without a journey in between, so when we pass from this life to the spirit world, we naturally embark on a journey quite unlike any other we have made.

To the scientists, however, many of whom don't believe in life after death, the out-of-body phenomenon is a difficult puzzle. They can't dismiss hundreds of ordinary people unconnected with each other as liars or frauds, as they can mediums.

So there can only be two explanations. Either these people really did go on a journey as they described or they were suffering from some kind of hallucination produced by a dying brain.

The scientists tend to prefer the hallucination theory. Now, I'm not clever and I don't have any technical education, but this explanation seems a bit strange to me. Is it likely that every dying brain in the world is programmed to produce an identical hallucination?

No two people dream the same dream. No two drug addicts or alcoholics suffer identical hallucinations (as far as I know). We are all individuals from the moment we are born to the moment we 'die' – so why should we suddenly, on the point of death, succumb to a mass delusion?

The arguments are too academic for me. Instead, I decided to carry out my own little survey. In my last book, *Voices of Love*, I asked readers who had gone through an out-of-body experience, to write and tell me about it. Here are extracts from some of the letters. Read them and make up your own mind.

Dear Doris,

   In *Voices of Love* you say you would like to hear from people who have experienced a return from the dead. I had this happen to me when I was about ten (I am sixty-five now). I did not mention it to anyone until about twenty years ago and was met with scorn so I've not mentioned it since but now I'm relieved to know it was for real.

   When I was ten I got rheumatic fever and was confined to bed not long before Christmas. How I passed the time I really don't know. The following summer was hot and my bedroom window was wide open day and night.

   One morning as I lay in bed listening to the voices of my friends playing in our back gardens I wished I could be out there with them and tears of self-pity came into my eyes. It was the dustman's day to collect and the noise of banging bins and their cheerful shouts and laughter came nearer until they were right outside and then gradually the noise faded as they went on up the street.

   The sounds of children at play also faded and finally I could hear music and choirs singing, no words, just a swelling and fading of sound. I thought it was Mum's radio, or wireless as we called it then, but I quickly remembered it was not powerful enough to reach upstairs to my bedroom.

   The music faded but the choir grew stronger and my bedroom seemed to have a bright, white mist in it except for the area immediately around me.

The mist gradually passed to leave a tube of light from me to somewhere in the far, unseen distance, light that grew brighter as the choir grew louder. I had the feeling of floating through the tube which was lovely. I wanted it to go on for ever. I felt warm and free of pain and quite indescribably happy, a happiness I've never experienced since. It surrounded me like a cocoon of embracing arms.

Suddenly the shouting returned, the light began to fade, I felt heavy and the pain was returning. There was a thump and feeling very surprised I opened my eyes to see our family doctor leaning over me slapping my face and shouting, 'Arthur! Come back! Come back!' My mother was rubbing my feet and legs and sobbing loudly, tears pouring down her face.

The pain and weight of the sheet which was all that covered me was so great I heard myself scream, then I fainted. When I came round the efforts of doctor and mother were still going on and I fainted again. Eventually I came round and the doctor was saying, 'It was a close thing but he'll be all right now'.

I only remember a feeling of bitter disappointment which lasted for days and days.

It was winter again before I was allowed to sit up, then weeks later I was allowed to put my legs to the floor. Obviously I made a complete recovery in the end but that was my experience of dying.

Mr A.H.
Somerset.

Dear Doris,
I've just finished reading your latest book and see you want to hear from readers with 'death' experiences.

Having had five operations I know you do not dream under anaesthetic. In May 1962 I was in hospital having a kidney removed and had been returned to my room.

Suddenly I was aware of my bed being pushed forward and I went along a dark tunnel and entered a vast cavern of light, warmth and peace.

My father, who had died four months previously from cancer, was sitting on the right-hand side of a presence who I knew was God.

This presence was again a vast area of light and I tried to look behind the light but knew I wouldn't be able to. My father, looking well, relaxed and much restored, glanced towards the presence, looked back at me and smiled, but shook his head.

I was withdrawn from the scene. No word was spoken but we understood, and I was in no pain there.

I thought my father had come through to me to let me know there was life after death. Although I thought there might be, I don't think he did!

I was awakened by a terrible scream and remember thinking, 'My God, someone is going through it here.'

There were four people, nurses and doctors, round my bed and one was shouting, 'Come on, breathe!'

I had been taught to deep breathe before the operation and I did my best. Then I felt the pain and I realized it was me who had screamed, then I fell unconscious again.

I thought they had jolted me bringing me back from the theatre and putting me in my own bed and had woken me – but the pain and the scream were in the wrong order, if you follow me.

It wasn't until years afterwards I was reading a book about life after death and read of people either leaving the body or going through a dark tunnel that I realised in a flash that I had probably 'died' for a moment and they were fighting to bring me back.

There is absolutely nothing to be feared of, it was a most beautiful experience and I feel privileged to have been there.

Mrs M.N.
Essex

Dear Doris,

I have just finished reading your fifth book (hope you write many more). You say you would like to hear of experiences of 'dying'.

My husband passed over in 1981 but about three years before then he had pneumonia and at his crisis point he 'died'.

I was sitting by the bed holding his hand. The room was quite dim (it was evening). There was just a small bedside lamp on for me to watch him. He suddenly put his hand up to his eyes as you do in bright sunlight. He said, 'Isn't the light bright, it's wonderful.' Then he said, 'There's my Gran and Ron amidst the flowers. I wonder where all the flowers are from, they're so beautiful.'

A little frightened, I shook him slightly and squeezed his hand. He opened his eyes then and was surprised to see me there. From then he began to improve until he was as well as he could be as he had a heart problem.

When he was well he talked to me about his experience. He said it was wonderful and the light was so bright and warm, yet nothing like sunlight. He saw his Gran (who died when he was a young boy) and Ron, his friend (killed in the Second World War), standing on the opposite bank of a river. All he had to do was cross the water after coming down a rather dark tunnel. His Gran however put up her hand and said, 'Not yet, son, later.' He thought he must have opened his eyes then.

He often said to me after, 'Don't ever be afraid of dying, it is a wonderful experience and so warm and comfortable, nothing to be afraid of. You know, if I go first I shall be waiting for you when your time comes as my Gran was waiting for me.'

Mrs W.A.
Staffordshire

Dear Doris,

The main reason I'm writing to you is because you say that you would be interested to hear from anyone else who had 'died'. This happened to me, also whilst under a general anaesthetic, and it was a most revealing experience which I am only too pleased to tell you about.

At first everything was dark and there was no noise and I thought, this is it, I must be dying. Then suddenly there was a bright light which seemed to be taking me forward and I thought, why is it that I can still think? Will something switch off my brain like a light being switched off?

The light became brighter then seemed to rise like a curtain and there before me was what seemed a never-ending, green, open space. This was still and quiet, just complete stillness, and suddenly I realized I was completely alone and had lost all contact with the human race. I was alone and isolated yet not at all afraid.

This journey I had to make entirely alone, as I did when being born came to my mind, and then I thought what a shock it would be to my family who would not be expecting me to leave. It was as if I had just walked out on them without saying goodbye.

The thought of having upset them made me sad and there was no way I could apologize to them, but soon my thoughts ran on as to what happens next. There was no one in sight and still not a sound so I did not know what to do and just stood there looking around thinking, it's best to wait.

Suddenly the light came back and blinded the view, it became brighter and brighter then suddenly vanished and I was in darkness again. I couldn't see but a voice called me, then again. I wondered if I could put a hand out which was possible, and I realized I could hear and the voice was right beside me now. After a while the blackness lifted and I could see who it was and the person was saying, 'You are all right, it's over now.'

A few days later I plucked up courage to ask if by any chance I had nearly died in the operation. They said no . . .

But when it is time for me to go, I shall go willingly as I know there is nothing to fear, in fact it is a journey to look forward to when the time is right and I feel honoured to have had this experience.

Mrs E.H.
North Cornwall

Dear Doris,
In May 1963 I gave birth to twins, a boy and a girl. The boy was stillborn, the girl was born alive and well.

I had a very bad labour. I had to have forceps and I

was very torn inside and I lost quite a lot of blood. I was so ill I couldn't be moved for quite a while.

After my baby boy was born I just screamed when they told me he was dead and then suddenly I felt so happy and safe I was smiling. I went down a very long, darkish path and I went through a gate at the bottom of the path into a garden full of beautiful flowers and trees.

There was lovely green grass everywhere and as I turned I saw seven mountains with a stream running below the first one. It was the greatest feeling I've ever experienced. I knew that if I went over the stream I would not be coming back.

All of a sudden I was aware of someone tapping my face and I was back giving birth to my beautiful daughter.

Whilst I was recovering in the operating theatre there was someone watching over me. He was standing in a corner all dressed in black and I knew that while he stood there I was safe. When they decided to move me he disappeared.

Mrs V.F.
Leicester

My last letter, from Mrs J.W. of Hertfordshire, tells of the time she had a wisdom tooth out under gas, twenty-five years ago. At first she had a very unpleasant dream, something that's happened to me too under gas, although my dream was quite different from Mrs W.'s, but then suddenly the night-mare evaporated and:

'. . . there I was in the spirit world pleading not to return. The spirits filling me with a warmth and love I'll never forget, telling me I had to return. I argued, as was my wont, wanting my own way until finally I was told it was God's will.

I turned and there was this vast light and a feeling of power and might and strength against which you did NOT argue. I went to a kind of opening flanked by four spirits (two either side). I asked that I might be gone for not too long and would someone be with me.

I was assured I'd be looked after and the feeling of love and caring from those spirits was something I'd never known. I wanted to stay.

The next thing I knew I was with my spirits in the top corner of the dentist's room looking down on myself, still enjoying the peace and love of another world. Then I heard my mother calling my name, three dentists departing from the room and the awakening from the depths of a very deep sleep . . .

Mrs J.W.
Hertfordshire

I have even received a poem on the subject from Mrs Angela Ray of Buckinghamshire. Mrs Ray writes with such authority that I feel sure she too has shared this extraordinary experience.

The Land of Eternity

What is 'Goodbye'? just a word that makes us cry,
When a soul like a ship, pulls from shore,
In a place where I've been just last night in a dream,
They don't use that word anymore.
Shimmering flowers, every hue, radiant faces I knew
Each saying, 'Don't cry for me,

For I'm waiting for you in this world of Summers blue,
The Land of Eternity.'

When I asked, 'Can I stay?' they led me away
Saying, 'He says it's not yet your time,
There are songs you must sing, seeds to plant in the
    Spring
And words to be made into rhyme.'
Wide awake in my room, where they'd left sweet
    perfume,
Life's purpose seemed clearer to me
Than it would have been, had I never seen
The Land of Eternity.

Well, there you are. Fact or hallucination? It's up to you
to decide.

As for me, I am quite certain in my mind that these writers
have experienced the journey to the very edge of the spirit
world.

This is a very difficult thing for sceptics to believe, I know,
because if these people are recounting true experiences and
not hallucinations, then there must be life after death. But
if you admit there is life after death, then you must also admit
that there must be some truth in what we mediums say and
do.

Yes, it's a real problem for the sceptics, and the debate
continues.

10

'More tea, Mrs Stokes?'

The steward, immaculately dressed in a white jacket trimmed with gold braid, leaned forward and placed a large silver teapot on the snowy cloth.

It stood there solid and elegant, its highly-polished surface reflecting the chunky silver cutlery, the slender vase of fresh flowers, the cut-crystal glassware and the pretty little table lamp.

Now that's what I call a properly laid table, I said happily to myself. I leaned back in the winged armchair and gazed around again, determined to etch every detail indelibly on my memory: pale carpet that squashed gently under foot, glittering brassware, and walls panelled in teak, mahogany and rosewood inlaid with marquetry that glowed softly in the lamplight. Outside the window, the Kent countryside rushed by.

'We've done some things in our time,' I said to John, 'but this takes some beating.'

We were spending the afternoon on the Orient Express – the unusual setting for the launch party of my last book, *Voices of Love* – and I must say it was one of the most exciting afternoons of my life.

What a magnificent train the Orient Express is. I'd heard so much about it beforehand that I feared the reality might be a little disappointing. How wrong I was. We set off on a dreary November day and from the moment we arrived at Victoria Station and saw the midnight-blue and gold train standing there like a splendid ghost from another age, it was like stepping into a dream.

The staff, all dressed in smart twenties-style uniforms, treated us like royalty. The carriages were like exquisite drawing-rooms and even the loos were splendid affairs of mahogany with solid brass fittings and lavish mosaic floors.

All afternoon I felt like a film star! It was wonderful. What's more, the party was great fun too. Celebrities such as Pete Murray and Rusty Lee mingled with publishing people and journalists, and we all sat down to a 'High Tea' of turkey and ham and salad, scones, jam and cream and a selection of delicious cakes.

I'm sure it would have been wildly fattening were it not for the fact that I could hardly eat a thing since the cutlery was so heavy for my stroke-weakened right hand that I kept dropping it. In the end I gave it up as a bad job, but it didn't matter a bit. There were so many people to talk to I scarcely had time to finish so much as a cup of tea.

The Orient Express is a legend, of course, and I was very interested to learn a little of its history. Apparently it was conceived by two men, Georges Nagelmackers and George Mortimer Pullman, and it made its first journey in October 1883.

News of the train's luxury and elegance rapidly spread and in those days before air travel, the Orient Express, which ran from Paris to Constantinople (Istanbul as it is now known) quickly established itself as the only route for the discerning who wished to travel between East and West.

Kings, maharajahs, generals and millionaires regularly used the service and the things they got up to en route make ordinary journeys by British Rail seem very dull. One maharajah was so pleased when the chef agreed to stop the train to take on board four sheep carcasses for the maharajah's curry that he gave the man a handful of pearls, rubies and emeralds as a token of appreciation.

On another occasion King Ferdinand I of Bulgaria, who as a small boy had clearly cherished a dream of becoming an engine driver, insisted on taking a turn in the driver's seat when the train passed through Bulgaria, on the grounds that it was his country and he could do as he liked. He made such a hash of it that the brakes were damaged and the train was delayed for four hours.

Then there was the famous dancer Isadora Duncan, who mesmerized the staff by wandering the corridors to the shower dressed only in a veil – 'the size of a handkerchief' according to one eyewitness.

And we mustn't forget the spies. Unable to leap on a jet in the modern manner, famous spies like Mata Hari and Sidney Reilley set off on their missions in a much more civilized style, aboard the Orient Express.

Yes, the history is really fascinating and if you'd like to know more about it, it's worth reading *Orient Express* by E.H. Cookridge.

With all those strong and often ultimately tragic personalities associated with the train, I wondered if any of them had lingered to the present day. Would the train be haunted? But as it turned out there was much too much bustle going on for me to tune in and no lost soul drew itself to my attention. Yet there was something left over from the old days. A powerful atmosphere still clung to the train, too strong to be explained merely by the beautifully refurbished carriages and the period uniforms of the staff. An indefinable air of glamour and of old-world elegance hung over the place like an echo . . .

The launch party raced by. It quickly grew too dark to see the countryside outside the windows but nobody minded. And nobody minded where we went. As it happened, the train chugged smoothly down to Dover, stopped a while in the station and then chugged back again, but we hardly noticed. Everyone was touched by the special magic of the Orient Express and when we finally pulled into Victoria Station at the end of our trip, we were very reluctant to leave the train.

'I shall never, never forget it,' I said dreamily to John in the car on the way home.

'Neither shall I, love. Neither shall I,' he agreed.

Often, after a really wonderful outing like that, day-to-day life can be something of an anticlimax, but on this occasion I was lucky. Just a few days later there was another special event. I did a demonstration at the Barbican on Remembrance Day. Now I visit a few theatres for demonstrations and I'm happy to say that I've never once had a miserable time (I'm nervously touching wood here). The audiences are always marvellous and the atmosphere fills with love. But that night at the Barbican really was something special.

Ever since a sell-out visit last year, I'd been promising to return to the Barbican and when Laurie was organizing my schedule he realized that November was the likeliest month.

'What d'you think about November, Doris?' he asked.

'Suits me,' I said. Then I had a thought. 'I know, let's make it Remembrance Day. After all, the demonstrations are all about remembering loved ones who've passed on.'

'Well now. Let me see,' said Laurie, getting out his diary, 'I'm not sure what date Remembrance Sunday is this year.'

'No, no, not Remembrance Sunday,' I said. 'I mean the real Remembrance day, November 11th.'

When I was a child, everything came to a halt on the eleventh hour of the eleventh day of the eleventh month; trains, buses, people walking down the streets, we all stopped for a minute's silence to remember those who had given their lives in the war. Maybe I'm old-fashioned but I don't like the way they've tinkered around with Remembrance Day in recent years, moving the ceremony to the nearest Sunday. To my mind, it's just not the same if it's not the eleventh day of the eleventh month.

Anyway, Laurie thought it was a marvellous idea and we decided to add a few special touches to the normal demonstration, in honour of the occasion.

We decorated the stage with poppies and white chrysanthemums and then, when everyone was seated, the lights were turned down low. A single spotlight illuminated the stage and into it marched a lone bugler from the Royal Artillery in full dress uniform of navy blue trimmed with red and gleaming with brass buttons.

The chattering died away as he lifted the bugle to his lips and you could have heard a pin drop as the poignant notes of the 'Last Post' reverberated around the hall.

It was a moving start to the evening. There was a short silence, the bugler marched smartly off, then the mood changed as my 'signature tune', 'One Day At A Time', came belting out and I walked onto the stage in my pink 'rent-a-tent', as Terry cheekily calls it.

As I was getting ready earlier that afternoon I'd tuned in to see if I could pick up something to start me off. At first nothing happened but after a while I heard the faint words '107 Andrews House' and the name 'Dolan'. Then the phone rang and somehow from then on the house was so chaotic I didn't get the chance to concentrate again.

'I normally try to tune in before the evening starts,' I explained to the audience, 'but today, what with one thing and another, I'm afraid I didn't get much time. All I picked up was part of an address I think, 107 Andrews House – or it could have been Andrews Place – and the name Dolan. Can anybody place either of them?'

My first message is always greeted by a sort of stunned silence. To most of the audience it means nothing, of course, and the person it's intended for is usually so amazed to find herself or himself singled out, that they are rendered momentarily speechless.

Undaunted, I waited patiently and after a minute or two a fair-haired woman in a blue jacket picked her way carefully down to the microphone.

'My name is Dolan,' she said, with a rather bemused expression on her face, 'and my brother lives in Andrews House.'

As she spoke a woman's voice came in clear from the other side. 'Tell her to remember me to Lillian and to John,' she instructed me.

'I've got the names Lillian and John . . .' I began.

'Yes. Lillian lives at 107 and John's my son.'

But the lady in my ear was rushing on. She was giving me some sort of number with a seven in it.

'Hang on a minute, lovey,' I begged her. 'You see, she's talking about John and she's giving me a number. Part of an address, I think. Seventeen, seventy . . . it's not just seven is it?'

There was an invisible sigh of exasperation.

'It's not an address, it's a birthday,' I was told.

'Sorry, it's a birthday,' I relayed obediently.

The woman at the microphone nodded. 'That's right, John's birthday is on the 7th.'

I don't think I ever did work out whether I was talking to her mother or her grandmother but it didn't seem to matter. The lady was too busy getting in as many family details as she could to waste time on enlightening me. She mentioned her daughter-in-law, Jan, and her granddaughter, Joanne, and good old Uncle Charlie.

'I was very lucky,' she added. 'I went over very quickly. I just went to sleep and woke up over here.'

I thought she meant by this that she'd had a stroke, but no. Apparently she had suffered a sudden heart attack after breakfast one morning and was whisked straight over. That's the way to go.

In the background I could hear other voices queuing up for a chance to speak, but the lady stayed firmly on the vibration.

'Yes, all right, I won't be a minute,' she told them. 'There's just one thing I must say,' she turned back to me. 'I'm sad because X is feeling guilty. There'd been an argument you see and we hadn't made it up. She's been feeling guilty ever since. Will you tell her I'm sorry. It was so stupid. What a waste of good time. Please send her my love and ask her to forgive me.'

I passed this on and the woman at the microphone nodded.

'Do you know what I'm talking about?' I asked her.

'Yes, I do,' she said. 'She'll be very pleased. She has been feeling guilty.'

This message had obviously been crucial to my spirit visitor and once she'd got it across, she was willing to melt into the background and let other voices take over. There were dozens of them, all eager to talk to their families and friends. So eager, in fact, that for the next few minutes I had a right old mix-up.

I ended up with two young girls at the microphone, one dark haired and bubbly, the other blonde and tearful. The dark-haired girl had a mother in spirit who was most anxious to talk to her, while the blonde had a father on the spirit side who felt the same.

They both decided to talk at the same time and the messages came out in a tangle. In the end the conversation went backwards and forwards between the two of them like a tennis ball at Wimbledon.

Basically, it seemed that the father of the blonde ('Call her Nelly and make her laugh,' he said. 'Her name's Ellen.') wanted her to know that although he, too, had died unexpectedly young of a heart attack, he was now well and happy on the other side with Ellen's grandparents, Frank and Ellen. 'We're looking after him, girl,' Frank told his granddaughter. 'Dry your eyes.'

The brunette's mother was keen for her daughter to understand that she was still around and knew exactly what was going on.

'She's moving, you know,' she told me, settling down for a bit of a gossip, 'and they're knocking out the fireplace.'

'Well, we're hoping to when we've moved in,' agreed the daughter.

'And she's getting a new washing machine.'

'I'm not sure about that,' said the girl.

'Yes she is, she needs one,' insisted her mother. 'Her old one was second hand. It only cost £70. It did her a good turn but it's past it now. She needs a new one.'

'Well, your mum says you're to have one,' I told her.

She went on to send her love to her other daughter, Cheryl, a hairdresser, who'd been a bit unhappy lately.

And so it went on. Many of the contacts had a few light-hearted words to cheer their relatives but some could not hide the sadness surrounding their passing.

One pale, drawn lady in sombre clothes was overcome to be reunited with mother hen. She was only thirteen years old when her beloved mum passed over.

'It shouldn't have happened. Something went wrong,' complained the mother.

Apparently, she had gone into hospital for an operation which appeared to be successful, and then a few days later she suddenly became ill and died. Nevertheless, she had stayed close to her daughter all these years, she'd watched over her little grandson, Robert, when he was born and now she brought back with her a beautiful two-year-old girl with auburn hair to show me.

'Did you lose a child?' I asked the lady at the microphone.

'Yes, I had a miscarriage.'

'Well, it was a little girl and she's got auburn hair,' I told her.

The woman gasped. 'My little boy's got auburn hair,' she said.

'So has your little girl,' I explained.

'We've called her Claire,' put in the proud grandmother in the spirit world. 'And there's no need to worry because I'm bringing her up now.'

There were quite a few young people who'd passed at a tragically young age. The most horrifying of all came right at the end. A boy whom I at first took to have been murdered moved in close.

'Ireland,' I heard him say. Then I felt a stabbing sensation. Immediately I had the sense of a lung being punctured and filling with blood, followed by a choking, drowning feeling. He had drowned in his own blood.

Putting the two together, I jumped to the conclusion that the lad had been murdered in Ireland.

The elderly, white-haired lady who'd claimed him, hitched her blue cardigan more comfortably round her shoulders and shook her head.

'No, he wasn't murdered,' she said. 'He did it himself. He'd just come back from Ireland.'

'He did it himself!' I was so shocked that for a moment I was speechless. Of all the ways to take yourself over, what a dreadful thing to choose. The boy was obviously very, very sick at the time.

'They tried to save me,' he said regretfully, 'but by the time they got me to hospital it was too late.'

It was a downbeat note to end the evening but fortunately there was a happy surprise in store for the audience before they went home. Sally Whittaker from *Coronation Street* had come along to give out the flowers, a little ceremony which has become a permanent fixture of these evenings. She moved tirelessly up and down the stage, distributing bouquets to people who had received messages, and shaking hands.

I hope the recipients think of these flowers as coming not from Laurie and me, but from their loved ones on the other side who would jump at the chance to give them such a gift if only they could.

Sadly, I couldn't hang around chatting for long after the show because I had to dash home for a live phone-in from Australia, but even though it ended rather abruptly as far as I was concerned, the evening stands out in my mind as a special one. It would be nice to do a regular November 11th appearance every year. I know we remember our family and friends in spirit every day, but Remembrance Day seems particularly appropriate.

It wasn't just me being sentimental. I think some members of the audience sensed the special quality that was in the air that night because, afterwards, a lady called Pam Lyons sent me a beautiful poem she'd written immediately after the show. Apparently she couldn't go to bed until she'd written down the words that came into her head, inspired by the events of the evening. The poem goes like this:

Step across tomorrow, past all your yesterdays,
Feel their love surround you in soft caressing waves.
Know that all who've gone before
Walk with you hand in hand
For they are ever watchful, in a place called Morningland.
And sorrow cannot hurt you, and grief it does not last.
But Love endures forever,
Though eternity should pass.

I travel to a lot of theatres these days and inevitably one occasion tends to blur into another in my mind. Every evening is a marvellous experience because the people are so warm and make me feel so welcome. Yet, just as in any other job, I find that some nights things work better than others.

It's a bit like driving a car. Some days you get in the car and although you feel perfectly well, you can't seem to do a thing right. Your co-ordination's a little bit out; you stall at the traffic lights, make a hash of reversing, crash the gears like a learner and fail to overtake when it is perfectly safe. Other days you jump in the car, pull easily away and everything falls fluidly into place; you sail along, smooth as a dream, the controls just extensions of your own body.

It's just the same being a medium. There are nights when I have to struggle for every contact and sort through a jumble of messages as confusing as tangled knitting; and there are other nights when one message flows easily into the next, clear, precise and accurate. I don't know why it should be like that but it is, and obviously it's the extremes that tend to stand out in the memory.

I had a wonderful evening recently when I went to Lewisham. I tend to appear at Lewisham Theatre more frequently than anywhere else because it's my 'local'! I don't have to spend hours on the motorway to get there and I don't have to book into a hotel for the night or worry about packing cases for the visit. It might sound dull but, quite honestly, at my age these benefits are becoming increasingly attractive.

Anyway, once again I was standing on the familiar stage at Lewisham and suddenly, almost as if my brain clicked into overdrive, the voices came flying through.

To open the evening I got my first contact to pass with AIDS. I suspect I'm going to get a lot more of these in the coming months but this was my first confirmed case. The poor lad, Simon I think his name was, came back full of love for his boyfriend who had nursed him devotedly through the terrible ordeal.

Simon mentioned a great many family members and friends but most of all he wanted to reassure his lover that he was now fit and well and happy. They were obviously very close indeed and he promised that he wouldn't move on in the spirit world. He would wait faithfully for his friend and then they would progress together.

Alarmed as I am about the spread of AIDS, I feel nothing but pity for the sufferers. I can't understand how people can be cruel to these poor victims who often go through agonies before they pass, and I made a special point to ask the red-eyed boy at the microphone to make sure he stayed behind to collect some flowers from his friend.

After a long chat, Simon stood back to allow other voices to come through and immediately a little girl piped up:

'I'm Michelle and it's my anniversary this month and my mum and dad are here.'

When spirit people talk about anniversaries, they mean the anniversary of their passing which to them is like a birthday.

'Does anyone know a Michelle who's got an anniversary coming up?' I asked.

Down in the audience I saw a head bob up and a woman hurried down to the microphone.

'Do you know a Michelle, love, and is there an anniversary?' I asked.

'Yes, she's my daughter and the anniversary is today.'

'Tell her that Peter's here with me,' said Michelle. 'Oh, and there's my dad.'

I glanced up as a man started threading his way along the row of seats to join his wife at the microphone.

'Peter's with her,' I continued to the woman.

'That's my father,' she said.

By this time the man had reached his wife and I was just about to go on when something struck me about the faces of the couple. They looked oddly familiar.

'I've spoken to you before, haven't I?' I asked.

'Well, yes you have, Doris,' they admitted. 'We came to see you last year.'

I had no idea they were going to be present that night and I had no idea of the date of Michelle's passing. In fact, I could remember nothing of the sitting apart from the fact that the little girl had passed tragically in some sort of accident. When you talk to as many people as I do, you can't possibly remember the names of their families and friends and all the intimate details they tell you. Nevertheless, it was only fair that I told the audience what had happened.

'Well, Michelle,' I said when I'd finished explaining, 'you'd better tell me about things that have happened recently or I'll be accused of just remembering what you told me last time.'

'Mummy and Daddy have bought a new car,' she volunteered.

'Yes, we've bought another taxi,' her father agreed.

There was something muffled about a move.

'Her friends have just moved to a new house,' said her mother.

'And Daddy bought Mummy a new watch.'

'Yes, he did.'

'Then there's Billy.'

'That's my little boy's little friend.'

'I didn't know him before but I do now,' said Michelle. 'He's always into things and my brother gets the blame.'

Very faintly beside Michelle I heard another voice. It was so indistinct I couldn't tell if it was male or female, but the person just managed to get over that they'd passed with lung cancer.

'Oh yes,' said Michelle's mother. 'My aunt died two weeks ago.'

'Don't forget Joyce,' said Michelle.

'No, Josie,' said her mother. 'That's her friend round the corner.'

'Sorry, Michelle, my mistake, I thought you said Joyce,' I apologized.

'Josie's got a new dog now,' said Michelle. 'Well you did

want to know what's been happening lately. And Mummy's had her ears pierced.'

'Yes, I have,' gasped her mother, her hands going involuntarily to her ears.

Michelle started giggling, so loudly in fact that I couldn't make out her next words. It was something about painting and George. 'George did it,' was all I could hear clearly.

Her mother laughed. 'Yes, I know what that's about. George is her uncle and he is painting the house for the friends who've recently moved.'

'Then there's Patrick.'

'That's a friend at work,' said Michelle's mother.

'Mummy works in a . . .' It went a bit muzzy. 'Hospital,' I thought she said. But just as I was about to say it I caught a glimpse of a pretty child with the most beautiful copper hair. She put her hand on her hip in exasperation and wagged her finger at me.

'You're not listening, Doris,' she complained. 'I didn't say hospital, I said school. Mummy works in a school.'

'Yes, I do,' said her mother, 'I clean a school.'

And so it went on. Michelle was able to communicate well because she'd done it before and that helps. It's almost as difficult for them as it is for me. We have to work very hard at both ends to get the message across. But although it's easier when the spirit person has communicated before, it's not essential. If the link of love is strong enough, if the need is urgent enough, the spirit people get through.

And get through they did that night. Very little went wrong.

Towards the end there came another daughter tragically killed. Eighteen-year-old Susan had passed in a road accident. Her face hadn't been marked but she was in a coma.

Apparently for forty-eight hours the doctors thought there might be some hope, but then she sank deeper and they realized there was nothing they could do.

As we talked, Susan showed me a picture. I was looking at a gravestone in the shape of an open book, and written on it I could see the words 'Safe in the arms . . .'

'Yes, that's right,' said Susan's mother when I described what I had seen. 'That's her grave.'

'It's very nice,' said Susan, 'and I sit with Mum when she goes to visit it, but then I go home with her again. She doesn't have to go to the grave to talk to me, I'm with her a lot.

'You know what's really been bothering her? Just before it happened I was a bridesmaid and now she keeps thinking of that song: 'Always the Bridesmaid, Never the Blushing Bride' – and it upsets her that I wasn't ever a bride. But it doesn't matter at all. I'm happy here.'

Like most spirit people, Susan had looked in on her own funeral and she was particularly proud of the cross of white flowers given to her by her family and the heart of flowers from her boyfriend.

'But, you know, all you need to do is give her a fresh flower by her photograph,' I explained to her mother. 'She'll be happy to see that when she visits you at home.'

And of course to start her off, I gave her some flowers from the stage.

The voices went on and on. While I stood there under the lights I felt as if I could go on all night. I was so full of energy and strength I thought I could do anything. But what a shock I was in for when the evening finished. Nothing's for nothing, as they say, and I had to pay for all that energy I'd used. Suddenly I was so exhausted I had to be helped back to the dressing-room and I sat there for ages like a wrung-out dishcloth, too tired even to talk.

I was weary for days afterwards, but I must say it was worth it. Long after the memory of exhaustion has faded, I shall remember that wonderful evening at Lewisham.

11

John Morley, my accountant, shook his head.

'Really, Doris. Your phone bill. It's astronomical.' He leafed disbelievingly through the blue and white sheets. 'You'll have to do something about this you know. You'll have to cut down.'

I stared sadly at the little heap of bills. 'I know. It's awful, isn't it,' I said, 'but there's nothing I can do. Often I just have to phone people urgently.'

How could I explain to my accountant the sort of letters I get which just cry out for an immediate answer? Only a few days before, for instance, the post brought me a desperate appeal from a lady who had murdered her baby when it was only five months old. She had been in purgatory ever since.

Even before I finished reading the tragic lines, I sensed Ramanov with me, urging me to pick up the phone and dial the number printed at the top of the page.

The poor woman was in a terrible state. When I tuned in, her relatives in the spirit world told me that she had been suffering from post-natal depression and wasn't to be blamed. In fact, even in this world she wasn't blamed and people had tried to help her.

'I know,' sobbed the woman, 'that's what made me feel so guilty. Instead of being punished, people tried to help me. I should have been punished for what I did.'

She had been carrying this dreadful burden around for years. It took quite a while for the spirit world to convince her that she truly wasn't to blame because she was sick, and that even her child didn't blame her.

Obviously, as this emotional call went on the little meter was ticking away, but what can you do? These things are important.

Then there was the case of a poor girl who was highly distressed because a medium had told her that her beloved husband was in 'limbo'. Once again I felt compelled to phone her and it was a good thing I did. She, too, was in a bad way.

She wasn't very old and apparently on her birthday her husband had taken her out for a treat. They had a nice evening, came home, and the husband sat down on the sofa while his wife put the kettle on. The next thing the girl knew, he'd keeled over, collapsed and 'died'.

Naturally she was distraught. There had been no hint of any ill-health in her husband and he was still a young man. What's more, the couple had two small children and they had looked forward to many happy years ahead with their family.

Shocked and unhappy, the young widow consulted a medium, hoping for comfort. What she got was an increase of agony.

The medium told her that because her husband had passed so suddenly and unexpectedly, he was in 'limbo' and for this reason the medium was unable to contact him. The poor girl came away almost out of her mind with worry, imagining that her husband was floating around aimlessly somewhere, belonging neither to this world nor the next.

I felt desperately sorry for her and furious with the medium. Honestly, I don't know where some people who call themselves mediums get their ideas, I really don't. This theory about limbo goes against everything I've been taught by the spirit world.

Anyway, I telephoned the girl, tuned in and her husband came to us straight away. He wasn't in limbo, he was safely in the spirit world and his only worry was the distress his wife was suffering.

He gave me his name, which was Ashley, if I remember correctly. He talked of the way he passed, of his family and of someone called John who had been a godsend to his wife and helped her sort out the complicated business that always accompanies a bereavement. Just as we were winding up, he said, 'There will be some flowers.'

But I thought no, that's your mind butting in, Doris. Earlier I'd been thinking what a shame it was that there were no fresh flowers in the house. I'm letting my own thoughts intrude, I said to myself sternly. If my concentration was going it was just as well the little sitting was over. So I said goodbye to the girl who was now more cheerful and I didn't mention the last bit about the flowers.

As usual, though, I shouldn't have doubted. The following Monday morning a beautiful bouquet arrived with a little card from the young widow thanking me for all the comfort and strength I had given her. That last message had been from Ashley after all.

Not long after this I had another query about limbo. How it seems to worry people. A lady wrote to say that her husband had passed over and left instructions that he should be cremated. She had respected his wishes and had the body cremated but afterwards she was very upset by a remark his sister had made. Apparently the sister was of the opinion that her brother was now in limbo because his soul had been burnt.

I've never heard such nonsense. You can't burn a soul. It's simply not possible. All you burn when a body is cremated is the soul's old overcoat for which it no longer has a use.

'I don't know, John,' I said, when I'd finished reading the letter, 'this limbo bit again. We're going to be cremated, aren't we? Our old clothes won't be any use to us when we're away. When medical science has finished with my body I don't care what happens to it.'

For some reason this episode set me thinking about funerals and the things people have written on their loved ones' tombstones as epitaphs, and as these thoughts passed through my head, I suddenly heard a spirit voice recite the perfect epitaph:

'Your work on earth is finished, Your life in spirit has begun, When you stand before the master, We know he'll say well done.'

What a beautiful verse, I thought, and how wonderful if it could be true. It's certainly something we should all aim for.

So you see, when I sat there listening to the accountant taking me to task over my phone bill it was impossible for me to promise to mend my ways.

'I know it costs a fortune,' I explained, 'but there's really nothing I can do about it. The phone calls are part of my work and I have to make them.'

But you don't have to be a medium in order to try to live your life well and make your spirit people proud of you. We can all do our bit in our own little way and it's amazing how one kind act can spread and spread.

My father always used to quote the old song: 'If you have a kindness shown you, pass it on. It's not meant for you alone . . . pass it on.'

And it's so true. It's quite extraordinary what happens when you start passing kindness on. Recently we had this demonstrated in the most practical way.

Tom Johanson from the SAGB (The Spiritualist Association of Great Britain) phoned Laurie to ask if there was any way in which we could help with the renovation work necessary at the Association's head office in Belgrave Square. The building is very old, it requires a lot of looking after and money is tight.

Well, first of all, Laurie and I suggested that we pay for a room to be decorated, providing materials and labour. Tom thanked us but explained that they had quite a number of volunteers going in at weekends to help with the decorating. No, what they were in desperate need of, he explained, was some new chairs for the restaurant.

Naturally, Laurie and I agreed to buy the chairs, and somehow we ended up buying the tables to go with them as well.

When Tom wrote to thank us he explained that after receiving our gift, Fulham Church had got in touch with the news that they needed new tables. So Tom gave them the old tables from SAGB, together with the new tablecloths they'd bought, because the tables Laurie and I had sent didn't need cloths. What's more, he added, since then SAGB had been given another forty chairs.

Hardly had we finished reading the letter when someone rang up from Sheerness with another plea. They had been given a building for a church and did we know anyone who'd got any chairs?

The upshot was that Terry went to SAGB, loaded the

spare chairs into his van and drove them down to Sheerness where they are now installed in the new church.

That one act of kindness resulted in three churches benefiting. It just shows that good deeds aren't wasted.

Mind you, you don't often see such a clear-cut case as this. Most of the time, I know, it often feels as if there's so much wickedness in the world that good doesn't stand a chance. New horrors seem to crop up every day and the latest dreadful worry is AIDS.

Jean and I were talking about it not long ago. As I think I've explained, since my stroke all the strength seems to have gone out of my right arm and it shakes quite a bit so I've had to get someone to help with the housework. Jean is a marvel and recently she's become indispensable. She's started coming to theatres with me to help me with my zips and the unpacking and repacking of my long stage dresses. On the last journey she even ended up doing the navigating.

'Is there no end to your talents, Jean?' we teased, as she successfully guided us into the town centre despite one-way systems and all manner of fiendishly confusing traffic signs.

So brilliant is Jean in every way that we've jokingly nicknamed her 'Treasure', and it's caught on to such an extent that now at the theatres everyone calls out for 'Treasure'.

Anyway, this particular day the subject of AIDS came up and Jean said how worried she was about it, not for herself, but for her grandchildren.

'I'm well on the way now,' said Jean, 'but what about the young people? What's going to happen to my grandchildren? The way things are going they could all be wiped out.'

I brooded on the question long after she'd gone and I got myself pretty depressed. It began to seem as if God had got fed up with us at last and this was his punishment.

The idea frightened me so much that that night when I

sat down to tune in to my guide Ramanov, I had to ask him about it.

'Ramanov,' I said, 'I've been thinking about this terrible AIDS epidemic and all the suffering it's going to cause. Is God punishing us?'

'No, child,' Ramanov replied in his calm, reasonable way, 'it's not God punishing you. You are punishing yourselves. You each know your own moral responsibilities. You know your responsibilities to your families and to the world.

'If you ignore the rules then this is the sort of thing that happens. It's not God. It's a weakness in mankind. You don't have to behave the way you do, you are free to choose. But if you knowingly take the wrong path then you have to accept the consequences.'

I wasn't sure whether this comforted me or not. Once again, it seemed, innocent people were going to suffer for the mistakes of others. Life is very unfair. Thank goodness you don't get this sort of injustice in the spirit world.

I try to tune in to Ramanov every night and he always comes to talk to me. He must be a saint because sometimes I'm sure he gets fed up with me forever whingeing about something. If I was him, I'd have earache by now!

Recently, I was moaning on about a very hurtful article in a newspaper. It was my usual theme to Ramanov about working so hard and yet being so misunderstood.

'I don't know,' I went on, 'I sometimes wonder if it's worth it. All this aggravation and worry . . .'

'Now look,' interrupted Ramanov in the nearest he ever came to an impatient voice, 'I didn't promise you roses all the way, did I? I didn't even promise to take the stones out of the pathway.'

'No,' I admitted reluctantly, 'you didn't.'

'Well then. These difficulties are there for you to over-come and to grow stronger in the overcoming. Anything worth having is worth fighting for. So long as you know within your heart that you are doing the right thing and you are playing fair with the spirit world and being honest – then that's all that matters. You will triumph in the end.'

Well, that was me told in no uncertain terms. I didn't dare complain again for at least a week after that!

Ramanov was certainly right when he said that anything worth having is worth fighting for. I seem to have been fighting ever since I was a medium. It was only after he'd given me his little lecture that I remembered I've always suffered various kinds of aggravation ever since I've been a medium.

Maybe it's because I'm a bit of a rebel and I've always gone my own way, but somehow I was always getting myself into trouble.

When I was a young medium living in Lancaster I used to work for the local spiritualist churches. Occasionally though, people would ring and plead for a private sitting. Some of them came from as far afield as America or Egypt and it was very difficult to say no. I couldn't understand why I should say no. They needed help and I was able to give it. What on earth could be wrong with that?

We were very hard up in those days because John with his war wounds couldn't earn much money and his pension didn't go far, so I used to charge one pound for my sittings. These days, thank goodness, we don't have to struggle and I don't charge at all for the few sittings I'm able to do, but back then the money was a great help.

Anyway, I did my sittings but for some reason the church didn't like it. How they got to know I can't imagine, but I can guarantee that within a day or two of a sitting a letter would arrive from the secretary of the church committee:

Dear Mrs Stokes,

It's come to my notice that you have been doing private sittings. If you continue to do private sittings I'm afraid we will have to expel you from the church.

Yours etc.

It was like being back at school but as an ex-nurse I had a healthy respect for authority and these letters used to frighten me. Afterwards, I would do my best to tow the line, until the next desperate appeal landed me in trouble again.

I just couldn't understand what I was doing wrong. If I'd turned up drunk at church meetings or used foul language or had an affair with someone else's husband I could understand the committee feeling it had to take a stand, but what could be wrong with helping people?

The last straw came when a family arrived on my doorstep frantic with grief over the loss of a son. The sitting went very well and they left my house like different people. Heads held high, tears gone and a new spirit of hope in their step.

Two days later I opened the mail and there it was:

Dear Mrs Stokes,

It has come to my notice that . . .

I was furious. I was so incensed that there and then I phoned the late Richard Eldridge, then president of the National Union.

'I'm ringing to tell you that I'm sending my credential cards back,' I told him. 'And as far as I'm concerned you know what you can do with them.'

A medium is awarded her credential cards after passing a strict test. These cards permit you to work in spiritualist churches and with the public. No medium is considered qualified without her 'credentials'.

Richard, who probably scarcely knew who I was, was rather taken aback.

'Why's that, Doris?' he asked mildy.

'I'm just a little bit tired of the church committee interfering every time I try to do something to help people outside the church,' I exploded.

Richard was very good. He soothed my anger, calmed me down and then got me to explain slowly just what had been happening to upset me so.

When I'd finished, he promised to look into the matter. Sure enough, after that, the unpleasant little notes stopped. But what a shame the situation had had to reach that pitch. The energy I wasted in indignation. The energy the committee secretary wasted writing those unnecessary letters. And the years that were wasted when I could have been going forward and helping people but was held back by stupid rules and regulations.

Sadly, it still goes on today. I'm afraid we still get a few self-important people trying to push the youngsters around and coming out with a load of nonsense in the process. A few years ago, when I lived in Fulham, I used to run a teaching class for developing mediums.

I sat in a circle with the kids, we said a prayer and then we tuned in. One day, just as we were settling down, one of the boys said:

'You have to keep both feet on the floor, you know, or it doesn't work.'

At his words the years rolled back and I remembered being told the very same thing myself.

'That's what I was told, too, son,' I said. 'And it's not true. It doesn't matter. You can take your shoes off, sit on your feet or stand on your head, if you want to. It doesn't make a blind bit of difference.

'I was also told that you needed a dim light and a bowl of clear water in the room. It's a load of nonsense. You can tune in at any time, in any place, so long as you can concentrate.'

Perhaps I was teaching my youngsters to be rebels too, I don't know. My only thought was to make sure their heads weren't filled with a load of rubbish.

Funnily enough, even today at my age I still have problems from time to time with the spiritualist 'establishment'. I was expecting a lot of criticism earlier in the year when I agreed to appear on the Jasper Carrott show.

It was Jasper's producer who first contacted Laurie to ask if I would do it. Laurie's immediate reaction was no. He tends to be very protective of me. Jasper's show is a satirical programme, after all, and mediums are fair game for being sent up at the best of times without actually setting themselves up for it.

'It's very kind of you,' said Laurie, politely. 'But I really don't think it's Doris's cup of tea.'

The next day, however, Jasper himself phoned me at home.

'Doris, I've been following your career for years and I've got the greatest respect for you,' he said.

I listened carefully for a mocking note in his voice but I could detect nothing.

'We'd really like you to do this,' Jasper went on. 'I'll send you the script and if there's anything you don't like, you can change it.'

He was so charming I could feel myself being persuaded.

'You promise you're not going to send up spiritualism?'

He promised. And he was as good as his word. When the script arrived I saw that the scene they wanted me to take part in was an amusing sketch about British Telecom and how difficult it is to get through to directory enquiries. It takes a medium to get a reply, they implied.

No-one with a sense of humour could object. There was nothing offensive in it. The only thing I didn't like was the fact that they'd got the medium working in a darkened room. I never work in the dark. All that darkened room stuff is just part of the old superstitious mumbo jumbo. The brighter the sunshine the better it suits me.

'Yes, I'll do it,' I told them when they phoned to see what I thought of the script. 'The only thing I don't like is the darkened room bit. Everything I do is in full light so I would be very pleased if you cut that out.'

There was no fuss. They agreed immediately and I had a very enjoyable time. Jasper came to see me on set. He kissed me and asked if everything was all right, whether I wanted to change the script in any way, whether there was anything I wanted taken away or added.

'No, it's fine now, Jasper,' I assured him. 'Now they've taken out that darkened room bit, I'm happy.'

Throughout the show everyone treated me with the greatest respect and when I eventually saw the finished product on screen I still thought it was amusing. The whole thing went so well that if there's ever anything else I can do for Jasper, I'd be glad to.

The day the programme went out I waited for the criticism but, surprisingly enough, there was hardly a murmur. Perhaps the dour members of the 'establishment' don't watch Jasper Carrott. Or perhaps they have acquired a sense of humour at last.

Whatever the reason, I'll never again let them put me off
doing something I believe is right. It's lonely going against
the group but I'll follow Ramanov's advice from now on. If
I know in my heart that what I'm doing is right, if I'm being
fair with the spirit world and I'm being honest – then I'll go
right ahead and do it.

Incidentally, just to prove that I'm not the only one who
gets encouragement from the spirit world, and that you don't
have to be a medium to hear voices, I must tell you a lovely
little story.

The other day I heard from an elderly lady in her eighties
who was very puzzled and somewhat alarmed to hear a disem-
bodied voice speaking to her.

As far as she knew she wasn't psychic, and she'd never in
her life before had an experience like this. Nevertheless, one
night just after she'd gone to bed, she distinctly heard a voice
speaking to her from somewhere behind her head.

The voice was definitely outside her head but there was
no one else in the flat and the people next door had gone
to bed long ago. The voice was very beautiful, though she
couldn't really tell whether it was male or female and she
was quite certain she'd never heard it before.

'The waters of the Lord floweth over me,' it said. 'And I
was made whole.'

That was all it said and then there was silence. Now the
lady puzzled over those words for the rest of the night. They
sounded almost like a quotation but though she scoured her
Dictionary of Quotations very carefully she couldn't find the
source. She began to wonder whether she was going mad,
and that's when she asked what I thought of the matter.

Well, of course, I knew straight away that she wasn't going
mad but I could understand how she felt. Hadn't I often
feared that I was going round the bend in the early days

when spirit people kept talking to me and my family thought
I was peculiar?

'No, dear, you're as sane as can be,' I assured her. Had she
been ill recently, I wondered?

It turned out that this lady had been suffering for months
after an unpleasant operation. Often she got very depressed
about it which wasn't at all surprising.

The answer was clear to me. The spirit world knew what
she was going through and were trying to reassure her that she
wasn't alone. Despite her trials and tribulations she was
gradually getting better and must not lose heart.

I thought it was a lovely story and it just proves that when
we are most in need the spirit world doesn't let us down.
Not everyone will hear voices of course; some might feel a
loving presence, others might be mystified by peculiar happenings in the home or a chain of coincidences too unlikely to
be called coincidence.

The spirit world finds many different ways to put its message
across. The important thing is that we are not alone and
when we need help we need only stretch out our hands and
it will be there.

Just to cheer me even more, I heard, about this time, from
a Roman Catholic priest who became a member of my Sod-
It-Club last year.

I was in hospital when I met him and the poor man was
terrified because he had cancer in the leg and he dreaded
having the leg amputated. He was talking to me about it one
day before his operation and I said, 'Father, why don't you
join the Sod-It-Club?'

He looked a bit taken aback. 'What's that, love?' he asked.

So I told him the club's history and how Diana Dors and
Pat Pheonix, among others, had all found it comforting.

'So when you go down to theatre say, "Sod it! I'm not

going to lose my leg. They are not going to take my leg off,"'
I finished.

The priest roared with laughter and agreed that, put like
that, you couldn't really call it swearing.

Anyway, he had his operation and, after they had wheeled
him back to his bed, the sister who'd been in the theatre
with him popped her head round my door.

'Do you know, after his pre-med when he was floating on
air, all we could hear was this mumbled voice saying, "Sod
it, they're not going to take my leg off. Sod it, they're not
going to take my leg off." The surgeons couldn't believe it
from a priest!'

Months later the priest phoned me.

'I just wanted to tell you, lovey, that it worked,' he said.
'I've got a stiff leg now but I haven't lost it. I put it down
to the Sod-It-Club!'

12

Once again this year I've been inundated with poems. What a talented lot my readers are! I do enjoy reading them. Somehow you can sum up in a few lines of poetry sentiments that would take pages and pages of ordinary prose. A couple of verses on a single sheet can make you laugh, make you cry or can give you something to think about for the rest of the day. It's amazing the power of poetry.

As I've explained before, I simply haven't the space to publish all the works I'm sent. There's only room for a tiny selection to whet the appetite and, with a bit of luck, to inspire other budding poets to put pen to paper.

Ann Fairman sent me this first one. It's a humorous poem and I must say I particularly enjoy these. I come across so much tragedy in the world that laughter is a specially precious gift to me. Nothing is quite so bad if you can have a laugh. Even when you're ill, laughter makes you feel better. Frankly, without a sense of humour I don't know what I'd do sometimes.

Our Doris

A medium known as 'Our Doris'
Made contact with Great Uncle Horace.

He said, 'Hello, dear. It's lovely up here
And today I met my brother Maurice.
He passed on in his sleep as he lay in a heap
And I greeted him on his arrival,
He said, 'Hello, Mate,' as I opened the gate,
'So this is what's known as "survival".

'Well isn't it nice! So warm and loving,
All pain and distress left behind.
And here's Auntie Lil and our Uncle Bill,
They've both come to meet me, how kind!'

Now I don't wish to gloat 'cos I've shed my old coat,
But there's nothing to fear, that's a promise,
If you want to know more then pop down to the store,
And buy all those books by 'Our Doris'.

                                        Ann Fairman

Ann has certainly captured the spirit of 'survival' without preaching to anyone and I must say I can't argue with the sentiments in the last line!

This next poem made me laugh too. Unfortunately, it's become detached from its accompanying letter so I don't have an author's name or a title, but it's such fun that it seemed a shame not to share it. So, with apologies to the author, here it is:

I dreamt of heaven the other night
And the pearly gates swung wide
An Angel with a halo bright
Ushered me inside.

And there to my astonishment
Stood folks I'd judged and labelled
As quite 'unfit', of little worth,
And spiritually disabled.

Indignant words rose to my lips
But never were set free
For every face showed stunned surprise –
Not one expected me.

You can't help smiling, can you, yet in twelve short, amusing lines the author has created a lesson for us all. I'll have to bite my tongue before I have a moan about anyone again.

Now if the inclusion of *Medium Rare* seems like sheer indulgence, please forgive me. All I can say in my own defence is that people like me have to take a lot of stick. You expect it, but it still hurts however much you try to pretend it doesn't.

Some black days it seems as if all people want to do is criticize, no matter how hard you work. On days like that you tend to think, is it worth it? Maybe I should retire and escape all this stress and heartache. Then the post arrives and out comes a poem like *Medium Rare* and suddenly everything's all right again.

Many thanks, Rene Stanton, for this uplifting poem.

Medium Rare

Platform idol to so many folks
Is lovely, natural Doris Stokes.
Sense of humour, with serious side,
Talent spread so far and wide.

Health setbacks are overcome
Conditions that would silence some.
Doris tho' springs back with ease
Surely everyone agrees
She has no need to 'act a part'
Sincerity comes from the heart,
Long may she reign and gather strength
To live a life of greater length,
Scattering comfort on the way
Like sunshine in a sky of grey!

                                        Rene Stanton

Well, I don't know if I can live up to all that, Rene, but I'll certainly try.

Many poems, of course, are very serious and some of them are truly inspirational. I particularly like this one by Lily Godliman. Her daughter, Kathy King, from Basildon, sent it to me with the following letter of explanation:

Dear Doris,

This poem was written by my mother, Lily Godliman, years ago. My mum died in November '85. She was only sixty-one years old. My sisters and I stayed all night at the hospital and she died at 9 a.m. the next morning. We went back to my sister's in great shock and grief. My sister got the poem and read it to us and it was like Mum wrote it for such a time.

Mum could write lovely poems and she always wrote in cards when she sent them. She was a nurse and very caring. She would always sit with someone when they were dying and comfort them.

Her kidneys packed up and she was too ill to be moved to London for a kidney machine. We were shocked that there were none at Basildon Hospital.

We have been raising money for kidney research and are going to send it on the anniversary of Mum's death. It makes us feel better to try and help people the way Mum would and it makes life feel worth while.

I would be very happy if you used this poem in your books.

God Bless,
Kathy King

Well, I'm more than happy to use Lily's poem. I think it's beautiful.

Life is just a testing time while we are here on earth,
The pain and grief, the obstacles
Are all to try our worth.
It's very hard not to succumb
When things are getting tough
But you must fight and overcome
Just coping's not enough.
For living's really wonderful
The good times and the bad.
Who'd appreciate the happy days
If they'd never known the bad?
Listen to the birds at dawn
Or watch a rose unfurl
Gaze on a baby's sleeping face
Or touch a tiny curl.
So when you're feeling down and out

Your spirit is depressed,
Just look around at everything
With which you have been blessed.

                              Lily Godliman

Even if Kathy hadn't written to tell me of her mother's warm and loving nature, I would have known from reading these lines what a very special person she was and still is, of course, on the other side. The poem shows great spiritual understanding and it's quite clear that Lily went over so soon because she had little left to learn. She'd acquired a great deal of wisdom in her sixty-one years.

Just reading her poem does you good. I'm no angel and like everyone else I grumble now and then about my troubles. But when I read Lily's work it reminds me to count my blessings. After all, life is wonderful and we shouldn't take it for granted.

Some poets write to entertain, some to inspire, while others write of deeply personal and often tragic experiences as if the very writing of them helps ease the pain. These poems are often sad, yet reading them it becomes clear that the writer, in the midst of his or her grief, has stumbled across a greater truth, a greater strength, which helps him to cope.

This poem, untitled and unsigned, is about the special grief that accompanies a stillbirth. Reading between the lines, I would say that the author must have had direct personal experience of such a tragedy, in order to write so movingly.

The mother of a stillborn child goes through a unique kind of agony and I know it well. Years ago, on a cold, bleak February day, my longed-for daughter was born 'dead'. As well as the grief it's a very lonely time for the parents because people who haven't experienced it can't understand why you mourn so for a child you've never known.

The writer of these haunting words sums up, far better than I could, the terrible sense of loss and grief for what might have been. Yet, for all that, it's a comforting poem:

> God has a special place for stillborn things,
> The things that never were and should have been:
> The little songs no singer ever sings,
> The beauty of a picture hung unseen,
> A noble heart that loved with no return
> And deeds well meant which somehow turned out ill,
> A lovely flame that vainly tried to burn
> But could not last, though all the winds were still,
> The early flower that no one ever sees
> Making its way through ground iced hard with sleet,
> A leader to whom no man bends his knees,
> The Christ-like smile that greets each fresh defeat;
> God treats them very tenderly, for he
> Knows what the pain of stifled things can be.

I know that this is true. God does treat these little ones with special care and they grow up happily in the spirit world. Away from the spite, the petty meannesses and tensions of our earthly world, they mature into truly beautiful men and women.

I was privileged to see my daughter, now grown up in the spirit world, and I couldn't believe that this lovely creature with the long, chestnut hair curling round her shoulders, could actually belong to me. I was so proud of her.

People find it easier to understand the grief of a mother

who has lost a baby born alive, but destined to breathe only a little while. Yet even the understanding of family and friends doesn't seem to ease the burden. Strangely enough, a poem can sometimes help where all the well-meaning attentions of friends do not.

Mrs T.C. of Middlesex told me her sad story when she wrote to say how comforting she had found a poem given to me by the spirit world and printed in an earlier book.

Dear Doris,

First of all I would like to thank you for your poem *In A Baby Castle*, which has helped me enormously in the last seven months. It has helped me accept my baby's death.

Seven months ago I had a baby boy called Daniel, who was born premature at twenty-six weeks. I prayed so hard that he would live, so did my family. The doctors and nurses did everything they could to save him but sadly there was nothing more they could do and after five days he passed away.

Those five days I sat there watching my son fight for his life were the worst. Just sitting there knowing he was going to die and not being able to do anything for him. I felt so useless.

On the fifth morning the nurse came to get me and said it was getting near his time and asked me if I would like to hold him for the last time on my own in a quiet room. I agreed because I knew he was going to die and I couldn't cope waiting any more. I went into the other room and five minutes later she brought Daniel to me. That is a memory I will treasure for ever. He was so beautiful.

I miss him very much and wish I could have him back. I've always wanted a child of my own and now the hospital isn't sure if I will be able to have another one but I'm going to try.

I am sending you a copy of the poem I wrote for Daniel a few weeks after he died. I hope you like it, I just wrote down how I felt one day and my mum suggested I sent it to you.

Yours sincerely,
Mrs T.C.

Darling Daniel

You're all we ever wanted, but it just wasn't to be.
But we were together for a few days
Just you, Dad and me.

You made us so very happy
And proud that you chose us,
And we will never forget
The happiness you gave us.

When we held you in our arms
I can't explain the love
Never wanting to let go
Although we knew we must.

So beautiful and perfect
In every single way
But we'll be together again
All three of us some day.

Though our hearts are aching
And we long to hold you tight
We'll visit you in our dreams
When we go to sleep at night.

So many things we want to say,
To show how much we care,
And in our minds we really know
That you will always be there.

So please don't ever forget us,
'Cos we will never forget you,
We just hope that you are happy
In everything you do.

So 'bye now our darling
We'll see you again some day
When we can tell you all the things
We are really trying to say.

Love Mum and Dad

My eyes fill with tears whenever I read that poignant poem and I marvel once again at the courage and dignity of so called 'ordinary' people. I know just what those poor parents are going through and I'm glad that at least they have the comfort of knowing that their little Daniel is not lost and gone for ever.

Mrs D.M. of London sent me another moving poem on the same subject. She lost her little son after just twelve short hours and has suffered years of turmoil and heartache ever since. But at last she has come to terms with the tragedy.

Do you ever wonder why he was born so very small,
And do you ever ask yourself why he was given to
you at all,
Do you ever wonder what you did to deserve the
pain,
And was it ever really worth the strain,
Did you ever feel alone and think that no one cared,
And knew they really wanted to but never really
dared.
Do you ever wonder why you still cry so many tears,
And never thought the hurt would last for all those
many years.
Do you ever feel that your life keeps going wrong,
And wonder what it is in you that helps to keep you
strong,
Do you ever ask just why it should have happened to
you,
And will the memory of then, remain your whole life
through,
And even if you could turn back time and had the
chance to erase that day
You know that even with all the hurt – you'd have it
no other way.

But it's not just bereaved parents who need our love and
understanding. We should also spare a thought for the parents
of handicapped children. I particularly liked this poem from
Mrs D.W. of Llanelli, who wrote: 'All children are special,
Doris, but the handicapped child gives so much and asks for
so little, only love.'

The Gift Of A Special Child

A talk was held quite far from earth
'It's time again for another birth.'
Said the angels to the Lord above,
This special child will need much love,
His progress may seem very slow,
Accomplishments he may not show,
And he may need much extra care,
From all the folks he meets down there;
He may not learn nor laugh nor play,
His thoughts may seem quite far away,
In many ways he won't adapt
He will be known as handicapped.
So let's be careful where he's sent
We want his life to be content.
Please Lord find parents who
Will do this special job for you.
They will not gather right away
The leading note they're asked to play,
But with this child sent from above
Comes stronger faith and richer love
And soon they'll know the privilege given
In caring for this child from heaven
That special child so meek and mild
Is heaven's very special child.

I get a lot of poems about children but they don't make up my entire postbag by any means. Recently I've been very pleased to see a great feeling for old people reflected in the lines. Pleased, not because I'm getting on a bit myself these days(!), but because of the dreadful attacks on pensioners that we keep reading about. I really can't believe some of the things that happen now. Twenty years ago the most hardened villain wouldn't stoop to attacking a defenceless old lady. How things have changed.

Yet, judging from my post, I know that old people are still loved and appreciated in many, many homes. Mrs C.W. from Sussex sent me these charming verses:

My Gran

I wish my Gran were here with me
And not gone into Heaven,
She'd be quite flabbergasted
How I've grown now I am seven.

I 'member how she used to say
That I was just knee high
And how she wiped my tears away
When people made me cry.

My Grannie never made me cry
She kissed my tears away
And it was lovely when she said
'My dear, let's go and play.'

I 'member how she used to wear
A funny little hat
And she wasn't 'zactly thin
And yet she wasn't 'zactly fat.

But she was round and cuddly
Just like my teddy bear
And I'd climb upon her lap
When she sat in the big armchair.

She'd throw her arms around me,
Give me such a squashy squeeze.
If you're listening Jesus
Oh do send her back – oh please.

I'm sure that you don't need my Gran
As half as much as me
There must be lots of other grans
Up there for you to see.

And never any tears for Gran
To wipe away up there
'Cos no one cries in Heaven –
Well – perhaps they mustn't dare . . .

I'm glad to see that elderly aunties are also appreciated.
Mrs E.O. of Devon was inspired to write this poem on the
very evening that her much loved old auntie passed over.
Invisible Me shows great understanding.

Invisible Me

You think that I am gone, because you cannot see
Or hear the footfall that was me!
I am only near,
I can see and I can hear.
I wish that you – when you think of me
Would speak to me and say my name and see
There is another life for you and me.
You cannot see the air or touch the breeze,
You cannot touch the wind but hear it in the trees.
You know it's there because you hear and feel
But in God's good time, he will reveal

All these wonders to you, dear.
So do not be afraid, be of good cheer,
Your loved ones are waiting for you here.
The Lord's my shepherd and He's yours,
He opens all these doors.
I have simply left you for a while
And you cannot see my smile
But when you need me I'll be there
To help you and show you that I care.

So think of me as I used to be
When I was young, well and free
From pain, infirmity and age
Which held my soul within a cage.

The Good Shepherd held the key
And only He
Could open wide the door
And set me free.

A little while I am with you,
And then I go to those I knew
So many years ago
Who shared my life and loved me so.
So do not grieve for me, my dear, as on your way you go.

My last poem has the rather sombre title of *Death*. But don't be put off. Once again the work is unsigned, but the words suggest to me that they were written by someone who has been very close to death and has good reason to know that it is nothing to fear.

Death

I lie here on a bed of leaves
Watching birds fly thro' the trees
Autumn will soon be here they say
With falling leaves which soon decay
But though these leaves are dying fast
Death itself – it does not last
All living things that grow and thrive
Will never die – all will survive
There is life in another world
Where joy and love are all unfurled.

Many of us fear to die
But this is truth – it is no lie
Do not fear death, it is not bleak
Just drift into a nice warm sleep
I tried it once, but doctors fought
To save my life was their one thought
Now that I am fit and well
On these thoughts I should not dwell
But all of you who fear to die
Believe me now, I tell no lie
I do not mean you to deceive
But in these things I do believe.

When I was very close to death
I could feel its comfort breath
It's warm and gentle, sweet and soft
Death itself holds no wrath
And so you see, when death is near
I'm sure that you will have no fear
Then you will only wish to die

And let your restless spirit fly
To learn of many things untold
As slowly wonders will unfold
I wish that this could comfort few
Who'd not fear death if they just knew.

So there we are. I hope you've enjoyed this selection of poems as much as I have.

13

'Now, Doris,' said the nurse, 'where on earth are we going to put these?'

She was carrying the most enormous basket of flowers, nearly three feet high and absolutely stuffed to bursting with pink and white blooms – a beautiful gift from Terry.

'This place is like a flower stall already.'

'How about there?' I suggested, pointing to the shelf that ran parallel to my bed. 'If we move the cards and shift that chair a bit . . .'

The nurse bustled about and, a few deft moves later, the basket was safely installed in pride of place only inches from my feet and the cards were squashed together at the other end of the shelf.

Yes, as you've probably guessed by now, I'm finishing yet another book from my hospital bed and this time I seem to be worse than ever.

To tell the truth, I haven't been well for some time, but there have been so many bugs going around that I assumed I was falling for one thing after another. After all, I do seem to have this nasty habit of catching everything going.

I even began to wonder if I could be suffering from a form

of agoraphobia because my symptoms became dramatically worse when I went out.

Not long ago I was thrilled to be invited to a royal film première. I was so looking forward to it. It's been years since I've seen a film at the cinema and this affair was to be much more exciting than an ordinary night at the pictures. The Royal Family and countless stars were to be present, all dressed up to the nines. It would be a truly glittering occasion.

I treated myself to a beautiful new dress made of real silk, I had my hair done specially, my nails painted and, although I don't wear much make-up, I spent ages fiddling with my powder and lipstick.

By the time I'd finished I looked pretty smart considering, and John, too, was elegant in evening dress. We certainly wouldn't be letting the side down when we mixed with all those posh people.

But it wasn't to be.

During the afternoon a fuzzy headache had come on and I wasn't feeling 100 per cent but I put it down to excitement.

'You'll be all right when you get there, Doris,' I told myself firmly. I was quite determined to go.

Well, admittedly, I did go. It was just that I didn't stay!

Hardly had I sat down in my plush cinema seat, than the room started spinning and I felt so ill I thought I would pass out.

'It's no good, John, I'm going to have to go home,' I whispered to John who was sitting beside me. I would have sobbed with disappointment had I not been feeling so dreadful.

So John helped me to my feet and I struggled back up the aisle and out to the foyer where the stars were still arriving. I was just in time to see Joan Collins waft past in something extremely glamorous and then I was back in the car, heading for home.

Instead of hob-nobbing with celebrities in my silk dress, I spent the evening with my feet up, drinking tea in my dressing-gown. I never did get to see a single frame of the film.

Yet the next day my faithful doctor couldn't find anything obviously wrong with me.

'It must be all in the mind, Doris,' I told myself. But it was hard to believe. The symptoms were so real and physical. 'Yes, but that's what happens,' the nurse in me replied, 'the symptoms are real enough but your mind brings them on. I wonder if it could be agoraphobia?'

Now I believe that this is exactly what can happen in some cases of agoraphobia but in my case it wasn't agoraphobia. Over the next few weeks my health see-sawed wildly. One minute I wasn't feeling too bad at all, the next I could hardly move. After a while, though, I couldn't help noticing that the trend was downwards. Sittings and public engagements had to be postponed and the doctor gave me antibiotics because, on top of everything else, I seemed to be suffering with a sinus infection.

Then at Easter I collapsed again. It had reached the stage where I was so dizzy I could hardly stand up. I thought the infection must have spread to my inner ear, which affects balance, but the doctor was not happy.

'You can't go on like this, Doris,' he said. 'You'll have to go back to hospital, and this time you must stay there until they've sorted you out.'

By now I felt so awful I was willing to agree. So back I went to hospital, and after a couple of days of tests they finally discovered what was wrong with me. I had a brain tumour.

At once everything fell into place. The out-of-character fainting at Christmas, the dizziness, the headaches and all the peculiar illnesses that had plagued me ever since. They all stemmed from the same cause.

I had a brain tumour. They are frightening words, brain tumour, but these days surgeons are so clever and it seems I am lucky. My tumour is operable. So here I am sitting in my hospital bed waiting for the operation.

Fortunately, I had just about finished this book when I was admitted so that's a load off my mind. I'd hate to be late for the publishers' deadline.

What's more, the rest has done me good. The nurses are very kind and under their gentle care I've been feeling better.

Flowers and cards have poured in and I don't have time to be lonely. I've had loads of visitors. Derek Jameson and his wife, Ellen, called in a little while ago with a lovely teddy bear to cheer me up because they knew I'd have so many flowers. Freddie Starr has promised to fly over in his helicopter and when I'm short of official visitors the nurses pop in for a chat.

One American girl was so excited when she heard about my work that, even though she wasn't on duty, she came to see me. She was fascinated to hear more about the spirit world because apparently on a recent visit to a supposedly haunted house in London, she photographed her sister standing next to an ancient fireplace. When the film was developed they could clearly see another figure standing beside her, even though there was no one visible at the time.

'Yes, that's quite possible, love,' I told her, and I went on to explain about the christening photograph in which a likeness of John Michael as a baby showed clearly in the air between me and the child who was named that day.

All in all, it's not too bad here in hospital. I can't pretend I'm not nervous about the operation. I expect I shall be out of action for quite a while afterwards and they will have to shave my head, which is upsetting for any woman, even one of my age.

Still, I won't be beaten. I've ordered a set of the prettiest turbans and the next time you see me I expect I'll have an exotic eastern look.

Wish me luck!

Doris passed away peacefully on May 8th 1987, nearly two weeks after a six-and-a-half-hour operation to remove a brain tumour. She never regained consciousness.

Two days before the operation she was still working on this book, organizing her family and bravely trying to keep up her own spirits and those of the people around her.

The operation was scheduled for that Saturday.

'Oh well, on Sunday I shall either be here or I won't,' she said cheerfully.

In fact this was one of the few occasions when Doris was wrong. On Sunday she was here, and yet she wasn't. She survived the operation only to slip gently away thirteen days later.

Despite her brave words, Doris was frightened at the thought of this operation. She wasn't afraid of dying. As she always said: 'There is no death. You can't die for the life of you.' No, what worried her was her possible condition after the operation. She had been warned that her memory might be impaired for a while and that, temporarily, she might be unable to speak.

Doris was no fool and she was also a trained nurse. Reading between the lines she feared that she might be left blind, dumb or 'stupid'.

Had any of those things happened she would have faced them with the courage and humour with which she faced every problem that came her way. But inside she would have been crying.

How much better this way. After all the illnesses and oper-ations she had endured, she finally slipped away without further pain or suffering. Now we can only hope that she's happy at last; walking with her father and John Michael, the beloved son she missed so much, in the bright fields of the spirit world.

Epilogue

Throughout her life, Doris brought comfort and hope to thousands of bereaved people. She also gave generously of her time and money to those in need. But perhaps the best possible tribute to Doris is to let her work speak for itself.

Here, with the kind permission of Mrs Carol Harrison, is a transcript of Doris' last sitting. Mrs Harrison lost her son, Stuart, in the Zeebrugge ferry disaster. When the sitting took place on April 8th 1987 Doris was already very ill but she was determined not to let the family down. Her only worry was that her health might spoil the sitting. This is what happened:

DORIS: They're singing Happy Birthday so there's a birthday coming or a birthday just been.
CAROL: It was my birthday a couple of weeks ago, on March 13th.
DORIS: He's singing Happy Birthday. He's only young. Possibly about nineteen. It's a very young voice.
CAROL: He was seventeen.

DORIS: Something about he shouldn't have been there. Does that make sense to you?

CAROL: That's right. He didn't have permission from his college to go.

DORIS: Who's Betty? He wants to send his love to Betty.

CAROL: Betty is his grandmother.

DORIS: Who's David? It's a 'd' sound, 'd', 'd', 'd' . . .

CAROL: Dean. That's my son's best friend.

DORIS: He's talking about someone called Anne. You've been talking to her about him.

CAROL: Yes, Anne's my friend.

DORIS: The awful part is that I needn't have been there, he's saying. I nearly didn't go. He went to please someone. So whether he wanted to keep someone company, I don't know. There were five of them.

CAROL: He went to please some friends but there were four of them not five.

DORIS: Oh there were meant to be five but one didn't go.

CAROL: That's right.

DORIS: We're all right. That's what he wants to get over. It all happened very quickly. Now that was something to do with an anniversary coming. It's someone's anniversary. Who's Paul? I've met Paul.

CAROL: Paul is my friend's son. He died when he was six and a half. His anniversary is coming up on April 19th.

DORIS: Doesn't he get excited? He's talking very fast and his old hands go. Who's Tony or Tommy? Tommy's been talking about me, he says.

CAROL: Tommy's a friend.

DORIS: He's met Bill or Bert over there . . . it's a 'b' sound. That wasn't Bernard, love, was it?'

CAROL: Bernard was the pet name of the friend who died with him.

DORIS: He's talking about someone called Alison. She was talking about him. And Mark or Martin.

CAROL: Alison is my niece and Mark and Martin are his stepbrothers.

DORIS: (*To Karen, Stuart's sister*) Are you going to get married soon?

KAREN: No.

DORIS: I'm sure he said you were getting engaged.

[CAROL: Karen has since got engaged.]*

DORIS: Who's Annette? A . . . A . . .

KAREN: I know an Angela.

DORIS: No. No, it's not Annette, it's Andy.

CAROL: His stepfather.

DORIS: Why didn't you say your dad? Oh, you didn't call him Dad, always Andy.

CAROL: That's right.

DORIS: He's a lovely-looking boy with such a cheeky grin and a dimple here. He says, I was a bit of a bugger sometimes but I did love you all. The point is, you don't know till you come this side. They never say I love you. They think it's sissy. It's only when they get here. I know, lovey, and they do understand. Who's Rose or Ron . . . ?

CAROL: My aunt and my grandmother were both called Rose.

DORIS: He's telling me something about a watch. Was he wearing a new watch? He's a bit annoyed about that. I'd just bought a new watch, he said.

---

* Square brackets indicate comments added by Mrs Harrison since the sitting.

CAROL: He did need one.

DORIS: I don't suppose it'll be any good now, love. Who's Claire? Susanne . . . Try that again . . . Susan . . . all I can hear you going is ssss. She's on the spirit side.

CAROL: Our friends' daughter was called Samantha. She died the Sunday before Stuart. He went to her funeral the day before he died.

DORIS: You tell Sam's mum that she's all right. Julie . . . There's going to be a baby born and he's laughing his head off about this. She doesn't think he knows.

[CAROL: Julie is his cousin. She's now pregnant.]

DORIS: He's a very caring young boy. He said, will you please tell my mum and family . . . You're a bit embarrassed, love. Go on . . . Don't let them spend a lot of money. I'm not there. You know I'm alive and our love's alive. Don't spend a lot of money . . . He bites his nails, doesn't he? And you're dark but he's sort of sandy. I can see him.

KAREN: Ginger.

DORIS: Well, I wasn't going to say that because I thought he might be offended. Strawberry blond, he said. Who's Phillip? Try again, I haven't got it right . . . Frank . . . no, you've missed it, darling. Don't worry about it. It's a bit confusing because he keeps dashing off to have a look what's going on. I was so angry at first when I got over, he says. He'd some nice friends at last because deep down he was very shy. Gary – who's Gary?

CAROL: Gary was his other best friend.

DORIS: Tell him I've been back, though he'll never believe it! Oh. I don't think I ought to say that, darling. Well all right. He says, the old fella (he thinks the world of you), he needs a new car, you know. Well when you get that money, you buy yourself a new car for me.

If I have had to give up my life, then for God's sake let me help the people I love. So will you promise me that, Dad? He's never had a new car in his life and I'm going to buy him one.

[CAROL: My husband did need a new car, but Doris wasn't to know that as we turned up at her house in my daughter's boyfriend's new turbo.]

DORIS: That was a name beginning with P . . . a girl's name . . . Penelope . . . no, Pauline.

CAROL: Pauline is Samantha's mum.

DORIS: Then there was a 'b' sound. Who worked in a shop? He's here too, so don't think the boy's on his own.

CAROL: My uncle had a butcher's shop. He died a few weeks before Stuart.

DORIS: I don't know, sweetheart. Did you? Now I don't want to harass you but I think they would like me to ask you this one question, then we'll leave it alone because it's going to be bad enough over the next few days. Was it very long? Mum, I've got to be truthful, he says. I was very frightened and I got separated. I think I was holding onto Nicola for a while, then we were separated. I remember we laughed at first. We thought it was funny when the ship started tipping. Then it happened so quickly, but I know you have been asking. It happened very quickly. The cold and no air and I quickly went to sleep. We had been down to the car and I went off and that's when we got separated.

[CAROL: Our neighbours who took Stuart were in the morgue when we went to Zeebrugge, but Stuart wasn't found until five weeks later.]

DORIS: Who's Amy or Ada? It's a short name, only three letters.

CAROL: Ivy, Stuart's grandmother.

DORIS: Oh, that's it. He's got an accent, lovey. I'm not being rude.

[CAROL: Stuart had a Somerset accent.]

DORIS: I can't very well say that, either. They get angry with me but they forget I'm a stranger to you. Can I be personal, love? (*To Karen*) Have you taken a ring off? Were you engaged before?

KAREN: I was nearly engaged before.

DORIS: That's it because he wasn't very happy about that. He's glad you finished with the boy. Who's Ed?

CAROL: Ed is Samantha's dad.

DORIS: Will you tell Ed that we've been back. He's going on about that new car again. He's determined you're going to have it. He loves you. He said, I wasn't demonstrative, Doris, I would just say, 'Cheerio,' and half the time I didn't even say that, I just used to go. I regret that now. I didn't go up and give Mum a hug. It's a pity you have to come over here before you can say the things you want to say. Listen, he says, and he's pointing at me. Never be afraid to tell people you love them because when anything like this happens and you come over this side it's too bloody late. My dad's so easy-going he never used to chase us up. Why didn't I tell him how much I appreciated him? He was always there. He never pushed me. I had a marvellous family. Well I still have. Yes, you still have, love, but you get it off your chest, that's what we're trying for. Don't keep wandering, sweetheart. I hope I've got that right, lovey. Forgive me if I haven't but it's a bit difficult with this pain in my ears. Sometimes I don't hear so well. They all came from the same place so they're all going to be together. It will be rather splendid, he said. Yes it will, love. We have heard them discussing it and everyone's in agreement that we all be put to rest together. Is that right, love?

[CAROL: They were all going to be buried together. Both families wanted it. We had already chosen their plots before seeing Doris.]

DORIS: Tell them all that's only our old overcoats and we'll all be there to make sure you do everything right. He's laughing. He's got a real old belly laugh and he makes it light. Tell them I've met Arthur.

[CAROL: This name meant nothing but my husband was adopted and did not know his family.]

DORIS: They don't know Arthur, love. Something to do with a solicitor . . . I think you've got yourself in a bit of a muddle, love. Or it might be me. Now that was something to do with cooking. Do you cook for a living?

CAROL: Stuart did. He was training to be a chef.

DORIS: Oh that's it. He keeps saying cooking, you know, for a living. He didn't say it was him. Oh, he says he was going to be a steward.

CAROL: He wanted to be a steward on a liner. He told us that a few weeks before he died.

DORIS: He was looking forward to this. Then that was Alec or Alan.

CAROL: Allen is Dean's surname – his best friend.

DORIS: (*To Carol and Andy who are getting emotional*) I know, love. Don't think I don't feel for you. I have lost four children myself so I know what it's like, love. I don't care what anybody says. You can lose a father, a mother, but until you have lost a child no one can tell you. Nobody knows. D'you know, John Michael would be forty-three on August 7th and there's never a day goes past without me thinking of him. Even with all I know, there's always an empty place there. But the sun does shine again. Honestly. I promise you. Now he's saying, stop being morbid, you. There's no need to be morbid. They've got enough on their plates without you being morbid. What were you going to tell me, love, then I will listen to you? You always wanted to travel so it's not been wasted. I can go anywhere in the world, look at anything I want to look at. Who's James? J . . . J . . . Joseph . . . John. It's John living. I can just hear the J.

CAROL: His stepfather's real name is John.

DORIS: I know you are very quiet, love, but there's such a bond between you. You shouldn't tell me that, love. He says, I wasn't meant to happen. The point is, love, you had a good life. I was a bit difficult at times, he says, I was no angel. It took me a little while before I settled down. Then this had to happen. It's not fair, is it? No, I don't think it is either, love. Who's Bill?

CAROL: A family friend.

DORIS: And Kathy?

CAROL: My friend.

DORIS: Who's Barry?

CAROL: His uncle.

DORIS: I think that was Stephen. I was not sure about that . . . S . . . It couldn't be Stuart, could it?

[CAROL: At this point, Doris didn't know Stuart's name.]

DORIS: That's what I've been waiting for. I'm all right, Dad. I'm not dead, honest. I know it's a great wrench because, let's face it, I was a bit of a trial sometimes, but you never ever grumbled. Thank you for being such a wonderful family. Now don't cry, love, or you'll upset me. Not bloody fair, he keeps saying. He uses bloody quite a bit, doesn't he, love? They told me before you came to be brave for the sake of my parents but it's not bloody fair. I know, love, but you will be able to help the others a lot. You've got me crying now and usually I can manage to control it. Sorry about that, he said. But I know what you're going through . . . Believe me, the sun does shine again . . . I don't know how long it'll take . . . I've been there. I know what it's like to get up in the morning and think, 'Oh God, I've got to face another day.' What you've got to remember, love, is you've got to take it day by day, one step at a time. And one day you'll wake up and, this I promise you, the sun will be shining again in your heart. You'll know with absolute certainty that your Stuart and all his friends, they are alive. But at the moment it's a cross that nobody else can carry for you. It's bad enough to lose a child without having all this agony piled on the top. At least I was able to hold my baby in my arms until my father collected him. I think they've already found him, but you've got to prepare yourselves for the fact that you probably won't be able to see him.

[CAROL: They had found Stuart the very day we went to see Doris. His face had been slammed against something and that is why they told us not to see him.]

DORIS: Don't remember him as you think he might look now. Hold a picture in your mind of the way he went out to work every day and think about how he was on the earth, because that's how he is now, lovey. You've already hung two new photographs up.

[CAROL: Yes, we had put up two new photos.]

DORIS: Oh yes, I know what you're up to, he says. One of them's not too bad but the other one I'm not so sure about, but me mum likes it. Don't you worry, I'm keeping an eye on you. He says, say hello to Paddy. Hello Paddy, love. He says, I'm not vindictive but you make sure they pay. They've got to be made to pay because that was sheer bloody negligence. When you went up to Stuart's room he said he'd been trying on sweaters and he's left two on the bed.

CAROL: Yes. Karen put away two sweaters that were on his bed.

DORIS: Sh . . . sh . . . Sheila. No, try again . . . Sharon.

CAROL: Sharon was a girl at college.

DORIS: Well I think you'll find you'll be hearing from her. It was so dark and so cold, he says. That was the worst part of it, trying to find each other in the dark. He held a child. She was only a toddler.

CAROL: Stuart would have helped a child. He loved them and they loved him.

DORIS: And then we got swept apart. That was the last thing I remember. I must keep this baby up . . . Oh what a dreadful shame . . . Well never mind, love . . . But there was one child left behind in Nicola's family.

CAROL: The son Patrick, aged twenty, was left.

DORIS: So his whole family's been wiped out. It breaks my heart. But I know that they're alive. You've only got to put your hand out and they'll hold on. I know it's the physical presence we grieve for. I'm just the same. When my babies died, and if my husband was to go before me I'd still be the same, as much as I know that we'll all be together again. But still you have to carry that cross. Don't bottle it up, love, because tears are God's healing gift to us. Bottle it up inside you and you'll go mad. It's not much consolation, I know, but at least you know there's so many people in the same boat as you. You're not alone and you know that each family is thinking of you as you're thinking of them.

Now why does he keep going on about the dog? It's the dog's birthday.

[CAROL: Karen had been singing Happy Birthday to the dog before we went to see Doris.]

DORIS: Give her a cuddle for me, he says, because he loves that dog. He idolizes Karen. I just said, isn't she a beautiful girl, and he said, I think so. I know, we all say things and do things and it's only when something like this happens we think, I shouldn't have shouted, I shouldn't have said that. But that's human nature, lovey, and they understand. When we go over there the love link gets stronger and stronger. Dad, promise me you'll get a new car. Get a good one and when you go out I'll be sitting there with you. Are you a hairdresser, Karen?

KAREN: Yes.

DORIS: 'Cos I said, what does she do, your sister, and he said, she works in a salon. She's a hair-dresser.

Well, I'll have to let you go, because if the doctor comes in and finds me working he'll do his pieces. But I couldn't let you down again. (*A previously arranged visit had had to be cancelled owing to Doris' poor health.*)

I'm sorry it's been a bit bitty but working through this pain has been difficult.

Carol Harrison sent Doris this tape with her love and thanks, for the hope and peace of mind she'd given the family. She also enclosed a poem which she thought Doris would enjoy. Strangely enough, unknown to Carol at the time she sat down to write her letter, Doris had already passed away. Yet the poem echoes Doris' beliefs perfectly. This is what Doris would have wanted to say had she been in a position to speak for herself. She couldn't have wished for a better ending to her last book.

Don't Weep For Me Here

If I should reach heaven before you,
Remember, don't weep for me here
For I shall be happy with Jesus
With never a worry or fear.

We journey along on life's highway,
The future unknown to us all,
We know not the day or the hour
The time when the saviour may call.

Together we've laboured for Jesus,
What happiness year after year!
So if I'm promoted to glory,
Remember don't weep for me here.

I'll watch for you coming to glory,
To be with my saviour so dear,
If I should reach heaven before you,
Remember, don't weep for me here.

☐ Voices: a Doris Stokes Collection	Doris Stokes	£8.99
☐ A Host of Voices: the Second Doris Stokes Collection	Doris Stokes	£8.99

The prices shown above are correct at time of going to press. However, the publishers reserve the right to increase prices on covers from those previously advertised without further notice.

———————————— sphere ————————————

SPHERE
PO Box 121, Kettering, Northants NN14 4ZQ
Tel: 01832 737525, Fax: 01832 733076
Email: aspenhouse@FSBDial.co.uk

POST AND PACKING:
Payments can be made as follows: cheque, postal order (payable to Sphere), credit card or maestro. Do not send cash or currency.

All UK Orders   **FREE OF CHARGE**
EC & Overseas   25% of order value

Name (Block Letters) _____

Address _____

_____

Post/zip code:_____

☐ Please keep me in touch with future Sphere publications

☐ I enclose my remittance £_____

☐ I wish to pay Visa/Access/Mastercard/Eurocard

Card Expiry Date [ ][ ][ ]   Switch issue No. [ ][ ]